The Navy Days

By Francisco A. Rivera

Francisco Rivera

A rainbow over the USS Arizona Memorial

Table of Contents

The Navy Days 1
CHAPTER 1. 1
Adiós, Douglas/Agua Prieta y Mi Familia 1
CHAPTER 2. 5
Hello San Diego 5
CHAPTER 3. 15
Manhood 15
CHAPTER 4. 21
Living My Best Life 21
CHAPTER 5. 25
Back to Reality 25
CHAPTER 6. 35
Preparing to Leave 35
CHAPTER 7. 37
Anchors Aweigh 37
CHAPTER 8. 41
Meet me at H.E.H. 41
CHAPTER 9. 45
Initiation to N.W. Australia 45
CHAPTER 10. 49
U.S. Navy Routine 49
CHAPTER 11. 55
The Civilian Life 55
CHAPTER 12. 59
Taking A Break 59
CHAPTER 13. 75
Finding My Niche 75

CHAPTER 14.	89
Preparing for Cyclone	89
CHAPTER 15.	99
Hawaii Bound	99
CHAPTER 16.	109
Visiting the Mainland.	109
Chapter 17	131
Hawaii Part II.	131
CHAPTER 18.	149
Returning to The Cape.	149
CHAPTER 19.	163
Leave in Perth.	163
CHAPTER 20.	181
Farewell H.E.H.	181
CHAPTER 21.	189
Hawaii- Part III.	189
CHAPTER 22.	205
Remain in Hawaii.	205
CHAPTER 23.	221
Hola San Francisco.	221
CHAPTER 24.	237
Bien Venido A México.	237
CHAPTER 25.	289
Getting Home.	289
Conclusion	303
Appreciation	1
Acknowledgements	2
*In Special Remembrance:	3

About the Author 4

CHAPTER 1.

Adiós, Douglas/Agua Prieta y Mi Familia

I'll start with a Welcome, and finding myself in Waikiki sipping Mai Tai's, watching beach babes, ships rolling and gorgeous sunsets! Nah! Kill this scene. Too juvenile.

Next flashback to the jungles of Viet Nam, during the hottest, most humid day imaginable and from our river boat taking pot-shots at Charlie (VCs'), who is well hidden in the lush tall grass sending bursts of return fire. That won't cut it. Hearsay. Not there. Next slide.

We're hunkered down in the cargo bay of the USAF plane in flight over the Pacific, munching cold rations, some chatting, sleeping or with our tape decks listening to Charlie Pride. A little better. Try again.

In my own mind hundreds of memories exist from my Navy time, I just have to pick the right reel, roll-it and away I go. You'll read this later.

Very honestly, I don't know how best to start relating, "The Navy Days of My Trilogy Series", to you dear reader. So, truth and reality are my best approach here, desde el principio. Aqui vamos!

It's about my joining the U.S. Navy and reporting for active duty on a hot summer July day in Douglas, Arizona, at the International Airport, with orders from the Naval Reserve Center.

I felt then like being torched or that the slings and arrows I imagined were flung at me. The emotions and feelings truly overwhelming, penetrating, heart rendering and tearing me apart.

Unlike before when I had flown to boot-camp, now it was for all the marbles, no quick return home. Many were there to see me off, board the bird that would fly me to San Diego.

Women were weeping, kids ran around, and the rest of the groups remained very somber, while I stood in my Whites, holding my tickets and papers.

Pobre Panchita, with her sisters and daughters to support her, held up fairly well. She had known for nearly three years that this day would come, as did others. She religiously prayed her rosary nightly and added a prayer or two for my protection. She even lit candles at Immaculate Conception Catholic Church for my guidance. Such guilt I had at leaving them, a betrayal on my part.

I distinctly recall the small gift, which I have since carried in my wallet, from mi Tia Ester Acosta- un pequeño cruicifijo, de hierro me supongo, y que seguido toco y digo oración. Mi tías y Nina blessed me then and there with it and said a prayer for the Lord, Holy Family and Angels to be my guardians.

This was very touching but did not lessen my anxiety.

I had some fears and reservations about my preparation for any new endeavors I'd be undertaking in the military. So much remained unknown. Only after processing in the next month or so, would I learn my new destination.

Breaking away though, leaving Douglas, the border, the desert, my job at A J Bayless also tickled my fancy, thinking about new adventures, peeking beyond the immediate horizon. I thought sadly de las amistades, los amigos y camaradas que se quedan, más seguros en su diaria rutina.

Yes, there was a bunch of mixed emotions tearing at me on that particular departure day. But let me back up a few days before my take off to the West Coast.

The Navy Days

I took a few responsibilities to heart. I bid farewell to my bosses at A J Bayless where I worked basically as a store clerk for nearly four years while attending college, where I also said goodbye to a few significant others. Goodbye as well to my mates at the Reserve Center.

Adiós también a mis vecinos del barrio, en particular a las Familias Meléndez, Arévalo y Valente.

Hice arreglos para disponer de mi coche. Asegure cuentas bancarias para depositar por correo mis ingresos. Le aseguré a mis Padres que muy seguido les escribire de donde yo me encontrara, así como también les prometí mandarles una mensualidad para su mejor sostén económico.

I got some great parting dates from girl friends from work as well as from college.

I did attend church and received a blessing from the Priest, who said men like me were brave, courageous and patriotic, and giving of themselves for our great Nation.

Back to the departing aircraft and final farewells to those in attendance there to watch me board and fly away to San Diego.

I had checked in, with my duffle bag already on board. Final call from the speaker indicated It's "Time to Go"!

A huge mess of hugs, kisses, handshakes and tears were next with me promising to write back. Saying also that I too would be close by phone.

All aboard and from my window I looked out, waved back to them to say Adios!

The cute young stewardess eyed me, winked and informed me that I had lipstick on my shirt collar, on the left side. From Mom, Sis y tias probably. I still didn't completely understand how the security and protection of our Homeland fell on the shoulders of a punk like me. This had at times been a passing thought, because after all you'd look at me and see an undersized, one hundred-ten-pound runt weighing that much soaking wet, and yet the Navy accepted me. It made a lot of sense. The rifle probably weighed more. So, I did not feel that confident that the USA could really be that safe with sailors like me.

But here I was ready for my big change, first time away long-term from home and Family. In the sky now, I pulled out one of those airline magazines that write little but advertise much about casinos and resorts, travel and such. A quick change over in Tucson and off again. Snacks were handed out, the usual, peanuts, chips and beverages.

Soon the hour was over, and we started our descent. The preoccupying thoughts being replaced by my concentration on the arrival at the airport and making my way to the Naval Base (the Base), very similar to the other times, like flying to boot-camp in 1967. I was alone this time, though.

In the intervening time since then, people who had heard our story were appalled that we only had about seven days of training during the Christmas recess from school. Yet, here we had to go on active-duty, likely live on a floating tin-can without much more preparation.

CHAPTER 2.

Hello San Diego

We touched down and the crew thanked us for being such good passengers and "Welcome to San Diego"! We went to baggage and I lugged my bag and carry-on stuff. I hauled it all to the bus and waited. No rush, it was empty. Once full, it would move. The civilian driver did not seem too interested, just bidding away the time.

After more passengers boarded, we got going, with the trip not lasting long at all.

I do not recall exactly how they processed me. I checked in and had my name crossed off a list and added to another, along with some instructions for the first day. I had my company number and was temporarily assigned a bunk and locker and to be ready at "0800 hours" tomorrow morning. I think that we could not leave the base, and to use the meal ticket for dinner at the chow hall.

More fun tomorrow morning.

I found my barracks, bunk and locker on the third floor, if I correctly recall, where other recent arrivals stayed. I received a few hellos and welcomes. The hall was half empty, but more men would arrive later. Still, the entire building had many empty beds.

Sailors, that is the enlisted men, would come and go beehive style. The main purpose for this set up I was in had to do with receiving men and to determine their next destination. Some went to school, others were discharged or waited for their ship. Medical orders held up some men, while a few landed in the brig.

In my case, my company would be recent arrivals grouped together, usually assigned their number by the date, such as Company 720, consisted of men getting there July 20th, and so on.

I stored some of my items and put the remainder of the duffle bag into the locker, with my old high school 'Masters' gym lock for security. I went to the office but they would not let me use the phones, I therefore got in a Ma Bell booth and dialed home collect to let everyone know I made it safely to California and that I'd be in touch often with them.

Next stop was the mess hall for dinner. This was nearby and fairly well packed mostly by enlisted men in dungarees. All sizes, races and shapes. They came off the ships to dine. Again, I was on a learning curve and being alone, I kept my eyes open and ears peeled to pick up valuable tips.

I followed this with a short stroll down Ships' Row and took a wider view of the base, then I turned towards the barracks, but before going too much further, I called a friend.

Ralph's brother Oscar answered.

The two were from Douglas and we grew up together. Ralph was in the Navy, probably now out at sea. Oscar, an Air Force Veteran, resided in the San Diego area. He worked as a civilian for the Navy doing jet mechanics on Coronado Island. His was highly technical work that kept evolving as electronics and computer systems changed. He repaired different aircraft on the carriers and if I'm not mistaken, he performed similarly on the helos.

He was happy to hear from me.

Over the years, Oscar to me seemed a happy-go-lucky fellow, working, on his feet and smiling. He looked or resembled a White Anglo American of medium height and build with his light complexion. I recall working with or under him in Douglas at his dad's shop, Electric Motor Service.

How long was I in SD? When can we meet? How about the weekend? He queried me. Despite the distance and infrequent contact, he was always there for family and friends from his hometown. Apparently eager to meet these folks.

We left it open for now, but we'd talk some more in the next twenty-four hours.

I returned to the barracks where some kind of racket was taking place. Security, Shore Patrol or whoever was dealing with a situation where someone's locker was busted and he lost money, wallet, etc. All in the blink of an eye.

We had been repeatedly warned, this happened often without any positive outcome, especially with so much transition. It was reported that even civilians posing as sailors got in just to rip-off the barracks.

By this time, more personnel came in with orders to report for duty. It was not just the rumor-mill, but it was July and the new Fiscal year, therefore, more men would be sent to serve their active-duty.

The overhead speaker went on, blaring "Lights Out", after a brief couple of announcements.

I saw the new stragglers walk in, loaded with baggage, probably hungry too, without having had dinner.

Sorry, I can't help you much mate, I just got here, so being new I knew little. Just make yourself as comfortable as you possibly can, find your pad to crash and we'll get it going in the morning.

There are some snack and coke machines downstairs, so help yourself. Phones are there too to call home.

The place seemed chaotic. At all hours men kept coming in, more like a train depot or bus station, they registered and were sent upstairs. Luckily, I was in early.

Right now, I write this entry or a portion on a somewhat odd or different manner, unlike my usual practice to my writing. Which people are starting to ask me about, who have recently read my stuff and musings?

Someone became surprised that I wrote in one day six- or seven-pages last summer (2017), when I vacationed in Boston and I was reading <u>The Last of The Dough Boys.</u> Writing for me mostly equals routine, an hour at the end of the day, or when the muse strikes, rarely now as I gain years.

After slumber of four-plus hours, I woke near midnight and here I find myself comiendo arroz con leche con galletas de almendra, que Gloria sabe bien me gustan y casi siempre las compra y escribo más.

She too finds it odd I do this but is unfazed. She'll never forget, she says, how I once labored twelve hours straight after work to re-do the kitchen plumbing and remodel, and then returned to my job with no sleep.

Maybe the reader by now knows I may at times go random, changing the pace and material differently.

So, it's past midnight, now dark and damp from today's rain and the city lights twinkle below a beautiful glistening view. Yes, I know, this seems farcical.

Returning to San Diego, the summer of '69, and on active-duty. I've talked with a distant longtime friend, Oscar, who in spite of his work either shows bohemianism, a bit beat-nik like style.

You'll read more about him in a few paragraphs.

It's morning the following day, my second one on active duty. Reville, the blaring speakers and the joker (it's the Master at Arms), all make us rise and shine. "Get Up! Get Up! Get Uppp"!!

What seems like a couple of hundred men hit the showers, got dressed in dungarees and made their beds. They walked to breakfast where there are mounds of eggs, potatoes, breads, cereals and more and don't forget the gallons of java- good strong coffee. The chow hall is packed.

By around eight, we are gathered in front and are ordered to fall In, stand at parade rest. Names are called, "Here", you respond, then follow your leader who'll be in charge of the squadron company, group or whatever it's called.

I don't recall much about the names or the souls in my gang, but we numbered about thirty who came in yesterday and now had to move forward and onto the fleet.

I say maybe seven new companies had recently been formed with the Reservists reporting for duty.

Our leader marched us out to a ramada to keep us from the sun. A young guy, maybe twenty-something, Second Class, who did not ride us hard. Easy talker letting us know what to expect, the process and procedures and to call him any time for anything. He said he'll stay with us until the last sailor from the squadron left. He'd then be assigned another company to command and start over.

He gave us handouts outlining activities to get done and places to go. For now, his orientation was brief, but the auditorium in an hour or so would fill and we'd have the real thing, such as Commanders welcoming us aboard.

We won't go hungry but get three meals daily, take physical exams, acquire more clothing, etc., were some of his answers to questions we asked. He stressed that we would be secure and taken care of and loans were available if we went broke. He added we'd be able to wear civilian clothes. Times up so we marched to the auditorium.

The atmosphere seemed relaxed yet quiet. Soon after everyone took a rest and settled down, the panel up front on the stage started talking mostly pablum. Maybe some of us could go to school for training, maybe most of us would end up serving in the Pacific fleet. Maybe a few would make a career out of the Navy.

Some gung-ho remarks were made, like we must fight for our Liberty and Democracy and contain the Soviet threat.

This panel of officers talked as if addressing middle schoolers, a kiddie-corps and hardly mentioned the damn War we were up against and where we could wind up, be killed or maimed........... a strong possibility, even probability!

They dismissed us and our guy said to take off, get something to eat and regroup at thirteen hundred hours at XX.

Our squad began to jell somewhat by now and familiarization started. Even first names were tossed around.

Most mates went to the chow hall and some hung around the barracks talking, smoking, sipping sodas or using the phones.

"Fall In", was the call after lunch. We were informed about what we'd do next- Admin tasks.

We went to a multi-story building where many operations were taking place, such as travel pay, leave, payroll and more. Once there we entered a section that took care of us new arrivals.

The large room contained about two dozen desks occupied by military and civilian personnel: young, old, male, female- more civilian females than others. Each desk had designation by letters, as I recall, meaning that desks handled the record or case by sailor's last name.

We spent most of the afternoon there being interviewed, and our files squared away. Documents were signed, such as life insurance and the listing of our beneficiaries. This took a good deal of time and had to wait it out until the last got done. Really exciting, hooray. But we managed.

After nearly two hours, we were sent to the barracks where our company received specific assignments of a more permanent nature for building numbers, bunks and lockers. This meant we had to move; therefore, we hauled our luggage and such to our new locale. Not a difficult transition at all.

We were free to go until morning once we completed this. This meant getting into our civvies, have dinner and go into town, if we cared to do that. It was Liberty Call.

Everybody did their thing; most went into town. On base one could go bowling, visit the library, be at the theater or work out at the gym. Plenty of distractions.

I had not found my routine yet and I stayed on base, but

The Navy Days

surprisingly I was called to serve. An Italian Navy Cruiser had arrived, anchoring nearby. These sailors had very limited practice with English and needed an interpreter. Voila!

I was asked if I could handle translating for them and I responded positively since Spanish and Italian are very similar. I had a blast talking with the Italian Navy men who were restricted to their ship and the base. I informed them where the chapel, the laundromat, snack bar, etc., were located. Nearly two hours later I was done. They wanted to pay or tip me, but I told them, "No Gracias", it was not necessary, that I enjoyed talking to them. They said I did a great job for one who doesn't speak Italian. Word got around on base.

The incident with the Italians did something. It brought me recognition that squad leaders and others thought it was cool what I did. Even an officer whom I never met nor knew passed along a favorable comment. I think this note was filed in my service record. Who knew? I did something simple, normal, natural for me and that's it. Others thought differently. International intrigue. FAR at your service!

Way later, I thought it was quite decent to be given this attention simply for being bilingual/bicultural.

Continuing with Navy Intro 101, on the third day, how the hell am I supposed to remember. Was it the day we were issued additional clothing, or did we go to the base dispensary for our physical exams? I know that in a few days after I checked into the base, I, along with my group, underwent our physicals, not far from our barracks.

Navy Corpsman and Dental techs prepped us and did the initial work and completed forms we had filled out earlier and submitted. Officers in the Navy Medical Corps then took over, like checking the hearts, lungs, ears, throats etc. Dentists looked at our teeth and mouth. Very cursory and everybody passed.

We'd return later for labs.

For the lunch hour everybody dispersed. Most went to the mess hall, after all it was free, so save your money. It was becoming apparent our squadron started to form small cliques, like the boys from the South hanging out together. Their accents and language would ID them.

In the afternoon, the auditorium held another pep rally for us with different speakers. The chaplain gave us his spiel. We heard from payroll and disbursing. This was amusing.

We were urged to establish a savings account, perhaps through the U.S. Savings Bond Program. They told us about deductions and additional pay for a spouse and dependents.

Of course, everyone had the opportunity to earn more by getting promoted. Time, rating, rank, etc., were explained as well critical ratings. Let's not forget re-enlistments with hefty bonuses. Hazardous pay, overseas duty pay and much more were explained.

I don't recall but at some point, perhaps here, we filled out our dream sheet, a.k.a., the wet-dream sheet. Where sailors listed their choice as to where to serve. Three state-side stations and three abroad. Not often does one get his choice.

I listed Spain, Australia and Japan along with San Diego, Long Beach and San Francisco.

In the scuttlebutt here and there, one listens and picks up valuable information, such as which bases and stations to avoid. Would you believe Hawaii was not a favorite, because it's too small and quite expensive, but there are many women due to tourism. Also avoid Alaska, it's too cold with long dark winters, yet men are sent to Adak and Kodiak, Alaska, which are okay if you like seals, polar bears and thermal underwear.

So, this sort of thing continued, that is being broken in and prepared for active duty, to be sent out to the fleet.

At day's end I figured I'd put on my civvies and go into town after dinner, maybe buy some magazines, shoot some pool, visit the USO or catch a movie. No big deal.

While having dinner I ran into a couple of buddies from the Douglas Naval Reserve Unit and we hit it off, just simply having a great time, a laugh a minute.

I didn't get their whole story and after a half a century, I can barely remember their names. But anyway, the two had put on some weight (from so much starchy potatoes), but they weren't complaining.

The two were on the same ship, an Oiler I think and had made Petty Officer. They completed a West PAC Tour and were in Nam and Hawaii. This lasted about six or seven months y poco les quedaba para salir, unos cuatro o cinco meces y regresar probablemente a Douglas.

Les explique que yo solo empiezo y no se a dónde me va a tocar. Me dijeron que evite el mar y lo barcos porque es una vida dura y pésima. Dios dirá.

Pero si pasamos una tarde inolvidable porque nos fuimos al EM Club y platicamos muchísimo, recordando la vida en la frontera, DHS, CCC, las novias, los carros, el deporte, más mujeres, el futuro y más.

Pronto se llegó la hora y salimos bastante atarantados, pero bien contentos. Nos dimos fuertes abrazos al despedirnos y dándole muchas Gracias a Dios.

More than once I've concluded that this single solitary life can lead down the road of debauchery. Based on some signs I've seen and experiences I've had, y, hijuela, que lindo ser libre y soberano aun algo pelado.

As if fighting a stupid senseless War of politicians and White D.C. men is any better.

Get over it and search or plan for a better destiny than be killed or maimed in battle.

So, I found the barracks, hit the sack and I slept the booze away.

The shower, coffee and pills made my morning better to continue the next day with more meetings or get togethers. More orientation and brain washing followed.

We talked about women and sex. Obviously, Uncle Sam does not want to have more dependents- wives and/or kids. Protection was over emphasized with lectures, films and scare tactics. We had more training on sex than training for the War. Stop venereal diseases, use Trojans, which also are useful in protecting against pregnancy and make terrific water balloons.

We were emphatically warned against getting married, especially overseas as many gals simply wanted a ticket to ride into the USA. Many examples were given that proved this point. What?? Guys have hormones too, get hard and drill. Sometimes there are consequences, sad but very true. These healthy men are in the military service and need servicing!

Another topic was automobiles, which some sailors wanted to bring theirs from home. Typically, the answer was to wait to get to your next duty station.

Staff told the squadron that in the next week or, so we'd be getting shots at Sick Bay (tetanus, malaria vaccines, etc.).

Also, some of us would be receiving our orders to our next assignment, along with funds, travel vouchers, etc. Mostly for sea duty, no training or school. Probably here in San Diego, in the bay, could be where one's ship awaits.

The squad would meet every morning and check progress.

Fall Out! Free Weekend! Liberty Call!!

CHAPTER 3.

Manhood

With the weekend here, I packed my bag with socks, underwear, toiletries and left my uniforms behind. I ate on base and waited until about five-thirty for Oscar, like we had pre-arranged our meeting.

I had a few bucks to last beyond payday, so let the party begin con gusto y alegria. Soon I heard and saw Oscar's green truck pull up, the same one I'd seen before, a little more ruined, beat up and noisier. I think he bought it at a government surplus auction. As long as it ran, was his motto, forget the appearance.

Oscar had already started his weekend and offered a beer, which he bought soon after work. We parked at this tiny Mexican joint because he wanted dinner. I ordered something light while he went full bore. The staff obviously knew him on a first name basis being he's a regular.

He mentioned what we would be doing the three days. This included drinking (and driving), some sightseeing, shooting pool, getting laid, some shopping as his fridge and cupboards were empty and that's not cool for hosting and partying.

Oscar was charming, charismatic, well liked and popular among the groups he hung around with, which were several. He could speak well and was not antagonistic, but he could easily defend himself. In fact, I saw him barge in to stop fights and calm the situation. People really had some respect for him, everywhere he went, like the bars and clubs we visited then and there.

He went around introducing me as one of his honchos from his hometown, a real Mexicano de Agua Prieta. It seemed he had become more Americanized, but Oscar easily reverted to his native tongue and liked talking Spanish with me. He really enjoyed colloquialisms sprinkled with his favorite profanity. When we rode in his truck, he had Spanish radio music broadcast from Tijuana.

That Friday night we ended it late at about three a.m. at his apartment with his biggest grin as they showered together for more fun.

We had breakfast- grilled tortas, cafè y pastel and cleared out of there by one or so. The three girls would return that evening.

He aimed his truck to Coronado but not before gassing up and more beer, chips, etc. He was in a terrific mood, whistling some Mexican tunes, como 'El Corrido de Juan Charrasqueado' y 'Amor Perdido.

Some side notes here. Oscar was a good friend and I looked up to him cuando viviamos en el barrio en Douglas. El mayor que yo por casi diez a doce años y me enseño cosas técnicas en el taller EMS de su papa, así como cosas de la vida.

Oscar siempre tenía novias y según su hermano Rafael que también vivio con él en San Diego, Oscar requeté bien sabia vivir la vida. Vivir para el placer. Sinónimo al corrido ya mentado, Juan Charrasqueado, un incomparable mujeriego asesinado en el amor.

I believed Rafael and now I became completely convinced with lessons from a true sybarite. Maybe not so much voluptuously as he's down-graded materially, but he was a believer and practitioner.

He really opened my eyes in many ways and educated me in ways parents would not approve. He encouraged me, Rafael and others to live it up. Forget the past. Especially since we were going to War and who knows what happens then. Could be tragic.

Further, he counseled us to change. He saw this in himself and left Douglas for the Air Force (he served four years). Once on our own, you shed your shackles and are free. The home and Family can abort your freedom and curtail your maturity and development.

Oscar believed that men were set up, in a manner that punishes men and he did not buy into the equation favored by the churches, government, religions, society, etc. What a crock he said, to be stuck with the load of supporting a family, basically becoming enslaved and indentured.

Food for thought by the ton. Decades later Oscar softened his tone and rebellious streak. He'd gotten older and I listened to him, learned something, joked and laughed. Time changed him, Ralph said, as did the cheap leaky condoms that had made him a dad.

So, we hopped on the freeway and proceeded to Coronado Island, across the bay. I may be a bit confused here, but I recall that we remained in the truck to drive it onto the ferry or barge, then paid the fee. After crossing, we landed in Coronado. Oscar might have used the pretext of work to show me his job, the garages, jets and more. Highly impressive armament that Uncle Sam kept. We toured some more and walked on the aircraft carrier, doing some inspecting of sorts.

Afterwards, we drove around and stopped at the famous Coronado Hotel and walked to the beach.

We followed this with a ride onto the bay bridge, which the old truck struggled to climb. Huffing and puffing, hissing and pissing, moaning and groaning, but it made it over the top and we coasted into the city and met the freeway.

I may be off, but I feel certain it was 1969, when this took place, the year that the Coronado Bay Bridge was completed. If not, it may've been later when I went to San Diego and again met Oscar. But fun, girls and partying with him a lo grande lo hicimos cuando llegue alli'.

Leaving Coronado Island, Oscar went for groceries for

dinner, buns, beer, beverages, steaks, meat, veggies, chips, etc. We went to his pad to host a party. We straightened the place and put on some music. Herb Albert was popular.

Guests arrived with dishes of salads, dips and such. A total I'd say maybe fifteen. Very casual, peaceful and relaxed. Oscar the chef grilled steaks, wieners, patties, and the girlfriends set up the kitchen with plasticwares.

We sat around inside and out on a beautiful southern California afternoon. Some drinking, some weed but all very cool, laid back and enjoying the music. Visitors served themselves potluck style with plenty of food to gorge on. All very delicious.

The whole experience was very enjoyable to me, but not entirely new and reminded me somewhat of my days at Cochise College when some friends hosted similar cookouts. Only here I was mostly among strangers ten years or so older than me. I held my own quite well, mostly speaking English.

Saturday night we took into Sunday morning so that by one or two a.m. most people had left, taking some food samples with them, because it made no sense to toss the leftovers.

Those six or so remaining paired off, and soon the bed springs were creaking and ohhh the moaning, until everybody passed out and welcomed sleep beyond the cool morning.

Sunday morning, I got up really early, freshened up, got dressed in my Sundays best and went like a good Catholic to mass. Not! Never!

We were all fairly well hungover and slept late. Showers and strong coffee with aspirin helped.

Oscar and I left once his residence was emptied of guests.

He suggested Tijuana for breakfast then changed his mind, too much traffic, the congested border crossing and our late start. Some other day he promised. Breakfast we ate though en un changarro algo inútil, pero con café super y sabrosísimo menudo acompañado con torta de queso, jamón, tocino o lo que guste uno.

El menudo tan tito rojo pero una pata deliciosa con tuétano ay, ni se diga. Para la cruda, no hay nada mejor que el menudo con Limón o lima, cebolla verde, cilantro y más.

Nos dimos un hartazón bárbaro y quedamos bien felices y muy satisfechos. Quien lo iba creer que un puesto junto a la carretera podía servir buenísimos platillos. Que ni se de cuento el departamento de salubridad porque lo cierran.

Nos dirigimos de tan fabuloso restaurante a varios sitios como Sea World and the San Diego Zoo, as well as some of the beaches which were crowded- normal for the weekend.

CHAPTER 4.

Living My Best Life

Oscar had other plans for the evening with which I went along, this suited me fine.

He picked up some wine, a pie and a cheap bouquet then we stopped at his house. He freshened up, splashed on some cologne and dressed in a nice clean light blue short sleeve shirt.

I packed my gear since I would be returning to the base, but not yet, not before dinner.

It turns out Oscar had a date con esta chava tan linda y elegante, en una vecindad HulaLa! Como grito cantinflas o uno de esos comediantes.

Nice towering condos with balconies and ocean views. What in hell was I doing here? Oscar con su diablura estoy seguro me trajo para tener más entrada con esta Doña. Whatever. It worked.

We dinied totally the opposite of how we ate breakfast this morning.

She was a very refined, educated lady from a well-off family back in the mid-west. I think she was in banking after training in asset management and accounting. Impecable manners. Que le vio a mi cuate, este amigo pelado de mi barrio. Even Oscar's gifts of wine, etc., looked out of sorts, beneath her tastes.

I had a ball entertaining her poodle, listening to classical music and taking in the seascapes.

The sumptuous dinner came right out of 'House and Garden', Julia Child's kitchen or the Waldorf- Astoria. Dios Mio. Como para un ejercito, tanto asi!

We started with a terrific cocktail of jumbo shrimp and a tray of hor d'oeuvres- olives, cheese, etc. The rolls were a bit like sourdough in taste but delicious. There followed a prime rib roast out of this world with some fancy red potatoes syrup and carrots. Ohhh My!

I tried out my best table manners, but these were lacking- elbows on the table, mixed up the silverware and dropped the cloth napkin. Duhhh!

Dessert was too much. Over the top, like swirl ice cream with a small souffle tart. Who eats like this?? Are we supposed to be impressed?! I saw the writing. The trap was being set to catch Oscar. The bearded goat knew the game well and played along.

This was my clue, my exit. "Sorry but I must excuse myself and return to base".

Oscar gave me a quick lift to the bus stop, where we bid adios. I retrieved my bag, thanked him and we'd talk and meet up again soon. He high tailed it back to the tower or condos. Well you can only imagine the rest of their evening, which Oscar later described as censored or some other terrific excuse.

What an extraordinary weekend. Unforgettable! Like Mr. Nat King Cole whispers with that smokey voice- I thought while sitting on a bench waiting for the bus back to the base.

Something like eight or nine when I walked into the barracks, where some guys watched tv in the lounge or were reading newspapers. Upstairs a few friendly card games took place.

One or two of the mates asked how my weekend went. What did I do? Where did I go, and they had noticed that I had been away a long time? Yep! I said, friends in town took care of me and showed me a great time.

Nothing much happened on base besides eating the sloppy meals, doing laundry, catching a movie and such.

Guess again! Some sailors did not return until morning, one or two of them slept in the drunk tank in Tijuana, where they lost their wallets and/or virginity.

What a weekend, Madre Mia!

CHAPTER 5.

Back to Reality

Monday started my second week of regular Navy and it sure seemed it had nada, nothing to offer like the weekend did.

For some reason some sailors seemed too beholden to me because I, Mexican, spoke Spanish and can instruct one on the ways of the south. That's because they wanted no trouble going to Tijuana. Tijuana starts with a capital 'T' and it means 'Trouble'! Be advised, Pendejos!

As if I'm the Oracle and can provide wisdom, guidance and the money exchange rate. I did what I could, which was very little to nothing.

But getting on, the squad was accounted for after rollcall and assignments were given. There was not enough work for everybody so I wound up in the lounge in the barracks. I had bet that we would be called, but it didn't happen.

For three seamen, however, their orders came in but the three remained in suspense. Yes, the orders arrived but they were not told where they would be going, when they'd be moving on or what their assignments were. Sort of like the policy of 'Hurry Up and Wait', that the military loves. Right out of Yosarian's mouth in 'Catch 22', by Joseph Heller.

Hence the squadron remained intact, but for three buddies

who could possibly leave in the middle of the night to who knows where, most likely Nam.

Meanwhile our group fought boredom. After morning rollcall. The assignments were killers of time picking up litter, washing windows, cutting the grass, if we weren't hanging around the barracks.

Towards the end of the week the squadron was hustled to the base dispensary. It happened in the morning and I'm fuzzy on the details. I think we carried our medical records. Whatever. It must have been the day for shots, not only for my men and I, but probably half of the fleet. Luckily, we got punched on the upper arm. Can you imagine having to view hundreds of butts or twice the cheeks? No thanks! That's pretty gross indeed.

Other than tv, the library, the EM Club or movie theater, not too much action on the base. I did take the bus into town, even had dinner there when Oscar picked me up mid-week and we went for burgers and fries. He asked and I answered, "no orders or assignments for me yet".

By the end of the week we lost a couple of friends who received orders for Nam, but only after a short-term school. Maybe three weeks, afterwards go deal with security.

Not much changed which by now was mid-July.

Oscar and I met that Friday afternoon and we drove south to Chula Vista and National City. We hung near there once he took care of some business. Simple, just dinner, some beers and shot the eight ball.

Llegamos a su chante- temprano, como entre las diez o once. This evening we had talked about me staying in San Diego to serve my time in the Navy. His brother, Rafael did a year or more with boot-camp, school and his assignment to a ship. Maybe it could work out for me, after all I did indicate San Diego on my dream sheet.

Oscar has been a Godsend, despite his flaws, also has a good heart, compassionate and generous.

I used his phone, if I recall correctly, to call Douglas and report my Navy story in San Diego thus far.

All were happy to hear from me just like I loved talking with Mom, Ed and Clara. Dad got very emotional mas que mi Mama, his voice cracked and trembled. This really touched me that I wished I could be there to comfort them and assure them all will be alright.

Maybe fifteen minutes and the call was over, with many thanks to Oscar de mi Familia y yo por el uso del telefono. I gave him a few bucks for everything- gas, food, phone, etc. He said it wasn't necessary, I insisted, so he took it.

Oscar tried to support me in several ways, be uplifting and offering much encouragement. The use of his vehicle alone was a time saver and economical.

The next day, Saturday, we crossed into Tijuana, probably about ten a.m. since sleep, snoring and dreams had comforted us sweetly. Quick showers, breakfast on the run and onto the freeway, then across la linea a Mexico.

"Don't Try Any Funny Shit"! Oscar warned me, with his best USAF Drill Sergeant, macho imitation (Lame). Debemos tener mucho cuidado que aquí sí que se ponen bien perros. ¡Abre los ojos!

"Y, además, no andamos en pinché Agua Prieta. ¡Acuérdate, cabron estas en el Navy y te pueden chingar a lo bruto"!

Oscar drove the point home. "Don't Fuck Up"!!

He gave other warnings/ instructions, kind of like what they told us at our Navy orientation. Civvies, not uniforms are better for the military in Tijuana. Secure your money, wallets, jewelry or risk losing them. Leave your compassion and empathy on the northside of the border. Careful what you eat. Whatever you do, forget the drugs and getting drunk, which many ignored.

TJ was crawling con Americanos, either pale or tan y hablando Ingles, milling mostly around shops, picking up leather goods, jewelry, trinkets and booze- Tecatè, Bacardi, José Cuervo muy populares.

Oscar knew the city well and the place knew him. He was on a first name basis with cops, merchants, putas, street vendors y Más.

We rolled around a while, watching kids hollering "bola", "chicle", or hustling newspapers, religious items and food.

Towards noon, Oscar fue a ver una de sus novias, que yo ni sabia quien, como, donde ni cuándo. Apparently, he was setting up a date for dinner tonight.

Muy guapa la joven. Esvelta, pelo largo y bien vestida. Girls from Mexico's interior move north with friends and roommates rent an apartment splitting the costs. They work at maquiladoras, retail, government jobs, etc. They intend to enter the USA by snatching un Americano anyway they can, and the men fall for it rather easily- muy facilmente. Oscar said he's seen it a thousand times or more over the years. "Gabachos Pendejos", he sneered, shaking his head.

He next took us to a shack towards the beach where he knew el cantinero, cocinero, músicos y toda la bola, un ambiente alegre y popular donde apenas empezaba el día. Pedimos cervezas y mariscos; el camarones y ostiones, yo siete mares.

Nos quedamos un rato, comiendo, platicando, viendo la plebe y escuchando las canciones.

El mar rítmico, con las olas y las gaviotas rompiendo el silencio o interrumpiendo el ruido.

By this time the tide began coming in, we started to leave to pick up his girlfriend.

We went upstairs and inside, a nice set-up and very clean. We stayed briefly and little did I anticipate having a date, thanks to my buddy, who chauffeured us four in his old truck to a restaurant bar set up with live music and dancing.

What a night! Very sweet girls with a great sense of humor.

All four of us and the large crowd talked, dined, danced and drank until the wee hours, fairly polluted. In Mexico some bars do not close, but we did and took our friends home.

Oscar and she disappeared indoors, but not before he tossed me some lids because he didn't think it be cool me becoming a dad'. Right, so she and I talked while in the cab.

I'll tell you what, GMC makes good shocks and springs with all our bouncing. After we went inside and I stayed on the sofa, she then joined me. Anyway, I didn't sleep much being afraid of getting assaulted. It was a terrific night even if I was on a blind date. Hey what the hell, I'm still learning, I'm not suave nor debonair. I was new at this!

Morning light hit me, and I woke up dazed, my mouth fully starched while I came slowly out of my confused and discombobulated state. I finally came to and heard some roosters crowing.

I waited a while and then gently rapped on the door to be invited in and offered rico cafè que hasta al difunte lo despierta. She looked prettier than before, in the light of day. Definitely, she'd find her Americano.

The other couple came down. More coffee for everyone y mas platica. They talked about morning mass which Oscar and I would pass, but we all went to breakfast. Afterwards near noon, we dropped the two at the church nearby.

For the next hour we rode around and ran errands as Oscar compro pan, chiles y latas. Luego le dimos al norte, pero nos tardamos en la garita con una línea larga de tráfico. Al fin pasamos y serian ya cerca de las tres.

De verdad pasamos muy buen tiempo. Oscar me dijo que a las dos damas él tiene tiempo que las conoce, pero no piensa en caso serio, solo la trata muy linda. Ella's piden mas.

We continued north on the freeway with him talking about his cat and mouse games.

The truck came to a halt near the Main Gate and I walked

onto the base, but not before I thanked Oscar. We BS'd a quick minute and he said he would call, or visa-versa. He wished me luck and to keep him informed.

I reached the barracks and crawled into my sack then passed out for a couple of hours or more. It was dark when I awoke to the noise of new arrivals reporting for duty. Paying no attention I went to the snack machine for a bite, then returned and done for the night.

A usual Monday morning. Up. Clean up. Shape up, then roll-call and roll-out. Some light work picking up litter, especially near the entertainment spots (EM Club, bowling alley), from the weekend. We filled up some plastic bags. The routine was nothing but dull and boring.

That evening I wrote a letter or two and mailed them. Not a happy Monday.

Tuesday morning however held different news. After morning muster, Andrew and I were pulled aside to meet with our squad leader for a few minutes.

It turned out our orders were in and both of us would be going off together to God knows where. Soon we'd learn something to get excited about, but not too much.

The other sailors querried us, but we couldn't say much since we didn't yet know our destination.

This is how Andy and I met and became closer, covering each other's back. We had seen one another but hadn't said much.

In fact, Andy is not his name, as I'm protecting him and respect his privacy. He may still be alive for all I know; I have no clue to where he's at this moment. We simply disconnected after the Navy, but I salute and thank him.

He was a strong, hirsute, dark, burly fellow who didn't talk much, joked little and seemed serious. We had the same age or close.

From what I remember, he had a semester of college and

The Navy Days

joined the Navy Reserve to avoid the draft like many young men (such as myself). He had a few jobs but not much to brag about, at twenty that's to be expected.

We would only become more acquainted with each other.

For whatever the reasons there was more togetherness and it was noticeable among the ranks. Such as toiling on the same work details, meals, etc., but still we weren't Mutt and Jeff, Batman and Robin or any of that. Andy was Andy from the south with a Mexican for a partner. Not the best match-up, but will it work?

By now our squadron had shrunk and men were leaving to/or for different assignments. Again, most wound up as grunts, cheap labor for the Navy and served on the ships in the harbor.

Around mid-week Oscar and I talked. When I informed him, I had my orders, he responded that my partner and I would probably be sent overseas, hence the delay with processing us. He was prescient.

That Friday Andy and I again were ordered to the office for a longer meeting to have developments explained. In a week or so, perhaps at the end of the month we would fly to Australia. First several things needed to be handled properly, such as air travel, money, lodging, etc.

In passing, someone mentioned that our dream sheet request had been granted. Nothing else to do but hurry up and wait. We couldn't take leave to go home and bid farewell to our Families, if my memory has not failed me.

I called Douglas para informar a mi Familia las noticias. Ellos triste, pero también satisfechas. Ed más porque yo no estaría en el mar tan peligroso y no me toco un barco, pero una base, quedándome fijo en unas barracas por casi dos años. Él no se sentía casi nada de pesimista y consideraba mi cambio como una aventura más en mi vida y desarrollo. Y me advirtió que siempre con mucho cuidado y con Dios en la boca.

Pues con ese pendiente empezamos el fin de semana cuando llego Oscar a recogerme en la base. Andy was not in this picture.

Over dinner and beers, we talked plenty about my going overseas. He made many valuable points by wisely noting similarities between his days in the Air Force and my time in the Navy. He said he did likewise with Rafael, our brother.

Oscar said to save some funds for my post Navy days after discharge. Be wise with the ladies, many who just want a ticket to America. Obey commands given and do not talk back or be a bad mouth. Man up, don't wimp-out or cry for mama.

Do Not Volunteer!

It didn't take long while we sat by the bar and ate when Oscar's friends stopped and greeted him. He mentioned to them I would be going Overseas with the Navy. People would pitch-in their two cents worth of advice, history, cautions and "congratulations", or "you lucked out- not Nam"!

Oscar said he'd pick me up in the morning at the same spot, but for now we had to go. Something I sensed, about seeing his girlfriend the accountant.

I asked to be dropped downtown. Dicho y hecho. Puro mata tiempo, sin que hacer. Pronto tome el camión a la base y me quede un rato en el club, solo, pensando temas pesados como mi cambio a Australia, la separación de mi Familia y cosas por el estilo. Calculando.

En la mañana Oscar me levanto y nos fuimos a Old Town donde comimos y turisteamos. Muy bonito lugar, estilo parque con mucho entretenimiento y diversión. Tiene un ambiente muy mexicano, con música, bailes folkloricas y otras presentaciones y mucha alegría.

I saw the chapel in or near Old Town, I believe maybe the Immaculate Catholic Church, as I visited and said a few prayers and sought blessings in my new ventures. Just being apprehensive.

We proceeded to Newport Village (or is it Seaport Village), where we ate al fresco- delicious seafood which we walked off by strolling around the park. Soon enough, just about everyone there admired a splendid sunset of orange, yellow, blue and turquoise lighting the sky.

The day was one of not doing much but lots of thinking and contemplation, being grateful for having a friend, someone like Oscar, to be there to bounce ideas around, with getting good and informative feedback. Crucial probably to enjoy such company when one is removed from home with tough choices ahead.

Sometime later before heading to Oscar's place, he showed me the Old Point Loma Lighthouse in the Cabrillo National Monument, but I'm somewhat vague on this, so kindly excuse me.

Once at Oscar's, he put some music on, got some chilled glasses and downed some Sangria.

Sangria was a favorite of his Mother's at the end of the day and that's how he acquired a taste for it, he told me.

We sat in the semi-darkness with silence between us, the soft music and few words. Oscar appreciated my situation and felt or knew that it's best this way without a crowd, noise or celebration.

I had mentioned to him that Andy and I would be flying together to Australia but stayed mostly quiet except for a few superficial questions about my fellow traveler.

Without warning I dozed off and soon went to sleep with a lot of help de la Sangria.

Morning came and not much happened except I tagged along with Oscar, who headed southeast on the freeway towards El Cajon but not that far. He had some affairs to deal with in one of those smaller towns surrounded by agricultural fields. He was in an abbreviated mood, not too talkative. His visit I gathered seemed work related.

At this point I felt Oscar was being supportive and being a good friend, knowing full well of our pending separation. His life would go on, back to normal and continue with its usual routine.

The companionship he gave me he provided to his brother as well.

This happens thousands of times daily, especially in very mobile societies not just America or Western civilization. I say this from experience and observations. The Rivera's left Mexico for the USA and along the way obtained support, help, advice, etc., from relatives and friends.

Many move from villages, small towns and other communities. Relatives and friends follow and are given a helping hand in finding jobs, housing and assistance in resettling. Similarly, with me who gladly received Oscar's kindness.

My life was unfolding in ways that were not fully known by me as I would be traveling far to the other side of the world, hopefully on safe voyage and be well received.

We returned to San Diego early having lunch and snacks as we rode in the truck.

I thanked Oscar for being such a great host and so benevolent, but he simply took it in stride. We realized that this was likely our last get together being I'd be leaving shortly with orders in hand, duty Overseas in Australia.

We shook hands nos dimos un fuerte abrazo al despedirnos at the gate to the base.

CHAPTER 6.

Preparing to Leave

In the next few days, probably by Thursday, Andy and I were prepped for send-off into the Pacific Navy. I don't have good memory of this nor the order of things, but I'll give it a shot.

With his notes and mine we only became more confused, such as what to wear. In San Diego, its American summer, therefore white uniforms, but in Australia it's winter so do we don our blues, which are thick, hot and heavy but much cleaner.

We were advised to take "American extras", because we'd be in an isolated location. Like deodorant, candy, sodas, etc., -where items or products were hard to find.

The dispensary gave us another physical exam, more thorough and I think more shots, probably to lower our libido because we'd be seeing very few females at our new station.

People joked with us and told us to get used to kangaroo meat, like steaks, hamburgers, sausage and even recipes. Even souvenirs that we'd bring back, such as koala bears- not teddy bears and boomerangs. We just laughed it off and enjoyed the humor.

But reality finally set-in with things no longer in the air, nor any plans. We received orders and the itinerary, with personnel, medical and pay records. Funds and plane tickets too.

The exact scenario is lost, but a broader sketch of those days included mis telefonasos a Douglas con mi gente. Tambien me despedí de Oscar. Algunos campaneros en San Diego les dije adios.

I did my laundry, turned in my linens and relinguished my locker.

I believe Andy and I were the last two remaining members of our squadron. It was now dissolved and only God knows where they went, stateside or overseas.

No recuerdo como llegamos al aeropuerto, pero tal vez, bordamos el camión o un taxi. There we checked in, like hundred if not thousands of military- Marines, Army and Sailors. Andy and I were hanging tight, within eyeball distance, but not even that far or apart.

Civilian aircraft (back then more airlines existed, and many have gone like the dinosaurs), possibly Continental, would fly us to Hawaii for our much later connection.

The airport lounge seemed no big deal and we waited for the "Now Boarding" call. How many times has the call been the last one for soldiers heading to Nam?

Many other authors such as Pat Conroy, (I thoroughly enjoyed his 'Prince of Tides', such great writing- the Nolte-Streisand flick wasn't bad either) would expound about us being cannon fodder, feeding the war machine, etc. But not me, not here. I lack that talent nor could I find a medicine man to tell me I had bad ankles and/or bone spurs. This is it, the real McCoy, but lucky enough to escape the rice-paddies and Charlie. Andy and I knew it and we most definitely counted our blessings and rosary beads.

CHAPTER 7.

Anchors Aweigh

"Now Boarding", one way or another we made it to our seats, side by side. I didn't bring much on board, probably just my pouch containing Navy papers and some candy, gum and flower seeds.

My first time on a larger airliner on a much longer trip, over the ocean at that. Soon we were rolling, and it seemed within seconds we were at our cruising altitude and had our ears popping.

The adrenalin was coursing through me and caused nervousness, excitement and anxiety that had to be controlled, quite thoroughly, in the tube with a few hundred passengers. No outlet existed nor found to burn off this energy or feeling. The fidgeting gradually subsided with the drinks of vodka tonics and some headphone music.

I read some of the magazines and newspapers, but then settled in when the movie started.

A meal was served afterwards, and this seemed right out of Swanson's frozen tv dinners. This caused drowsiness that led to sleep but only briefly. This flying affair was by now close to four hours, which meant that we would be landing in Hawaii earlier than anticipated or was it the different time zone.

Maybe we were indifferent, perhaps I was naive and did not know what to expect.

A lot less turbulence for sure, not what we had been told

back on the base in San Diego. Turbulence in flight and on the streets.

Royalty was not the treatment we were given but the times and our uniform made for, shall I say discomfort, after all, "baby killers", "butchers" and " war mongers", were terms the protesters yelled in public or on the streets.

We didn't ask for this and many of us were serving reluctantly, avoiding Canada or being arrested.

Touch down Hawaii.

FLASHBACK! WARNING! APOLOGIES!!

It's one of those mental lapses that occur and here goes- it's military related though sometimes the ideas go elsewhere, and they're not all unpleasant thoughts. Ask any old guy and he'll wonder y pensar de sus romances del pasado. Bonito!

So, I am officially working mid-week probably one o'clock, summer or so and feeling sluggish from lunch. Es hora de mi siesta, even if I'm in Australia, que no.

I must run an errand, I don't exactly recall where to, perhaps payroll or such. I tell the office mates I gotta go and they answer, "fine". I grab my hat and walk the hall, open the door and step outside.

OH SHIT!?%*%@#!!

It's the devil himself, herself, whatever. Straight out of hades!

The guys hear me and follow wondering what's wrong, why am I yelling.

I yell that the creature escaped paradise, leaving Adam and Eve and just arrived here.

Oh fuck! Wow! Damn! Everyone is saying.

After my nerves settled a bit, we kind of admired the serpent that's coiled in front of us. I recall it was a big fat snake common to the Northwest Cape. Quien sabe, maybe a creature of land, water or both. Probably more afraid of us sailors, than we are.

I checked my fruit of the looms, but luckily, they remained dry no hash marks.

We were prohibited from killing wildlife. I can understand why. Half the enlisted men would be dead from drinking, brawling, etc., but we couldn't touch the kangaroos, lizards and such.

So, I was instructed to proceed with my errands, but before jumping on my bicycle and taking off we figured the reptile was seeking shade, a cool spot and the air conditioner might have lured it to the door.

Nothing cool about me getting scared like that.

I completed my errand somewhat quickly and returned to the office, keeping an eye on the serpent.

The staff informed me security came and picked up the snake, put it in a garbage can, with a lid and hauled it away far into the desert.

Aloha! Whine! Grass skirts!

Yeah, yeah, yeah but not that big of a deal after departing from the big jet and the large crowd, we made it to baggage claims. We found our muletas verdes y nos fuimos al frente. He was always more gun-ho than me and now more so.

I feel pretty comfortable saying here that we had to be at the US Air Force Base, Hickam Airfield, but my timing seems off. I might have walked leisurely and done some sightseeing. Either way we arrived at Hickam and boarded a military cargo plane to Australia, or we waited a day or two at the barracks. We didn't get into any trouble but were simply following orders which specified certain hours.

The aircraft was ready and from the lounge they marched us up the steps and into the cargo bay, about twenty of us all in our various uniforms. This was way different, in complete contrast to civilian flights.

No fancy ramps, pretty stewardesses, elegant food or movies. Ni Madre. It reminded me of a tunnel-long dark and gray. Minimal lighting. Netting, pallets, belts and ropes galore. Plus, overhead wiring.

I'd swear that if I had to piss it would be in a bottle or a hole on the floor and let it out. That was my initial impression. Ugly, backwards, unimaginative was our observation, designed by Orville Wright.

I think that we got a bagged lunch- fruit, chips, soda and sandwiches. Not much. We sat on long metal benches with safety harnesses. Keep in mind I'm describing perhaps one model of aircraft, not all the military ones I flew on. Basically, generally, they were all alike. This was not Air Force One. I don't recall any weapons on these birds nor were we given a parachute.

Bear in mind the loads went in first, consisting of boxes, machinery, supplies crated and what not in the long-centered aisle from floor to ceiling. Tons of it! We sat like in an alley between tall walls and the cargo. Everything went through the back of the plane with huge hydraulic or pneumatic doors opening like jaws.

Damn, if the boxes shifted or became loose, we could be crushed, but all seemed very, extra safely tied down, bundled and held together in the nets and gray thick tarps.

We were told to not act foolishly and obey commands. Remain strapped for most of the flight and try to stay warm. The crew was then introduced.

CHAPTER 8.

Meet me at H.E.H.

A short while later the aircraft came to life by starting to shake, make noise and light up. It was a lumbering beast with a long wingspan and roaring propellers. The dark green/gray whale-like monster started slowly crawling into position for takeoff. Note: I'm almost certain it had propellers- not jet engines.

Given the thumbs up we gained speed, but it was hard to believe we'd take off because it seemed to me that we were traveling too slow to climb. Up, Up and Away!

Yet we succeeded and looking outside I could see how busy the Hawaiian skies were as it had a bunch of bugs flying around. The many airplanes reminded me of hornets about their hive.

I swear I even saw Cantinflas in his colorful rainbow hot-air balloon humming "Around the World in Eighty Days".

Soon enough the passengers started chumming-it up about this, that and many other topics. I experienced a huge ahaa momento porque realise algo demasiado significante que para siempre me afecto.

Tal vez seria debido a la altura, las nubes y los cielos tan azules.

Me supongo que Uds. no podrán definir lo que les voy a

contar aqui en el siguiente párrafo. What a blow! My ego zilch!

It occurred to me and me alone, not the others, that my days of speaking Spanish would be over for a very long time. As I was transcending almost totally and completely into the English-speaking culture of American, Australian and that of the British Commonwealth. Que chingas Madres!

Imaginense un Mexicano chatting the Kings English! Wow! What a trip! Yet this truly happened.

Nevertheless, I would later write letters in Spanish to my Parents weekly or more often as well as to some of my parientes en Mexico.

There were to be projects as you will read, where I employed my Spanish.

Hell, I even taught a little bit of Spanish to a few, the Australians and the Americans, both civilians and Navy men.

More about this later.

Back to our MAC Flight. Over the many times I watched these as a passenger and as arrivals on our base in Australia, that's the code word for military air command. Don't ask for more cause I'm no authority. No, they are not from McDonald's flying burgers and fries.

But anyway, we were huddled and had broken the ice, talking with one another- our hometowns, athletics and families. We had covered all corners of the USA. Very obvious was that none of those flying had wealthy backgrounds, nor were any connected politically such the son of a U.S. Senator. This scenario repeatedly presented itself and even today one sees this.

In our group were some Airmen who would be dropped off in New Zealand, where the USA has connections there as well as down in the Antarctic region.

Before we went there though the plane stopped at one spot or another. I think on my first trip over the Pacific we landed in America Samoa (Pago, Pago), and took care of whatever business was necessary. About a three hour stop-over where we ate, stretched and met the locals. A crowd of very large, solid, hefty people like some Hawaiians.

The time and length of each flight is not known, but these were of long duration between islands. I didn't recall when I flew that we encountered problems of bad weather.

We would fly, stop, refuel, replenish then aboard, then bored. Reading, music, sleeping occupied us while hurdling through space and the time zones.

On my first trip to Australia we had a few hours in Christchurch, New Zealand, I think. We made it across to Sydney and remained there overnight.

New Zealand was a drop off point for some four Air Force passengers who served there or went further to the South Pole.

Christchurch in particular was/is very pretty with scenic landscapes, manicured lawns and much greenery. Picture perfect with the people taking great pride in their country, neighborhoods and homes.

I recall how older vehicles, not antiques were everywhere, new autos rarely seen.

CHAPTER 9.

Initiation to N.W. Australia

Landing in Sydney did not take long, and we had an overnighter, the next day to our Northwest destination.

The several times I crisscrossed the Pacific Ocean, the itinerary was pretty much as described above with some variation of one type or another of course.

Sydney had a great deal to offer I'm sure that's the reason the Air Force pilots flew there. For the fun and the loving.

Keep in mind that the War in Viet Nam was going on, that soldiers were nerve-wrecked and exhausted. To provide some relief for them they were given R&R, rest and relaxation. Besides Sydney, Hawaii was another place where the military would send its weary fighters for well-deserved fun and recreation. Seems to make sense or does it actually do the opposite.

The costs are astronomical, mind boggling, beyond comprehension. I'd guess that my tour of duty up to this point cost in the millions when you consider the aircraft, fuel, personnel flying it and the numerous airfields where we landed, and much more.

But it was not for small minds like mine to reason why, but to follow orders, do or die. I think that's how the message goes.

I learned many officers and enlisted men in the military

loved a twenty-year career and pension. So do the big manufacturers and corporations getting fat government contracts that paid for weapons, food, clothing and other items of War.

I'm rather ambivalent about much of this, after all I served and paid my dues.

I cannot deny that I was learning much and having a great experience.

On to Sydney and talk about a great experience. It was likely on this trip that we rocked at the Kings Cross.

First of all, Australians then and now very much like Americans and the alliance is strong. In fact, Australians fought the Viet Nam War also at the same time.

Sydney was teaming with American soldiers on R&R at the Kings Cross when we flew in. Talk about debauchery, bacchanalia, whoring and such. Hell, the place was running out of condoms and sex toys. Booze was overflowing everywhere. Dollars were flying.

The Kings Cross of Sydney in the late sixties and early seventies was a small district or area in or around the vicinity of the wharf or water. Strippers, escorts, hell raisers- it was becoming seedier, noisy, raucous daily into the early morning hours, with a drug scene too. It was the time of the Beatles, free love, grass, LSD (laid several days), and whatever else, I'm glad I experienced it and tasted it. We all did: the fighting soldiers, local Australians, our flight crews and fellow travelers. It sure as hell reminded me a bit of life in my hometown and Agua Prieta.

Sydney and the Kings Cross out did them all in my humble estimation and experience. San Francisco my close second.

Many hours of sleep were lost, the hangovers lasted days if not weeks and hunger was unknown and who had time to grab a bite??

While at Kings Cross, I felt love and a marriage proposal.

I was in uniform and girls fell for mine. One seemed intent and serious after the loving, but I had a plane to catch nor did I feel the connection. More like she wanted a ticket to ride to the USA, and ride we did.

But this was fairly typical of what was happening in the Kings Cross, and I repeatedly heard similar stories which I did not write home about such accounts.

In those days I also learned about the unwanted pregnancies that resulted from such wanton disregard and sailors, the state departments, etc., having to deal with them matters of paternity, child support and such.

Luckily, I escaped.

The Kings Cross was not the only act in town. It certainly attracted the base or lower tendencies of men. For others, the coming attraction was the Sydney Opera House, a true architectural wonder near the water.

This cultural center is renowned throughout the world for its futuristic design, its events and crowning glory that it brings to that part of the world.

But for uncouth military guys like me who lacked culture, finesse, and better things in life, naw the King's Cross rocks.

I'll die and, in my grave, I will relive those few but terrific times I had at the King's Cross.

'Viva La Cruz Del Ray' the Hispanic G.I.s would holler. AMEN

CHAPTER 10.

U.S. Navy Routine

The MAC-Flight crew and remaining passengers were up and on time for morning take off, with everybody sucking coffee and another few their Camel's. We picked up half a dozen sailors heading back to their naval station in the Northwest. They had been on leave.

The long flight would equal one from Miami, Florida to Seattle, Washington one way. I'd say over three thousand miles and six hours flight time. I recall a stop at Alice Springs or somewhere mid-continent. My knowledge about this was that the pilots put in long hours, because after dropping us off they returned to Sydney that same day. Not always but most of the times. Some of these times and miles need some tweaking here for better accuracy, but I hope you get the gist of the flights.

One looooong, boring flight in a practically windowless plane. Like riding inside a bullet. Here and there I caught a view of the red dry terrain everywhere with little to see from our twenty-thirty-thousand-foot elevation.

We brought it down somewhere in a huge cloud of dust and I can't honestly say it was Alice Springs, but it was ugly with a Tombstone, Arizona territorial feel to it. I did not see any Alice spring, walk or run.

If King's Cross was the height, apogee or Zenith, mid-Australia was the low- Death Valley like in California.

Grin and bear it, that's where we were heading and where Andy and I wound up.

We talked with some of the Seamen we picked up in Sydney and they offered a few clues, such as a great place for a tan and/or skin cancer. You can get a nice-looking belt by skinning a snake. Seemingly Jaws was nothing compared to the monsters that lurked in the ocean under the pier. Or try this one, the fishing is simply terrific to put a positive on it.

We kept on winging-it and flying lower to our destination I could view large herds of sheep, thousands and thousands of kangaroos and green pastures for hundreds of miles.

Settlements of the aborigines could be sighted, some with a school or chapel.

The entire area to me appeared very primitive and undeveloped, with man's intrusion minimal.

Welcome to my new home!

I'd flown the whole of Australia from tip to tip, Southeast coast to the Northwest, while viewing Ayer's Rock, ranches, mining operations and such. Barren terrain throughout in all directions.

A note on Ayer's Rock, aka Uluru. It's a famous natural formation of solid single reddish rock, several square miles in size and it sits in the middle of the continent. That I can see, from reading or hearing about it; serves no purpose other than tourism and provides a great deal of shade.

As for natural resources, Australia has vast amounts of aluminum and is likely one of the world's major exporters of this light metal greatly utilized.

The supply plane landed in nowhere land, a long airship or runway with nothing there but asphalt or concrete. No buildings, lights or markings- nada but some trucks, a bus, military personnel and a few civilians and the cool, windy weather and quite sunny and very bearable.

How many of us were there? I'd guess about thirty, three dozen at most. With an equal number of new Navy personnel arriving and the same number leaving. Sadness and frowns on the former and smiles and laughter for the latter.

The storekeepers, forklift drivers and Sea Bees dealt with the loads and put these on flatbed trucks.

We waited for our baggage then hauled it to the nearby shuttle that looked like a school bus, but all gray. Exmouth, the local town, was next and it stopped there briefly.

At this point I noticed for the first time these tall antennas that scratched the clouds. They looked thousands of feet high, probably tickling the angels by the Pearly Gates. Who took care of these structures painted reddish orange with lights on them? Who would want to?

The driver returned and pointed the vehicle to the base, about three to five miles from town. The two-lane road immediately opened my eyes. I noticed we were on the wrong lane. How to describe it. Ass backwards. Americans drive forward on the right lane but over there they use the left lane. And the vehicles steering wheel is on the right side. One gets used to it and wheels around without a problem after a year of practice.

Except I did crash into some kangaroos when I was an ambulance driver.

The security guard opened the main gate to let us in. The band played and the welcome mat put out and the red carpet rolled. Very impressive indeed, except nothing like that happened.

I quickly rushed into the Admin office and placed a phone call to my Parents in Arizona to let them know I, we arrived healthy and well. Mentiras. Tampoco así fue.

Bueno, muy pronto di gracias a Dios por guiarnos en el largo viaje y llegar bien, seguido con un postal a mis Padres notificándoles desde Australia. That's how it took place.

Nobody seemed to give a rat's patootie whatever, not impressed just part of the weekly routine, some came in and others go out. No big deal- BFD. Easy come, easy go.

We were dumped on the street near the parking lot by Admin and our bags piled there too, plus told to proceed to personnel. The processing started by alphabet. Last name, A-G here, H-M there, you get the picture. Actually, the staff seemed pissed cause we arrived, plain and simple. They had to work and thus maybe cut into their suds time or happy hour at the E-M Club.

Really a warm welcome by terrifically, friendly people who had an actual interest in us and our wellbeing.

Further instruction was to drop by the chow hall, or we'd miss dinner of mutton or kangaroo steaks, sizzling and burned.

Some papers and forms we received included a map of the base and one for the outlying area. Also, an outline or schedule of orientation for the next few days. A W-D2 for payroll and an admission slip of some kind for the Master-at-Arms at the barracks for our bunks or lodging for the night. Just temporary until a more permanent spot could be found for us.

Andy and I semi-secured our baggage once we were excused by the office of enlisted personnel.

Believe it when I pronounce that the officers received preferred special treatment, whether new arrivals or otherwise.

He and I ate, nothing special- potatoes, gravy, rolls, a veggie, jello and a drink. Maybe added to a beef stew or hash. All not too appetizing or appealing.

Such a welcome. Surprisingly, we didn't have to wash our own dishes.

The Base, Naval Station, Compound, HEH, NCS and other terms will be used to identify our location, but first some explanation and additional facts about the place.

United States Naval Communication Station Harold E. Holt, I understand was the official name or title of the facility. Many commonly just said Exmouth, which becomes misleading because that is the name of the town nearby, a civilian community, not a military installation whatsoever. The two will be described accordingly as we move along.

But one thought I can gather somewhat easily as to the reason American sailors were there. They had orders to be there without question, but not the Australians. From my dim knowledge I never saw any Australian military presence, only civilians, quite a high number, likely a thousand I'd guess, who voluntarily lived there without duress or coercion.

Several reasons were stated but only one seemed valid- money. Some said to get away from problems (family, financial). To escape jail or legal issues, breakups like divorce or a partner, to save money and/or establish a solid footing or maybe financial plans.

The last had a solid basis. I seem to be moving from my main premise here but as I saw it, three main groupings existed in the population of the area. The military: the Australian citizenry and the immigrants, who seemed keener at accumulating the funds, especially the American dollars, thus sacrificing an urban or metropolitan lifestyle for the better wages paid in the Northwest Cape.

I had a similar intent, as you will read. The money was available, with the government willingly giving it away in just about anyway, manner or fashion.

Let me get back to HEH. Who was this Harold E. Holt character? I think he was the forefather of the Holtz Clan before it multiplied and pluralized and grew quick and big like mildew.

Truly he was an Aussie Prime Minster who drowned, the body never found. A politician with all the connections to get a Naval Base named after him, as well as an aircraft carrier or submarine. Sure he likely drowned and disappeared. Does your Mother wear burlap chones?

Look him up or google him to get the real facts and history on him.

Wow! Did I really say that? What a Patriot!

Sidetracked again, I got. But afterwards from the mess hall, we took to the barracks and I certainly died. The jetlag, long flight, food and different time zones and being at sea level took its toll on me. So much so that I was asleep before my head hit the pillow. Maybe like fourteen hours straight sleep. Did I really? Without once going to the head.

King Cross wiped me out, you think.

CHAPTER 11.

The Civilian Life

The next day was Friday and everyone was already in a TGIF mood since the day before, with not much getting done. By this I mean that the POD (plan of the day) did not apply and for new arrivals, just lay low until Monday.

A couple of items were crossed off the to do list, one being the assignment to the barracks. Andy and I split up though both wound up in the security division, the guys who handled shore patrol, guarded the Main Gate and investigated accidents.

Andy, a Seaman (E-3) in rank, remained in this division for a number of months until he made postal clerk and was promoted, leading to a position with the base post office and its services.

We learned about the shuttle into town and its different routes and schedules.

The weekend for me included the movies I think on Friday evening, or maybe Saturday. I found out more about what Special Services offered, such as the softball games in the evening between various teams. Similarly, for bowling.

The library drew my attention and I spent hours there reading, listening to music tapes and such.

I recall also having gone into Exmouth just to get an idea

about what that was like. The local pub and the most popular one was the Pot Shot Inn. The joint was a hole in the wall offering liquor, food, loud music, arm wrestling, darts and camaraderie.

The beach and the coasts were beautiful, plus the cool breezes made the heat more comfortable.

Hence the weekend turned out to be a 'look and see' exercise to find out more about my new surroundings.

My opinion and attitude weren't much better than that of the new arrivals including Andy, who all felt they landed somewhere in one of the infernal rings of Dante.

Monday morning, the time for our orientation to begin and doing so by introducing ourselves to he who led us.

We would be together about a week during which we would have speakers and tours.

First of all, we were told where we were and the name, the address so that we could correspond with the outside world, because of our isolation.

An hour into this, the XO (Executive Officer) showed up and welcomed us. He was second in command and the boss when the Captain/Commander left. The gentleman addressed the weather, pay and leisure activities and he warned us about the dangers of the wildlife, such as snakes, the ocean, etc.

He told us about our mission and purpose. Protect and promote democracy and curb communism by keeping track of the Soviet submarine fleet patrolling the Indian Ocean. And doing it in partnership and cooperation with the government of Australia.

I might have started daydreaming and lost my train of thought as I heard rumblings about SEATO or the South East Asia Treaty Organization. Comprised of France, England, Australia, the USA and other nations. It's an alliance similar to NATO. President Eisenhower pushed for the creation of SEATO in an effort to keep communism and the Soviets in check. Not the most exciting stuff. He finished and we went on break.

The Navy Days

Who or what was next? I can't figure it, but we heard from the Special Services people, which included civilians. They offered the E-M Club and its activities- the library, the hours, etc. The movie theater, the swimming pool, bowling alley and more.

Competitive sports (basketball, volleyball, softball), were mentioned and the equipment that could be checked out.

We knocked off at about eleven for the lunch break, to regroup at thirteen hundred hours at the same spot/building.

This meal consisted of eating at the chow hall (sandwiches, pizza, soups, fruit, drinks and more), or junk from the PX (post exchange) chips, lunch meats, cheese, candy and sodas.

Some preferred liquid lunch and drove to town to indulge hurriedly then return to the base.

During this week of getting acquainted and hearing different speakers with all kinds of messages, I think now the top one was a tour of the town of Exmouth. The locals are/were a very proud crowd and preferred to call the place, the base, etc., 'The Cape', or 'The Northwest Cape'.

In fact, the base initially went by 'U.S. Naval Station Northwest Cape', though later changed to Harold E. Holt (heh, heh, heh), after the Prime Minister's demise.

Exmouth was first built around the 60's to accommodate Naval personnel with families and dependents including an elementary school. Older youngsters were sent to boarding schools in Perth, Sydney, Melbourne, et al.

Off base housing consisted of flat roof, solid reinforced concrete block buildings, because of likely natural disasters such as the cyclones with powerful, ripping winds and flooding.

There could also be found trailers, mobile homes and campers, indicating a roguish, rough lifestyle with much drinking and celebrating and a low drug scene.

One could find a small shopping center, an Aussie bank and hardware store, but not a whole bunch more. Maybe a couple of breakfast/burger joints commonly called the Greasy Spoons. Indeed, be prepared, le ptomaine o la muertè.

Was there a church or chapel? I can't picture it other than the one on the base.

Exmouth was not a military installation but it certainly resembled one. It just needed a tall chain fence around it and security. The place was laid out in grid formation, very straight and clean. Almost nothing out of place. Mowed lawns, swept sidewalks, spic-n-span.

I heard people were written up if they messed up and could lose their residence, sort of or worse than a HOA. Big Brother Watching.

On other days you'd see kids running around, yelling, roughing-it up, Americans and Aussies.

Then the ubiquitious moving van bringing household items for new arriving families.

CHAPTER 12.

Taking A Break

The van took us here, there, nowhere, and the passengers queried the driver. Where are the women? Very few. How late does the Pot Shot stay open? Till it closes. Does it serve American beer? Some sometimes.

We left Exmouth and turned in the direction of the base, or so it seemed, at least for the first mile. The ocean appeared next after we got onto the dirt road and the brush.

The beach was pristine, without a soul almost. Quiet, peaceful but for the noise from the waves and seagulls. We got out of the vehicle and puttered around while the chauffeur made a few points.

One could see some launches and small boats but nothing to call home about. This was a poor man's paradise without yachts, speed boats or marinas. We did see some off-road vehicles and a repair shop or garage where a couple of mechanics worked and welded on a small, white gray and blue skiff.

We took-off along the beach then jumped back on the asphalt, leaving the base behind. In a blink, the pier showed up before us, one that's long enough but not like the one's I saw in San Diego or Long Beach.

The pier handled mostly large incoming loads for the

operations or communications center without any Navy or fleet ships, just commercial ones. You'd see vehicles being unloaded as well as household goods of dependent families, once in a blue moon, a couple of times a year.

The wagon took us on the t-shaped pier and passengers got out and stretched our legs. Looking down into the water I saw various sea creatures I didn't care to get near to. The beach had some litter (bottles, plasticware, fire pits), indicating it was a place for recreation and/or social activity.

Moving-on and returning to HEH, we didn't but instead, the next treat was the base of one of the huge antennas, which was not at all anything exciting or fun. We probably became radioactive.

We finally arrived at the base by way of a trail near or around the warehouses and shops- where the Sea Bees hang out. One could see heavy equipment, quite a bit of it, large spools of wire, lumber, ladders, big trucks and such. I couldn't figure out what some sailors were doing, but some were just loafing.

This was the real male domain: smokes, ash trays, decks of cards, Playboy and such items.

Before turning the page on orientation week, there were some presentations of some significance, such as naming our beneficiary: in the event of our demise, they'd receive a monetary award or an insurance of some sort.

We were given the pep talks on re-enlistments or extensions of Naval Service.

The Legal Department, though very small, sure packed a punch. It started with getting our American passport if we wanted to travel in Australia or is it out of Australia.

The topics continued with acquiring a vehicle and all the requirements of registration, liability (mostly insurance), driving privileges and license. Importing an American vehicle versus purchasing a local Aussie or American car was discussed.

Matrimony was tossed around but by the tone of the

speakers this was not encouraged, though there were a few new unions during the year, as there were divorces as well. Both were quite complicated and the best advice to come out of this was avoid the former, and the latter won't happen.

On the criminal side of the law, also an interesting but very complex matter- "Stay Out of Trouble and That's an Order". The military side of the law and the Australian code both commonly had to be dealt with. One example given was an arrest on a public road, not the base, for a DUI. Don't do it or go there because the penalty- OUCH! Loss of driver's licenses, fines, incarceration and God knows what else.

But let me get off here on a tangent- what else is new or who knew. I don't know about the following and if you wish to believe it, fine. It is surreal. You'll be entertained. I'm reporting only what I read in a newspaper or magazine, a reliable one with UPI or AP bona-fides, not a tabloid or trash rag.

It was around the 1990's in the Northwest Cape of Australia, U.S. Naval Station H.E. Holt. You can read that I was long gone, no longer stationed there. The place had the evil spirits in it from what I heard and observed having been there, as you'll read later in these pages. Some things the aborigines reported.

So, there was an American military couple, from what I remember in the article from the Daily Star or the Tucson Citizen (now defunct).

Marital discord prevailed but were they American or perhaps Filipino, or a couple of mixed backgrounds. Were there children? Again, I do not recall.

The newspapers reported that she had disappeared from the base, Exmouth and the immediate vicinity and people noticed her absence though the man continued as usual. Again, I'm not certain if the two were married.

An investigation followed but took some time and many loose ends resulted, but there was enough there for an arrest or indictment of the poor fellow, with a trial in the months ahead.

I wish I could corroborate this reporting instead of simply relying on my memory, but I did not succeed with the newspaper, library, google, Wikipedia, etc. I believe it happened and think the news was accurate and verifiable.

It turned out that the man was convicted of killing her and feeding her to the sharks. I believe she was never found, nor did I find out on what basis they prosecuted the bloke. Or what was the sentence? I wish I had more details, but I don't.

The matter piqued my interest after having been stationed there and I read the article with interest, because it was another strange incident among several that took place there.

It strikes me as very weird that's what happened to the Prime Minister Harold E. Holt, who drowned and disappeared, never to be found. Imagine that, a prime minister disappearing, like George Bush or Ronald Reagan vanishing while out toiling at their ranches, sure- also happened to this woman.

But the aborigines I had occasion to chat or interview, not very long or thoroughly, spoke of spirits and evil. They sensed the changes brought about by White people- intruders. Upsetting the natural flow of the ambient surroundings. Hence, the intruders were punished for wrecking the peacefulness of the environment.

This makes little or no sense, and maybe I did not explain this too well, but who knows, the aborigines with their beliefs may be right and two intruders did disappear. Spooky. I think so.

I couldn't help but make the comparison. The aborigines were ostracized and segregated.

We experienced similarly down by the border of my home place, Douglas y Agua Prieta.

Another interruption before getting back to the orientation business, which was the mail from Douglas and boy was it just truly wonderful to hear from the folks back home. To learn how everyone was doing. They said they missed me big time and that the town folk inquired about me. Like when Ed (my Dad) would go shopping at A.J. Bayless, the employees asked him about me.

People are shocked I wound up in Australia and added I was lucky to escape Viet Nam and the War.

I had given my parents my overseas F.P.O. address (Fleet Post Office). USNAVSTA H.E. Holt, hence the reason for the early letters.

I feel like Gomer Pyle; "Golly gee, Sergeant, so great to hear from you".

My sister Blanca had a baby, Lisa in June 1969, both were doing well with my Mom, Panchita, having a ball looking after Lisa and attending to her.

Many send me warm regards and best wishes, plus I'm warned that some people may write because Ed has given out my address and encouraged people to write me to boost my spirits, and do it in Spanish so that I don't forget my native tongue and culture. So now I have to answer, as my Parents have requested.

The guys here on the base went around kidding me that I was already homesick and receiving correspondence from home and pretty soon the goodwill package would be arriving, with maybe some homemade goodies como viscochuelos.

My Dad made one observation being that he reads the newspapers in English. The war was on and American casualties were too many and Dad felt grateful being in the USA despite the mess. Thankful for having me fairly safe away from the battlefield.

He lived my experiences vicariously, especially seeing how different my life was unfolding with college, the Navy and far away from home in comparison to how his young life turned out. He did not express too many regrets and did not disclose problems which would worry me, but I knew the health of both of them was in declivity.

He even added that he had a good harvest from his garden despite the hot weather.

Also, he inquired about Rafael, wanting to know where he was and what was he doing.

Getting back to our orientation that first week at HEH, Heh, Heh when we were listening to speakers from Legal Services.

Generally, not much took place as far as incidents where the law is broken and the Legal Beagle steps in. Small matters usually taken care of through a disciplinary procedure, such as a Captain's Mast and the appropriate punishment rendered, like a fine or a reduction in rank leading to loss of pay. Examples might be fighting, public drunkenness or petty thievery.

Very few have been the times when there was a court martial and even then, that may be held like in Hawaii.

The next topic was education, and this had three spheres, as follows: military, civilian and dependents, and here I offer a broad, rough sketch about what was offered.

For starters, the education office was led by an Australian civilian and he was like a U.S. Federal Civil Servant. He had even been to the USA for training in his specialization.

Education for the enlisted men consisted at this level, locale and time mostly of correspondence courses or base library in the education office. This can best be illustrated by example.

For the Navy man, especially those with a long-term career (lifers), promotions and upgrades are a BIG thing. Regularly improving, making grade means earning better pay. It is a process in place to reward the sailors.

A seaman can move-up the ranks mostly by completing courses. Such was the case for me, from Seaman to Yeoman without benefit of attending school. The grades run from E-1 (new enlistees), to Master Chief (E-9).

Interestingly, there is much discrimination. For example, the Navy values certain fields; occupations or ratings: An Electronics Technician in submarines will reach Chief (E-7) much faster and with more pay than a cook or steward elsewhere.

Next is civilian education and the Navy is much involved or connected with the United States Armed Forces Institute or USAFI, which in my service time had headquarters in Madison, Wisconsin. I have limited knowledge about this. It offers courses from USAFI itself, but also provides correspondence studies from other colleges or universities in the country. One can accumulate a number of credits towards a college degree but must be careful and select wisely and it may have a cost.

There is much here that can be addressed, such as attending college if one is stationed stateside. There are many options that can be explored if one desires to pursue higher education.

The third part is education for dependents and applies to a small number of seamen.

I never counted an exact number, which never seemed to be constant with families moving in and out. This was an expensive bill having to pay for the kids' schooling.

Exmouth had a small school, a public one I believe that American and Australian children attended, but I believe only through sixth grade.

Youngsters in seventh grade or higher attended boarding school, I am unsure of the exact cut-off grade. These minors went to Perth Brisbane, Canberra and other urban centers that measured quite equally to their American counterparts. Therefore, a student rarely fell behind when returning to the United States and re-enrolling.

I vaguely recall that there may have been some home schooling with American and Australian kids, plus there also were certified teachers in the area that taught privately.

Exmouth also offered some adult community night school for those wishing to attend, courses were quite diverse, from snorkeling to crafts and so forth.

A final note on education, a few chiefs and officer's also put their men through training, usually in small groups, in order to stay abreast with the revolution in technology, communications and computer systems.

Let's not overkill the week of orientation and all the blah, blah, blah.

Recall that this account or narrative covers a short period in 1969 and 1970 in Australia, a time during which its government policies were designed to prevent diversity and multiculturalism. In other words, simply put, keep it White. Do not let non-Whites into the country and such policy was enforced, because that was the law pretty much then down under.

This is important to know here because I am a minority, brown, not white, but a Mexican, naturalized to be an American Citizen and a Sailor in the American Navy.

Whose pawn was I, I mused. Maybe the American government, the Navy, that is, was using me and other minorities to piss-off the Australians. And I was not the only one who had been having these thoughts.

I heard mumblings and rumblings, rumors and gossip, mutterings to this effect. Mostly in hushed tones, sort of in a very cowardly manner. Basically, pointedly, I was not welcome, but what the hell, what's done was done and we had our thing to do.

In fact, the mailman or base courier liked to call me Spic or Spiky. We know what that means: an offensive term for a Mexican.

He was John, an Australian, pink as a lawn flamingo, six foot two, two-fifty in weight easily. He didn't like that I called him Fat John, Fatso, Lard Ass or JUAN.

So, it was more of this Sarah Marley crap when I was in grade school in Douglas. Not only were the Australians proving themselves to be bigots, but also the Navy or American government. By using us as pawns, along with this other cagada that differentiates between enlisted men and officers. Que Mierda.

It didn't take me long to figure this out.

I should point out that in the personnel record of every American Military person who has served is listed his educational grade, like twelve would be high school, or sixteen a college grad

The Navy Days

or close. Also, there's mental capacity (IQ) rating.

Mine read college level which didn't rest too well with many of my cohorts, who barely made it through secondary ed. I wouldn't say I was a marked man or a smart aleck, but word got around, that Mexican is no dummy.

Yet all this I lived through daily because of the scuttlebutt I heard mostly, and not because anyone would confront me.

For example, the driver's exam for an Australian license I passed easily, both the written one and the driving test on my first and only attempt. People were in disbelief and all the base and Exmouth knew it, while others had to take the exam repeatedly until they passed.

By the third week, which is after orientation, we had our work or duty assignments. Those on the MAC Flight were mostly going to the communications area which had radiomen, electronics, technicians, instrument men, etc.

Not the two of us. Andy and I went to the Security Division that's responsible for the Main Gate every minute of the day. A chief was in charge.

Security had mostly seamen, who would be E-3 and E-4. These guys worked on rotation eight hour shifts at a time and had shore patrol as one of their duties, after hours and weekends.

The perimeter of the base had to be secure, so they did this as well. Several times a day the gray security Ford trucks were seen all over the base, Exmouth, the pier and more. Security covered the entire area and they even went under water. I heard frogmen were available for example, to inspect under the pier. I think you get the picture here about the Security Division, which didn't do much because very little happened. A rarity for an unusual incident to occur.

Why did I wind up in Security? Snail mail, miscommunication, spitefulness and missing paperwork.

Back in Douglas I had taken the exam for Yeoman Third

Class E-4 and succeeded in getting promoted from Seaman E-3. This was while I was inactive reservist. I did this without benefits of schooling but through the reading and workbook, just studying while employed and in college.

A few weeks later I reported to active duty in San Diego, but the paperwork had not been fully completed. I had a form or receipt that indicated I was no longer a Seaman but a Yeoman Third Class.

Apparently, for whatever reason this was not acceptable by the Navy brass at HEH, but after a short while, I'd say a month or so, the situation was straightened out and I received my crow. I think there was a small ceremony for this award. Uncle Sam gave a raise with retroactive pay to boot.

So, I left Andy behind in Security and I went to work in the Administration Division and in doing so I raised a lot of heckles. Who ate crow now?

Change the subject. I don't want to get into admin just yet, but you'll get here some of what working in Security was like.

The worse part about it was the graveyard shift and the best part of it, the days off. Nothing ever happened. I take it back, perhaps all the dust was awful, riding in the truck.

The Security Chief and I had an ongoing friendly banter or feud, or he gave me some slack or literary license because I was a rookie. As required, the watchmen on security detail had to make an entry into the log every hour and report something like, "nudist or naked bathers/swimmers on the beach by the pier", "Jo and Jane fornicating doggie-style in lover's lane". Stuff like that made everyone laugh but were inappropriate log entries and the watchmen were written up.

There was no contest about which entries were the raunchiest or who was the best author. Just be creative, let the imagination run wild, simply go like hopping kangaroos. Here are a few of mine, which I was promised would be saved for posterity in the one and only HEH Hall of Fame. A court martial would be welcomed, then exit Exmouth.

The Navy Days

It's near midnight, about 11:41, on shore, and I glimpse a long cigar-like object, black or dark gray, its silhouette against the night sky and morning light.

I figure it's a Soviet sub, but I can't read Russian. My cheap binoculars don't help, but a small crowd of men stand by the conning tower and are waving at me, giving me the bird and other signs. Wait, a couple just mooned me. Boy, they got huge, dark, hairy dicks. I better call back up.

Frogman, Frogman

Full of sand

Carrying goggles, knife and spam

And tons of gear,

You get to reach

The sizzling beach,

You tried,

God!

You belong on land

Not water, Frogman.

I'll say that the insanity defense would not help me. We were all going nuts, in the outback. If you claimed insanity, then this was normal considering the isolation, heat and meaninglessness. If you said you're okay, not nuts, then you are crazy to put up with the lunacy of the Cape.

The irrational behavior of sailors will be addressed later, and you will be reading material that will boil your blood, make you cry or even change your mind and/or opinion of our American Military Forces.

Another responsibility that Security had was guarding the pier, which meant many things. Because it drew attention or attracted visitors, it required maintenance, such as collecting litter, covering holes and pits, securing boards and planks. People would run out of firewood and tear pieces of the pier.

One incident took place while still assigned to Security and I had an MVA, motor vehicle accident. A ship was being unloaded in the bright morning and there was much activity with trucks, forklifts, dollies, etc., hauling things and people moving around.

I had worked graveyard and after completing my shift I was instructed to drive a crew in the truck to the pier. My long night made longer. I had not slept.

After turning onto the deck to drop-off the sailors, I then had to make a turn to get back on the road. I barely scraped the truck's bumper against the siding and drove off, parked and rejoined my co-workers. We all did our job in the heat until early afternoon.

We returned to the base. I was tired and the Chief excused me, so I went straight to bed, exhausted.

In a few days I was at Captain's Mast after someone reported my accident. I did not deny anything but explained there had been no damage but a small scratch. I did not believe it needed to be formally accounted for and furthermore, I was exhausted from lack of sleep that I failed or forgot to inform anyone.

The Captain, who was the commander of HEH y muy importante en esta region, finally got to meet me and we chatted about our backgrounds. He considered me an oddity- a real Mexican in the US Navy in Australia. He dismissed the whole affair and said if I ever need anything to go talk to him. How about getting me outta here, to stateside. I didn't feel too bad about what had happened. Heh, Heh, Heh!

Time and again I've felt that meeting the commander, as described herein was set-up somehow due to his interest and to avoid the awkwardness of an officer "fraternizing" with the lowly enlisted personnel. Being such are the rules of the Navy and/or U.S. Military. Is that stupid?

It sort of, "let the grunts get hurt or killed while I sit back, plush, manicuring my fingernails". Maybe even my E-4 promotion

The Navy Days

might be at play, a ploy. Who knows? It stinks.

We are into late August or early September 1969, at Cape Fear.

My beef had been resolved by now and I went up a grade to E-4, that is, I became a Petty Officer Third Class Yeoman. This meant that the Administration Division (hereon Admin or admin), had to absorb me because I would be transferring out of Security, where I never should have been assigned to in the first place. Heh! Heh! Heh!

This change did not occur without controversy. I promised everybody they wouldn't get ticks, fleas, hoof and mouth or any other disease from me.

I didn't hide anything. Honestly. I didn't know much about yeoman ship, but mostly generally. Everybody knew I never went to Navy school to train for it and as a reservist, I had about zero experience since I had been on active duty about two months only.

The admin head, a lifer lieutenant commander ready to retire, kicked the matter to the personnel officer in charge, a small thin, mousy looking lieutenant female with more mustache than most sailors.

I remember a phone call while in the barracks and people were in a quandary. A billet for another yeoman did not exist. I was supposed to be a seaman, filling such position in Security. Supposedly it was like I threw a monkey wrench into the works or operation.

Some thought it was splendid how I had discovered a seam and rigged the system to get myself promoted, yet not to be able to do anything nor even know the job and be able to perform it.

Admin definitely did not care to have me at the front of the office. They would never tell me anything to my face, but I found out from secondary sources the rumor mongers.

As ridiculously as it sounded, Australian protocol dictated that only White individuals could man the area receiving or serving the general public. I was clearly none of that, so I was pushed to the back, believe it or not.

I really did not care, nor did I want to assume a role such as did Rosa Parks.

I figured I could easily hang in the outback a year and a half until I was out and, in the states, do the best I could and learn a few tricks I had already been witnessing.

Taking leave would also ease my term in Australia.

Admin became my regular gig, Monday thru Friday. Morning muster at seven-thirty, with roll call, plan of the day and comments, then dismissal to our stations or posts. Whatever it's called.

The first few days I worked in the actual Admin hole with about ten people: the female lieutenant, a chief yeoman with his five underlings consisting of two yeoman and three personnel men. Three female Australian civilian clericals helped us as well.

A distinction noted, yeomen served officers and personnel men handled the enlisted.

Admin also had a floating sub-division officed in another building on base, not far at all, I'd say seventy-five yards separated the two.

The executive officers had other personnel that reported to Admin. Another re-adjustment for me in several ways. Having been in Security initially, I had become acquainted with mates there and they were more of the rough and tumble, outdoors type who trusted me well, welcomed me and taught me a number of things.

Admin staff was indoor employees who rarely stepped outside but sat mostly throughout the day in cool air-conditioned comfort and pushed paper. We were called pencil dicks, pen pushers, office jocks, etc.

I got around to meeting my new coworkers, who by now knew more about me by having read my personnel file. These guys were of a competitive sort, trying to out-do each other in whatever way they could and be the Chief's brown-noses. Who could type faster? Who had the fewest errors? All BS it seemed to me.

I held no animosity towards them nor tried to displease them because I was there to get out, be discharged, gone. They found out I had a reservist's attitude and preferred civilian life, not a military existence. There were several reservists, I learned, in Admin and elsewhere feeling likewise, wanting out.

With my move to admin, I had to relocate barracks-wise being that I had been housing with sailors assigned to Security. This was the set-up, the way the base ran.

I went upstairs, second floor admin where journalists, photographers, yeomen and others bunked. In other words, medical, admin, cooks, sea bees, etc., were all segregated to occupy different sections of the barracks.

Life in the dorms really stunk in more ways than one and I'll have more on this later, which is bound to be delightful as the scenes unfold.

During this transition from Security to Admin I noticed a few acts of kindness or otherwise. The Security Chief wished me well when he announced at morning muster my promotion and move to Admin. Others were more reserved but were glad to see me go. Security was for bottom feeders, those at sea, chip paint, man the lines and much more. Men in the lower ranks felt threatened by a new arrival, a minority at that.

I did like the freedom Security offered by riding the truck like a cowboy rides his steed on the range. We had about a ten-mile radius from the base that we secured, from the outlying antennas to Learmouth where the airfield rested. What a ride!

In spite of the separation, I remained tight with my guys from Security throughout my days in Exmouth. I felt closer to them than the new crew in Admin. I don't know why but to this day I remember them first and best, playing cards in their section, shooting pool and drinking at the EMC.

Maybe if I had landed at HEH and went straight to Admin, I

would feel differently.

But move on, I had to and after a week in Admin I was sent to Educational Services, which building also held the offices for legal services, public affairs and photography. I would spend my remaining days at HEH performing my tasks as a Petty Officer Yeoman in education.

CHAPTER 13.

Finding My Niche

I did well, I thought, not exceptional or perfect but content while realizing that I had a job to learn. I would occupy the position being vacated by another Yeoman who was due to depart in approximately a month after completing his military obligation. He too was a reservist and not too happy at having to have served, especially in a hell hole like the Northwest Capes of Australia.

One of my first inquiries was to find a bicycle, otherwise I would be doing a lot of walking and Admin did not have a vehicle like I drove in Security.

I got around to meeting all the staff in the education building, with informal introductions and some handshakes, plus a brief description about the job that everyone performed or didn't.

Work was slow, workers laid-back and I'd even say lackadaisical.

OOOPS! Don't write me up Chief!

Letters started trickling in de mi Familia but who exactly, quien sabe, pero los incluidos serian Blanca y Clara, así como mis Padres que siempre me advirtieron mucho cuidado y con El Señor en la boca para que nos proteja hoy y siempre. Me daban gracias, Ed y Panchita por lo que les mandaba.

Con Blanca creo que a este punto ya habíamos arreglado mis asuntos tocantes a mis ahorros. Yo no quería llegar con las bolsas vacías a regresar al hogar en dos años.

Unas amigas del colegio también escribieron y es así como les puedo decir que de verdad se siente uno más animado y alegre con esta correspondencia de tan lejos.

Algunos de mis camaradas se sorprendieron al ver las cartas de México que recibí de mis tíos en Cumpas y Nacozari, más al saber que vengan escritas en español, muy formal.

Con esto ya tenía al menos tarea bastante para contestarles a cada uno de los correspondientes.

Y hablando de esto, pronto debía yo empezar mi comunicación con los colegios a donde pensaba ingresarme para continuar mis estudios cuando termine este servicio militar. Me debia dedicar porque será largo y duro el proceso y no nada más cualquier baba- require empeño para bien planear esta transición.

See, I didn't want to lose my culture, language and writing, so I toss you a paragraph or two en español, because being immersed among Gringos could rob me of my precious roots.

Yet some people on base were interested in my background, and I would not say amazed or shocked, piqued about life on the Southwestern border of the US, as well as in Mexico.

One question quite often asked was about Mexican cuisine and did I miss it. But of course, and I explained the different styles of food, preparation, distinctive regions and so forth. I threw out a few terms like tacos, tortillas, cerveza and entertained them and made people laugh.

Amazingly, these curious individuals were not the young punks out of high school, but those older more sophisticated ones intrigued by this different sailor amidst the crowd.

I was twenty-one and I did not like hanging around with the 'teenage force' but sailors, civilians and other sorts in their twenties and thirties. Can't explain it? More mature personnel maybe suited

The Navy Days

me better.

Allow me to welcome you to the offices where I'm to spend a major portion of my active duty enlistment, and again, the folks in the building had a good idea about who would be joining them.

Foremost would be the Education Department (which we kiddingly labelled ED, as in wet noodles, limp dicks and erectile dysfunction), or also commonly called Educational Services or Education Office.

Not a bad looking building but the interior was drab, as is usually the case with military furniture (desks, chairs, tables, shelves, etc.) in Army green or Navy gray.

Arriba! Arriba! Arriba! Arriba! The Tennessee nut-job just jumped into my recall center and pressed the button. This bright, smiling character made military life somewhat more bearable though he very much disliked the Navy and his duty. But of course, he was a potential draftee and avoided this by joining the Navy Reserve to wind-up in the Outback. We had this in common and he loved me for it. Two draft dodgers among many. Arriba!!

He was so hyperactive, attributable in part to his half dozen daily cups of java, just exuding tremendous amounts of energy that he called me Paco, Cisco, Don Pancho and yelled often, "Arriba Don Poncho"! I called him G.I.

The base journalist was his trademark and he managed to be fairly objective in spite of his craziness, style and fun. He published weekly by himself, as best I can recall. He had a keen intellect and inquiring mind. He probably became the one sailor with whom I'd share more working hours.

His newsletter gave him recognition, but few knew him like those who worked closely with him in the same building or in admin. More later.

Getting back to the organizational structure of where I worked. The Education Office occupied the largest portion of the building, more than half. It had the big classroom, a library and an office.

Part of my job became the cleaning and upkeep of the classroom being it was at times utilized after hours by one group, club or another organization. Even on weekends it saw some activity.

Oh! Don't let me forget. Next door, a few yards from us was the base chapel serving all denominations. In fact, I recall it as multi-purpose, but not often. For example, a baptismal followed by a short service and a small reception.

It had a piano, so one would hear people practicing their music there as well.

I must admit not many attended and neither did I, but another brief point here follows...

I believe it was at HEH, though perhaps other military intel stations (Hickam, Ford Island, etc.) are possibilities. A nerdy squeaky-clean sailor worked his post as a chaplain assistant or similar role. What's interesting is that he was a conscientious objector of some sort. Somehow an arrangement was worked out whereby be would avoid the brig or a bad discharge (bad conduct, dishonorable, convenience of the government) and finished his enlistment cleaning the church pews, mowing the lawn, polishing the chalice and such.

It's been such a long time, almost fifty years and some details are gone. This character was in the military, Navy and he had a change of heart and started wearing garb of a clergy, crosses and crucifixes, with his uniform and preaching. Maybe he wanted a Section 8 Discharge.

Sometimes the military keeps their guys in whom it has invested a bunch of money, with hopes of re-orienting them. We'll call it brain washing. Remember Klinger in the television series 'MASH'? That sort of thing but not necessarily punishable conduct or behavior. Let the Armed Force shrinks try to bring these fellas around.

Maybe if I had dressed like a Mexican bandido- spurs, boots, sarape and sombrero- I would have gotten out, avoided the draft. Maybe next time.

Anyways the above was but a thought that my mind tricked me into recalling who worked in the chapel next door.

WOW! The mind does crazy, amazing things and really just has a mind of its very own. Like it's supposed to be controlling the heart and cardiac system and the blood flow, lungs and oxygen levels. Along with the vision to monitor the environment while monitoring the digestion and sugars as one munches a sweet super syrupy mango and then bamo- the next thought or idea charges from nowhere in the galaxy, or a nudy of Raquel Welch or a very complex math equation interferes and takes over.

Like right now, the church and religion and the conscientious objector became master de mis pensamientos.

The brain is a terrific sponge of fat that boggles the mind, at least mine as I was saying about my job in Educational Services (ES), which were headed by an Australian gentleman supposedly with the knowledge about civilian schools, American and Australian.

We'll call him Gabe, to protect his identity. He was fifty-ish in the early 1970s, so he'd be about one hundred as of this writing. But then, there's those still alive who knew him, like his family.

He performed a fine job but seemed not too keen on it. He got things done. He was a biologist and I think a secondary Ed teacher before this position. He regularly reported to work as if on his way to the beach or a soccer match. Very rarely did he dress in slacks or long sleeves, like we did.

Gabe was the boss, but the Chief and Lieutenant were in charge. I never followed this ruling chain. Gabe took care of me in many ways and he always went around saying, "we'll make things work".

That was a great philosophy if you stop to think it through. We were in Bum Fuck Egypt, where people walked around barefoot and a G-string. There were shortages of everything, from food, to medicine, auto parts, you name it. In abundance we had sunshine, beaches, ocean and kangaroos. We improvised, used our creativity and noggins to make things work.

I showed up at the ES office per orders and went through our introductions. I quickly learned I'd be second fiddle, second banana- whatever it's called- until Gabe's yeoman departed. That meant three weeks or so before the position was mine, thus I learned from both occupants in ES.

The job was not complicated and easy enough and did not hold my interest. In fact, this seemed about true throughout HEH, where we were hanging on and putting in our time to comply with our duty.

The ES office or component was almost unmechanized except for phones, the electric typewriter, a slide and two movie projectors. Remember the old hand cranked mimeograph machines, well we had that plus we used tons of carbon paper for duplication, unlike today's copiers.

I heard that things had to be kept simple, otherwise highly technical machines would break down and fail with no one to fix them. Finding a repairman was impossible because who would travel from Perth, eight hundred miles away, to do a service call at HEH! Heh, Heh, Heh.

This was also the case with vehicles, but with these the part could be ordered by phone and delivered next day on the bus that regularly travelled that route.

We got along well, the eight or so of us in the building, except for the coffee making each morning. But it got brewed, though not the best tasting. Even the high-ranking JAG with us labelled it piss at times.

A small get together marked the occasion when the guy I replaced returned stateside. A bigger celebration took place elsewhere. Gabe and his wife and family prepared a weekend dinner for him. A few of us attended. The Admin boys also marched him out at the EMC with music, a kegger, munchies and some small gifts.

Now it was just Gabe and me at ES. I don't think others had much confidence in me when they made remarks about my siesta; not being speedy like Speedy Gonzales, etc.

The Navy Days

I performed the job, did the work and Gabe had no big complaints. He liked that I was punctual, kept the office and space organized and received visitors well. Maybe things went on behind my back and never up front, face to face.

I sensed people felt ill at ease dealing with a minority, like some folks among Blacks, in those decades, but anyways.......and then in Australia with its White policies and idiotology.

Onto a couple of developments. Gabe had many connections and one was a gorgeous blond, Vic (Victoria). Tall, tanned, married and smart. She worked in Special Services, though at times she rotated to other Admin positions when and where needed.

These Australian folks had their own 'network' and while true to their jobs, some shenanigans did take place, like equipment disappeared or shortages in the warehouse and empty gas tanks from government vehicles. Office romances. Who knew, but the rumors repeatedly surfaced often.

Gabe and the legal yeoman worked it very favorably so that his gal friend Vic in Special Services placed me in a part-time position as a librarian after hours. How sweet it was!

You see, I made no bones about it. I would be leaving the military to return to college under the GI Bill (in fact, some Aussies and sailors said I'd never make it, fail, flunk out). That's why Gabe helped me prepare financially with another job for extra income to save for school.

This was but one way or example in which the 'network' worked. Call it nepotism, favoritism, etc. Thanks. I benefitted.

Aussies were at HEH for the money. To save it and return home, whenever that was. They earned it in any manner they could while sacrificing themselves on the Northwest Cape. They reminded me of oil riggers who go out to the wells at sea, only because the money is soooo good. A very dangerous job.

Vic had a very personable manner and got along fabulously with everyone, with the officers like wolves around her. She was

HOT! Absolutely stunning in her swimwear when we were at the beach. A good sport and athlete too. I'd dream we went after each other in the library, sort of a la Mrs. Robinson with her yearning for some younger Latin lover.

She and I teased one another, touched, flirted and gazed. She taught me a lot about the business of running a library. People noticed and commented.

She and Gabe expressed pleasantly that I brought a different style and appreciated my background and struggles. The norm was usually White American kids from middle-class upbringings without many worries.

Definitely a big difference for me, because I hung around civilians whereas almost everyone had closer associations with military types. Examples follow. Gabe and I ate lunch in the office, or we'd join Vic, sometimes driving into town.

I'd be at Gabe's home for dinner, visit with his kids, wife and neighbors. We'd all go to the beach at times or out boating.

I would invite them to the base, the theater and watch movies or go fishing at the pier and enjoy a cookout.

Gabe and I would also leave work early to go visit the school, talk business with staff there and check up on the American kids.

The ES Yeoman's job was the job, but the job not always at the ES office or building.

Gabe would repeatedly take leave of the office, such as when he took vacation time. I'd stay behind and cover. At times, however, Gabe would be gone a week or two for work-related visits in Brisbane, Canberra, Melbourne and other cities for 'Inspection' purposes. Look at the boarding schools, interview personnel and students, review academics and such.

He'd call the office to check on how it was holding-up and perhaps offer encouragement, a pep-talk. I'm sure he called others to be double sure all was fine.

This aspect of ES work to me did not seem Navy or military-like, as I had once thought. It wasn't all or entirely McHale's Navy from television, but it was not the movie Pearl Harbor either. I came to learn about military operations necessary or vital to the missions of defense of the Homeland, whether it's stateside or in foreign lands.

I felt a new awareness, learning to socialize with a different population outside of my Hispanic culture, but in a semi-military setting of sailors and Australian civilians.

The hi-jinx continued whether the higher-ranking staff, the JAG or Gabe were in the office. Sometimes both would be gone for an extended period of days, and they also participated. The activities were nothing serious: darts, hangman and checkers. No one could say anything because the JAG was in our corner.

The second development concerned extra duty. In the Navy, not only in Exmouth but other stations, just about everyone and truer for enlisted personnel, had regular duty that would be the regular work. For me this was the forty-hour work week at the office. In an Admin this was steady, stable, Monday through Friday dayshift. Others, like Security, had rotating hours.

In addition, we were assigned extra or special duty, such as shore patrol, which this one-hundred-twenty-pound weakling performed briefly. Soon I switched and I became an ambulance driver out of the dispensary. Strictly after hours.

The interviewers asked about my background, driving, first-aid, etc. I passed. This was truly for slackers with plenty of time to write letters, sleeping, reading, cards and more sleep.

Nothing ever happened but the dust build-up on the vehicles in the carport, which I cleaned. I learned quite a bit about the dispensary itself and more the role of the EMT.

I shared this duty with a corpsman who regularly trained on life saving techniques or procedures. Infrequently one of the military doctors (MDs) or nurses would drop in to catch-up on their work.

Weekend and holiday duty was twenty-four hours. One could exchange or sell the duty, but I didn't with my library position.

I'll allow myself to briefly repeat the following incident which I described in my earlier writing. Some readers found it hilarious, our government at its most ineptitude level.

The Chief Hospital Corpsman and I had the duty and we had retired, already snoring when very early in the morning, about three a.m., a 911 call rang.

Dazed, fully unconscious, we learned of a male body on the side of the road near Exmouth. We dashed to the scene and on the way literally ran head-on into some kangaroos, I'd say fewer than ten. We didn't stop being we had a body to look after. It could be life or death.

The entire moving episode had the makings of an Abbott and Costello film, if you think about it and frame a mental image about what happened. Simply imagine a Navy ambulance, siren blaring, lights flashing as it speeds down the highway and smashes into some marsupials, which go flying every which way.

We located the bloke sprawled on the side of the road, as if dead. No, but terribly drunk and smelling awful, covered in filth and dirt, like having been in a brawl.

He was an American, a tall, lanky, pale Texan, knocked out but mumbling nonsense. Somehow or other into the wagon he went, and we returned to the base and dispensary. The Texan never lived down that night of drinking.

I went to bed, very quickly fell asleep and the other two soon followed. I think the Chief checked him over, cleaned him up a little, then put him to bed. Did I check the damaged ambulance after the impact? I can't think of it now, probably not.

Off duty, I went that morning and only later, after an investigation, was I questioned. The Chief Corpsman backed up my story, which cleared me, but I apologized for my forgetfulness by not reporting the accident.

The whole base laughed about what had happened that early morning and ribbed me, but hey, I heard the galley served tasty kangaroo burgers for a few days thanks to this careful ambulance driver.

So, let me report that having dealings with sick bay, as I did meant that the corpsman needed dummies to practice their skills, but few were available. Therefore, they used us drivers to check our heart rates, temperature, blood pressure and perform basic medical exams.

Another interesting tid-bit or two was that some of the married corpsman would at times have their family stop by to visit. They'd bring a dessert which I too enjoyed and got a chance to be entertained with the kids. Which I didn't hesitate to do or mind while the adult couples hid in one of the patient rooms for carnal pleasures, moans and groans and shrieks.

Who cleaned up the clinic, but janitorial staff, an interesting bunch that lightened the spirit, as you'll see?

I was the ambulance driver but once a week and full-time as Yeoman at the ES buildings. The same cleanup crew did several buildings, but I wasn't too concerned with their work.

These workers were foreigners and the four or so I regularly encountered came from Europe, the Slavic Nations, Yugoslavia, Czechoslovakia and others, in the early nineteen-sixties, before the breakup of the Soviet Union. I'm not certain about the names of these countries now.

Meeting these workers and trying to have a conversation presented difficulties due to their limited English. Tried teaching them some Spanish.

Naida or Nadia usually swept and mopped, she just popped up in my mind as I recollect that time and place, she and her companion, who may have been family or related, regularly worked together and did quite the decent clean-up of the building in their charge. The inspectors wrote favorable reports regarding the work and effort of these women.

Naida appreciated Gabe and I, such as by bringing her home baked pastries- European recipes. Not bad.

She identified with me- ethnics, not Australian nor American. She asked me many questions and seemed curious. We looked at atlases and National Geographic's to research our respective lands, birth places and bodies.

I even mentioned her in letters I sent home.

She dug into my background- my Family, education, interests, Mexico, my return to America, etc., when they came by the office, drank our coffee and so on.

Oddly, these European souls seemed beaten after years of struggling for a meager existence. They had poor posture, bad teeth and short stature, with dark hollow eyes. The gals wore no make-up and rarely smiled and wore old clothing, out of fashion.

But figure it out, they would rather be living in the nowhere land, the Outback of Australia than in Europe, their native country. Such were the conditions that drove them away, they said, they grabbed the opportunity to leave, even if it meant to this land of sheep, kangaroos, aborigines and sailors.

There were many like them throughout Australia and Exmouth had a nice small sampling of these kind, hardworking people I feel very fortunate to have met and shared my military experience.

Once, I happened to catch them in the chapel performing some of their usual but unusual, in that they were kneeling at the front and were in prayer. I heard that in their home country in Europe they could not do this freely.

Yet we as Americans take for granted our freedoms guaranteed to us by the First Amendment of the Bill of Rights in our Constitution. Moving on.

The Navy Days

Francisco Rivera

CHAPTER 14.

Preparing for Cyclone

Late summer, early fall, 1969, will be with me forever. Who knows, maybe I'm lying or mistaken about the exact time or months. It could be as late as November, but a scary time for sure, a certainty.

The hot weather changed. Thicker humidity, a rolling ocean, heavier clouds and more, meant hurricane season known as cyclones in that part of the world. No, I do not want any part of it. Quite the experience. They can have it, and all the natural disasters. I still have photos in my albums of those horrid days of inclement weather, the worse imaginable.

The main thrust lasted many hours, but the residual effects lasted much longer, and we were on lock-down for three days. Furthermore, there would be repeat performances during cyclone season. My mental picture fades, but I believe a large vessel tied up or anchored near our pier to avoid the storms. Maybe not.

Here are a few notes about the scene around Exmouth & HEH.

Some of the locals welcomed the change, because it broke up the monotony and the surfers loved the waves. Some trailers got tossed around and flooding occurred. There was no loss of life but a dog or two perished, as did some of the wild beasts. People prepared by boarding up buildings, staying in the school and gathering supplies. A contingent of the Red Cross from Perth showed up.

On base, the barracks, constructed of solid reinforced concrete blocks and tied/anchored with cables, shook and trembled like the quakes in California. We had boarded up all windows and entry ways. Vehicles were parked, no traffic except from Headquarter Control Central. "Restriction" was the word, the code. Few ventured outside except for the Sea Bees who worked to minimize the damage.

Rations in the dorms suited us, why risk life or limb by walking to the chow hall for a meal.

Amazingly, later, once calm returned, dead sea creatures could be found here and there, which we either buried or tossed into the sea.

Damage resulted in broken windows and shattered protective plywood covering from buildings, flooding, like a swimming pool and baseball fields. Projectiles such as branches, fences or lamp posts penetrating walls. I witnessed the spearing effects.

Once the storms passed, working parties took care of the clean-up and some of the repairing, such as roof leaks.

I don't know how many cyclones I lived through during my two seasons in the Northwest Cape, but the fear in us remained each time.

Give me the dry Arizona desert anytime, I would write home.

Our building and offices remained unscathed. I attribute this to the lack of windows. I had not paid attention to this but now it became apparent. It was a safety feature.

It was around this time, or not, that the ES Office became quite busy, because this was when advancement exams for enlisted personnel throughout the U.S. Navy were held. Whether for cooks, storekeepers, electricians, submariners, Airedales and Sea Bees

The Navy Days

from E-3's on up to chiefs. All over the fleet.

Lists had to be comprised of sailors seeking advancement and the tests ordered. All very top secret to prevent cheating or having the exams compromised, which has happened.

We made the necessary preparations and worked diligently to prepare and set the rooms per instructions, ensuring we had monitors and the clocks for timing. Bathroom breaks were closely watched.

Afterwards, elaborate or detailed, organized inventory, packaging and mailing were followed to ensure security according to plan. All kinds of seals, stamps and signatures were required.

My role in this was mostly to help Gabe and the Personnel Officer. I did little, mostly typing, filing and moving furniture. Contentment came acting as a gofer. This process repeated itself in six months.

The integrity of the advancement exam process was paramount. Scandals occurred repeatedly, such as paying someone to take the exam, bribery and so on.

I could see it, why some would cheat in order to advance. I had access to personnel records, all kinds. Some that I reviewed revealed sailors still or Seaman E-3, after six or seven years of service and unable to move up. How did they ever enlist and become Seaman?

Right now, I recall, four sailors who were in such straits. Stuck in Security without being able to advance. Regardless, the U.S. Navy needed them and relied on them to be gun-ho and ready to set sail almost at a moment's notice.

After a two-decade career or longer, if not busted or discharged, perhaps with luck on their side, they'd rise to maybe boatswain mate, Petty Officer 2nd Class.

Think deeply about the idea that sailors would be promised a promotion with re-enlistment.

All the dealings with the advancement exams for enlisted

personnel took place, a bunch of man hours at the time, but six weeks later or thereabouts when the results came in, more work for us, more than usual and there were some unhappy campers.

To illustrate, let's say an E-6 career Quartermaster almost ready to retire with twenty years of service, mostly sea duty, tries to pass the exam for the fourth time to upgrade to chief. He doesn't make it. Retiring as Chief boosts his pension, and his ego, not four times a failure. There are positives being chief- better uniforms, higher command, pay, etc.

Some sailors are firm believers in this pecking order, the re-enlistment, the twenty-five cent and hour raises with a promotion.

Yet the system has many flaws. Our Quartermaster here is near forty, ready to exit while a younger sailor of age thirty is already chief because of his critical rating as a radarman, plus he gets much higher pay and re-enlistment bonuses.

It may be different now, four and a half decades later. But in 1970, from the little I knew or observed, there was little incentive to remain or re-enlist.

I could not picture myself going through with it and extending my time in service. I witnessed a few of these instances, starting with badgering to renew the pledge to serve and protect the country, to promise offshore duty in Europe, as a civilian not in uniform. The money lured many, it seemed married men with dependents were easier targets with eagerness.

If a sailor wished to re-up with an elaborate ceremony, he got it: trumpets, color guard, music, a gun salute and family. Now that I wonder, had there been a Mariachi band playing at one of these shindigs?

There were many like me who just shook our heads and frowned inwardly. We could not speak out in discouragement.

Money was and is the motivator, not dedication, loyalty and it was far easier to earn it than by trading one's life away.

For me, the library gig paid handsome civilian wages. For

others, like the Sea Bees, they would work after hours repairing vehicles, clean-up and yardwork.

Ambition and motivation would take somebody far.

Having broached beaucoup the education theme, I'll provide some personal digs on the matter.

I had started considering about my return to civilian life in America and the schools to attend, with likelihood I'd go for a liberal art or a business degree. Something along finance, accounting or banking, in general, commercial, mortgage, government or investment. These were but the initial thoughts, first steps.

Another step I took was applying after preliminary research, for correspondence courses. I mailed the application to USAFI for a study of Russian history. The Navy said nothing, perhaps thinking I wasn't a commie.

Later, I dealt directly with UTEP with another correspondence course in literature. I did well in both and gave me something to pass the time away at the cape.

But getting smart and educated, as I've said before, does not entail just reading, writing and/or classroom work, but includes some practical application, live experiences and hands on dirty manual work.

This included field trips near HEH. Special Services offered a really great opportunity. It had three or four Land Rovers, which are Jeep-like vehicles but bigger, stronger and just as ugly. These could be reserved and checked out, boy they were in demand.

We borrowed one on a weekend and took off. I'm weak on the very particulars but I think the three or four of us went south, maybe a couple of hours driving with our target being Manilya, but I may have it misspelled here.

Minilya is a young, pretty native lass in miniskirts and goes by Leah/Lia. She inhabits the wild Outback. If you believe this you are one funny or sad, gullible bloke. Cheer up!

Minilya exists south of Exmouth, a tiny spot of civilization though the surroundings, I recall, were agrarian. Much brush and scrub, plus red earth decorated it. A very rustic place where one sees the aborigines, as I remember.

I think we stayed overnight, living off our ice chests filled with chips, bread, lunch meats, beer, drinks and ice. We didn't suffer at all and endured a different type of activity, not just the barracks.

Some of the Aborigines who came into the camp were really rough looking and scorched black from the sun and outdoors. We shared our snacks with them.

For me it was just remarkable, beautiful, a terrific experience. Others would go for night clubbing, drinking and dancing, that's good fun as well. Me, I'm a desert sailor, rural.

But being out with nature, the gorgeous starry night sky, getting buzzed while listening to the tales of the tribes and folks. It felt spiritual to me and then some of their rhythm and drums added to the great vibes (we had no radio or tv in the area for hundreds of miles).

I've had similar memories of back home, in the surrounding hot desert with its coyotes, owl sounds and bon fires.

The Aborigines have had a very hard existence, many, many times made worse by the invading White people who enslaved, abused, killed and stole from them. In the early 1990s, the Australian Supreme Court attempted to change the conscience of the country. They made a monumental decision by outlawing or reversing the many policies detrimental to the aborigine's population.

While change was made, a Labyrinth still exists to make things right for these people. The change is exceedingly slow.

The history is vast and very complicated. So, for a better understanding, which you won't find here, there are many sources at the libraries and internet. Dig in.

We drove around some more and did explore here and there. I recall a stream where we washed. Bear in mind, nearly fifty years ago the Outback was raw and wild, whereas now the improved road system makes the adventuring easier, especially with IT, phones, etc.

The return trip to HEH proved uneventful and we promised we'd do it again. Perhaps south to the coast where more scenic beaches, paradise-like, could be visited during a weekend, as long as the weather cooperated and remained pleasant.

Shortly after our arrival on base, we unloaded our gear and cleaned the vehicle because it became red from the desert dust. Then we turned in the Land Rover to Special Services, which did what it could to boost morale and lift our spirits.

The bowling alley, in the same building with the library had big crowds and leagues. Tournaments were ongoing, sometimes in the day for the night crawlers.

Back from our excursion in Minilya or whatever tiny locale we saw, back from the hills, back in the barracks.

I haven't addressed the barracks, have I? Here goes.

The description is a downer and hardly anyone likes it there, but the choices were very or extremely limited. Perhaps a self-built mud-hut off base would be better.

The buildings' age comes across with old coats of paint peeling. The graffiti shows, such as around the staircases.

The unpleasant life daily, hourly: janitors during the workdays. Lots of noise for those working graveyard who can't sleep in the day.

The weekends attract crowds when sailors are not working. Drinking, softer-noisy brawls, music, (all kinds; jazz, country, rock, etc.) gambling and laundry.

In the lobby can be found some magazines, music, games (bingo, darts, cards), hobbies (puzzles, arts and crafts, billiards and more). Mostly a nuisance.

The cliques are very obvious. The Black sailors number maybe eighteen total and they stick together. With a couple of married lifers with families, they gather at their off-base housing or residences.

The Filipinos have their own social style along with their own language, Tagalog.

Think about this, they liked me because we can speak Spanish which has similarities to Tagalog. This results from way back when Spain conquered the Philippines.

These sailors have mostly steward and storekeepers' ratings. The Navy recruits them out of Manila, many as steward to tend to the officers corps.

They love to gamble and were regularly seen in Exmouth in Navy housing socializing, enjoying life and partying. I went along but infrequently.

To add to the unpleasantness of dorm life, worse on the weekends, think of stopped toilets, trash, old food and flies, odors, stenches and awful smells.

Such were the crowded Navy barracks, with segregation by nationalities and occupations. Animal house almost.

All the excitement became past-tense and we started a new week, same-o-same-o, the old grind.

So many items to cover, what's the next big thing. Here is a morsel, a small jewel. I'm not too sure when exactly it took place, but I vividly remember the incident but for the date.

Periodically, maybe once or twice per month, a seven-man team (no females), would be formed to remove litter from the highway. Low ranking dudes chosen, me as the truck driver and of highest rank. I'd have six sailors maybe from the brig or on corrective conduct as disciplinary action.

We got going early, before it heated up along with some tools with the truck carrying ice, water, drinks, snacks, etc. Gloves, boots, music, long sleeves and big hats were required as protection.

The Navy Days

Also, plastic bags.

The pier was the starting point and into Exmouth we'd go at about a mile per hour. Five miles, five hours or so and we'd call it a day.

Past the Main Gate by a half mile or halfway on our trek, hell did not break loose. I drove with three guys on each side of the road slightly behind and the trash load heavier, then I braked and came out yelling, hollering and snapping. Chinque a su puta! Piruja! Madre! Pendejos! Brutos! Babosos! They weren't paying attention and I brutally tore into them, made each a new hole.

On the left side of the road, near the curb and pavement, Volpe (not his real name but I remember him VERY WELL), walked over a poisonous snake and if bitten he would have died very quickly. Missed it by inches and the viper slithered away.

Its been the only time that I can remember I utilized my rank and authority, with such force but for the good of the team.

I explained what happened and some saw the serpent, the slick quick moving kind. They didn't blame me at all, and Volpe actually thanked me after he calmed down, unbelievably scared about what could've been.

Not much later, maybe that same afternoon, the snake incident was in the rumor mill, growing bigger by the minute, to be expected.

I'm surprised it was not the Loch Ness monster.

CHAPTER 15.

Hawaii Bound

Not to startle you, alarm or surprise you, but in a few paragraphs, we'll take a major break from our time in Australia and head in a different direction. I'm just preparing you for the upcoming switch or transition.

Sometimes the daily, boring routine screamed for a change. The HEH sailors looked for or created ways to go about this in a quite crazy manner. The surest way was death as in danger to self or others. One sailor climbed the water tower and threatened to kill himself by drinking all the water! Gotcha! By jumping off. That was his ticket to be shipped out.

Another guy punched his hands through a glass window and slit his wrists. He too was saved and sent elsewhere. These were but two examples to illustrate the seriousness caused by the heat, isolation and family separations. These men suffered. For some it was a psychological war.

It was said men would brawl and get into fights to break a jaw with a good left-hook, only to be out of Exmouth and in Hawaii for surgery and treatment.

Being I was the ambulance driver and in the medical clinic, I witnessed some of this behavior. My turn also came to be shipped out due to legitimate health reasons. Or maybe they thought I was truly insane. Maybe.

This is when the big switch or separation occurred. My tour of active duty in Australia was interrupted, divided into 'before and after' this separation.

Somehow an optometrist checked us for glasses and referred me to HEH Physicians, who then diagnosed me with an eye problem they felt needed evaluation by an ophthalmologist. These doctors were only MDs, young, fresh out of school and inexperienced.

In a short time, maybe ten days, I had my ticket to Waikiki.

Gabe and I talked, discussed the ES operation, the office set up and where things were and how we stood. We trained a back up to cover for me while I was gone on medical leave for about two weeks.

I worked it out as well with Special Services to arrange for my time off.

I packed my belongings in the barracks, everything neatly arranged and secured my locker.

My contingency-plans took Andy into account as my confidant in the event I did not return.

My bank account was drained, and I bid farewell to mates Vic, friends and Gabe's family. I had intentions of returning but one never knows. Best laid plans like getting laid and not going away. Would you rather get laid or think about what could've been?

I didn't realize I had gained such popularity. Just about everywhere I went people wished me well and some even wanted me back, not risk danger elsewhere by leaving, especially by being out at sea with the treacherous and merciless ocean.

The day of departure arrived and the little I remember was that I did not get the time off. I think I worked because the MAC Flight always returned late to Sydney or Christchurch. The aircraft touched down, unloaded and the pilots took their break while crews restored and secured everything, then passengers went aboard, etc. Four to six p.m. by the time we left.

I dressed in my Blues, grabbed some grub, drinks, magazines, etc., and was set to go. I was okay, not shocked or in any discomfort, plus the doctors said I'd be okay.

The pilots preferred daylight for takeoff, not the darkness, so we were soon bound for Southeast Australia. We were about a dozen individuals, with five crew members and the rest staff from HEH.

Nerves kept me awake and jittery, not able to concentrate nor be able to read. I even got up, about ninety minutes into the flight, without permission and sat in the cockpit.

I interrogated the pilot and navigators like crazy for the half hour or, so I was with them. They were very understanding and kind. The two made small talk. Amazingly, they were aiming for the USA. They were due in California in a couple of days after stops in New Zealand, a Pacific Island and Hawaii and maybe some shut eye.

These flights, the military ones as well as the commercial. were beginning to give me wings, an old pro crisscrossing the vast blue Pacific, which I think is not so pacific. I'd rather do it flying than by ship- I am a landlubber for sure.

I returned to my seat and after a snack I got lethargic then dozed off, long enough until Sydney.

Almost with certainty, I want to say we stayed in Sydney overnight, but the mind is funny, then times are indelible for certain events and not so for others.

One thought started to occupy my mind and persisted more and more and more. That was visiting Panchita and Ed in Douglas, Arizona. That's correct, back home. I kept this to myself. Let's see what happens in Hawaii first.

I remember from orientation in San Diego, about six months or so ago in July, that it was impossible, for enlisted men especially, and the military frowned on soldiers going stateside. Death in the family, birth of a child, nothing worked. The Navy had this policy as well and stricter for the Pacific Far East. Yeah Right! I heard differently.

Guess what? Soldiers found a loophole, rather humorous.

Soldiers from Viet Nam on R&R (rest and recreation) in Hawaii, for example, avoided MPs (military police) patrolling the airport to prevent this. With airline tickets in hand they boarded the aircraft by being in disguise, typically dressed as long-haired hippies. As long as one did not appear like, resemble, or act military their passage was safe.

With short haircuts, spit-shined shoes, tattoos, soldiers were easy to spot and stop. But much harder if otherwise dressed as a war protestor, who the military did not mess with.

Getting back to our MAC Flight in Sydney. If we remained it must have been just a stop-over, nothing much, not memorable at all. Just simply to rest and sleep.

A few passengers stayed behind, and some new ones boarded, then on to New Zealand. Not much of a stop. We picked up researchers and scientists from the South Pole where they had been conducting studies, 'though not much fun in the cold and darkness', they stated.

Is this island hopping? Four islands: Australia, New Zealand, Hawaii and whatever other island we had to land on, Guam, Midway and Pago Pago.

Evidently, the MAC Flights had a different stop on this route because we were headed to Midway. A famous Naval Battle took place in World War II, near there. It was a turning point in the war. We knocked out three Japanese air carriers.

This vital barren tract of sand, a no man's land, serves America's interests in the Pacific. A trillion times worse than HEH.

You don't get mail but once a year at tax time. It's not on Santa's Xmas list. Not midway between crazy and the looney bin, but 100 % insanity, Guam is give up and masturbate. You can't even do that in Midway. You get the idea.

Welcome to America! To the American Outpost in the

The Navy Days

Pacific, the beautiful state of Hawaii. From way up at twenty-thousand-plus feet and descending. The views were magnificent, lower, lower and lower still, the earth became larger and I can't fathom this. The wheels grabbed the tarmac and burned rubber into smoke.

I felt giddy, inexplicably happy with a sense of accomplishment. Very difficult to describe, but here I was in paradise, as the islands are called (or pearls or gems). Ecstasy! Ebullience! Viva!

We came to a stop almost, and slowly made it toward the unloading area. It was like the firmament opened, once outside I saw and experienced wonders after returning from the wilderness. I stopped and turned around, got a good look- I'm back! I could not believe it and some of the others were jumping for joy, extremely jubilant in returning to civilizations, at Hickam AFB.

The feeling had to give way, pass, because we needed to remove our luggage and be processed. Some had to run to the airport to meet their commercial flight. Nos despedimos. Goodbye, farewell. Adios.

I remained at Hickam and registered. Arrangements of one sort or another had been made for me, but not my guys who were all horny gawking at all the females. Eighteen months away will do this, turn you rabid, tongue hanging out, dick in hand, playing pocket pool.

At receiving, the personnel checked me in and sent me to the lounge to wait, which I briefly did, then sent to some motel-like barracks. I registered and with keys in hand went to my room until further notice. I was free, alone in my room and could fart to my heart's content. Oh, what a feeling, unlike canned sardines in the barracks. I kept the key and never turned it in. The room was mine.

If you thought I was sky-high, feeling all juiced up. That was nothing compared to my Parents and Family in Douglas when they heard me on the phone. We all started laughing, yelling, crying and loving every nano-second of the moment. Of course, they wanted to know the reason for my being in Hawaii. I lied to put them at ease and not have them worry. I think I said R&R duty, because of our isolation in Australia.

We talked some more and caught up on numerous topics of this, that and the other. What a pleasure to exercise my native tongue.

We marveled at the technology, so advanced that made our communication fun, instant, possible, but the moment couldn't last forever. I promised to call again.

I had mixed feelings. Much joy hearing them, not with letters, cards or cassettes. But I lived and learned they're well health wise, financially and more. Sadness came with tears at disconnecting.

Onto my mission. I transferred to Pearl Harbor, the Navy Base- which is a short distance from the airfield- soon after- but I managed to keep my connection at Hickam.

I quickly was learning the ins-and-outs of living in the military while in Hawaii. Like shuttle services to avoid the public buses, free food and so forth, thereby saving a few coins.

Once on the Navy side, I worked sparingly after processing, because I was fully ambulatory and could perform several jobs. This consisted mostly as back up typing, filing, chasing records for office workers, both civilian and military. I still had my medical appointment to keep, which I waited for.

One of the sightseeing highlights nearby was the Solemn Arizona Battleship, which I visited.

I knocked off at four and by five I was in Honolulu, Ala Moana, Waikiki or elsewhere. Busy social life with a gazillion female tourists from throughout the world. Live it up!

In the early seventies, I'd say, Don Ho was the most popular in entertainment and his hit 'Tiny Bubbles', was off the charts. He would perform in various venues to the large adoring female crowds of all ages. Wow! Wow! Wow! Women!! Just unbelievable dating and pleasure. A 180 turn from Exmouth. Girlfriends galore.

The Navy Days

Finally, Tripler Army Hospital called with my appointment at the eye clinic, but details escape me. This medical leave seemed secondary to my Hawaiian vacation. Needless to say, I had to comply, my reason for being there.

The shuttle to TAH ran regularly or one could use the bus, taxi, etc.

Tripler sits on a hill and can be seen from a distance. It's a well-designed institution, pink, that provides a long list of services to Military Personnel, Veterans and their families. In my view it was quite modern then.

Later I will better address Tripler being that I will have spent more time there.

Several of us boarded the shuttle from Pearl to the hospital. We each had different reasons for going, in dealing with our medical concerns and/or health issues. The entire experience was foreign to me. Being that in my young life I very rarely saw a doctor, since I was blessed with good health, despite my size.

A good size crowd had gathered at the information desk, asking for directions, requesting records and/or visitation inquiries. Soon enough I easily found the eye clinic in the upper floors, where the kind staff attended to me and took my medical/health records.

They looked me over and gave me a cursory exam, then had me take a chair in the waiting area until I would be called. Many were ahead of me. I relaxed, read magazines and such until I heard my name.

The escort took me into the examining room and prepped me for the ophthalmologist. He took his time showing up, but the place was busy with many patients of all types.

He came in reading the clipboard and we introduced each other. He was an impersonal officer, just brass tacks and to the point. His exam was thorough, one I had never had before. I even felt burning in my eyes when he would shine his light there.

His report concluded that I had good vision with corrective

lenses, no glaucoma, cataracts and such. Though I had a benign growth, larger on the left eye than the right one. This could be surgically removed without too much trouble.

That was the gist of it. The physician concluded his summary and dismissed me, with a six-month follow-up. I was instructed to tell my military bosses this. No ifs, ands or butts. He would see me in half a year.

He assured me all would be fine and to resume my normal duties when I got back to active status.

The night life awaited, and I headed there once I walked out of the maze at Tripler. What a labyrinth!

I'll clarify one point here. My foggy mind clearly tells me I spent one Christmas season in Hawaii and another one in Australia, but I don't remember the sequence.

I celebrated my good fortune with the eye doctor giving me such good news after his examination.

Get ready for a jolt!

The beautiful lobby, the fine decor, the soft lighting and great tunes. I acknowledged how grand life can be, while I flew thirty-thousand-plus feet in the wild blue yonder over the Pacific in a new 747 beast of American Airlines. This huge carrier had very recently come off the production lines and were welcomed royalty.

Spacious, with double decks- the top one qualified as a lounge, bar and entertainment center, with a large crowd being served. Happier than happy hour. Food, drinks, music, movies and gorgeous hostesses. Everyone on the prowl, and me here!!!!

Forget Tripler and my bad eyes. I managed (not bribed), to get approval for my request for leave, and discounted airline fare for the military. I headed to California, Arizona and Mexico.

I won't say more because I could still be court-martialed and/or imprisoned, but it all worked out perfectly. I don't want the powers that be to get in trouble. As if.

The Navy Days

You can probably surmise and say that my whole Hawaiian excursion was a set-up, a farce, the hoodwinking of the military, etc., but I won't. Was Radar from M.A.S.H. always a straight arrow, on the up and up? That's how Navy Admin in HEH worked. Heh, Heh, Heh! Hawaii too.

I had a thoroughly fun time on the 747 and left with a remarkable gal to spend the night within her LA condo. The rest I leave to your imagination, dreams and history.

Francisco Rivera

CHAPTER 16.

Visiting the Mainland.

Exhaustion set in for us by morning from the jetlag, drinking and loving. When strong coffee, pills and breakfast eased the symptoms, then we bid farewell. She loved that this sailor was heading home to see his elderly Parents. She did her patriotic duty for sure in support of the military and I'm the proof.

I had finagled and schmoozed the airline tickets for a few bucks and caught a second flight to Tucson without any difficulty. It seemed to me that the soldiers received very favorable treatment from United, Continental, American and the civilian air carriers. I won't complain at all being I got along great with them.

My sister Blanca and her Family resided in Bisbee at this time and Ma Bell information provided her address and phone number. I sought her indulgence and contacted her to please pick me up at Tucson International Airport, my arrival from LA due near midnight.

She shrieked with joy, practically splitting my eardrum with her blast. She couldn't care if I was well or not or what happened. All she heard was that I'd be home.

Blanca knew that if anyone could pull such a stunt and return from down under, that would be me! "UNBELIEVABLE", both said, Raul and Blanca who had to gently break the news to

Mom and Ed.

That dark cold night in the lit parking lot both had waited for me until my plane landed, then she came and met me while Raul stayed with the kids in the gray Buick.

She ran, hugged and kissed me, tears streaming down her soft pretty rosy cheeks, overcome with joy. We couldn't let go of each other, so strong our familial bonds.

I had got my luggage from the carousel and we walked towards Raul who bear hugged me. The two sleeping kids in the back seat gave way to me, who soon joined them snoring.

We quickly drove the ninety-minute ride to Bisbee then we all sacked out. Raul had to get up early to go to work at the bank and I don't know what happened next, until four that afternoon. I had slept fourteen hours or more. I was dressed and ready when Raul returned from his office.

The Buick took the five of us to Douglas and my Parent's home on Second Street, two blocks north of the International boundary line with Mexico. ¡HOME SWEET HOME!

El gusto y placer, tan grandioso ese momento lleno de felicidad al vernos todos reunidos. Hugs, kisses and handshakes, while dinner was ready but getting cold. From the young Tony and Lisa, to the grandparents, all just ecstatic, ebullient and exuberant.

Vecinos, amigos y amistades se acercaron para verme y darme gran bien venida desde tan legos, del otro lado del mundo. ¡Pero que gusto! A Dios le dimos las gracias por esta reunión.

Supe después, creo, que Blanca le dijo a Clara (en su empleo) de mi regreso y ella le aviso a Ed y Panchita, que se asustaron bastante al recibir semejante notificación. Pero todo salió muy bien si no perfecto y con gran alegría.

Ed me aconsejo que a la otra les avise con más anticipación y no solo un día, pero si se quedó encantado. Clara agreed with Ed.

Quite the 'Hero's Welcome' I received, or so it seemed.

Maybe it's that you can take the Mexican out of the barrio, but you can't take the barrio out of the Mexican.

Actually, a very pleasant Homecoming it was. To me it boiled down to giving Mom and Dad a boost, a picker-upper to improve their morale. They were up in years and with that comes the downward health slide. Yes, you can come home again! Thomas Wolfe eat your words!

This trip also helped appease my guilt by having left them so vulnerable when I reported to active duty in July 1969. During the hot months when Blanca gave birth to Lisa, who was now a cherub, beautiful and quite big.

The get together lasted a couple of hours, the Cantua's had to return to their Bisbee residence but would return the next day.

We had dinner y también recibimos a los vecinos que vinieron a saludar a la Familia en esta reunión. Lo bonito que es el barrio, es casi como una gran Familia. Nos conocemos y ayudamos.

Al fin llegó la hora y se apagó la luz en nuestro hogar y dormimos, pero afuera y alrededor se dian los carros, la música de Agua Prieta y pláticas entre vecinos.

Me sentía rendido por el viaje tan largo que de vuelta no abri los ojos por diez o más horas.

Rico Café Combate en la mañana con un desayuno marca diablo- un rico menudo con tortas, frijoles refritos con queso- recién hechas al comal. Y todos muy agosto en pláticas de mis aventuras en Australia y Hawái.

Panchita noto que mis cartas de cada semana eran un evangelio para ella y toda la Familia. Con mucho gusto y a carcajados con lo que les contaba, como las hamburguesas de canguro y los nudistas nadando en el mar.

También tocamos el tema de nuestros familiares en Agua Prieta, Cumpas y Nacozari que seguido pedían noticia de mí y rezando por mi bien estar, que yo evite la guerra en Vietnam y que regrese pronto y sano, con el favor de Dios.

Pensé en como pasar el día, pero empecé con una visita a los Meléndez y discutimos temas, pero principalmente el servicio de Rafael en el Navy.

Tuvimos como una hora juntos, ellos ya habían ido a misa y desayunado. Don Antonio entro del garage where he was already at work, repairing a washing machine. Both were very pleased to see me and had a hundred questions for me about my Navy tour thus far.

They were very concerned about Rafael because he was serving in Viet Nam in non-combat status but was due out of there shortly. Who knew where he would be sent next, probably out to sea again?

We wound-up our visit being Mr. Melendez had work to complete but I promised to return before I went back to Hawaii.

Afterwards, I recall driving around but with vagueness. Whose car and where to, other than A.J.Bayless my former employer, to greet co-workers and friends. They were very surprised and pleased to see me again, they had many queries as well.

The old Navy Salts who worked there but had already served their military obligation- HELL!! I made their day, laughing and joking, in a state of disbelief at seeing me, y preguntando? Fuiste a la Guerra? Why are you back? What are you doing besides jacking-off? What ship are you on??

It was a short but sweet reunion with invites to return de unas mamacitas.

I stopped at the bank to withdraw a few funds and review my savings, the money I mailed from Exmouth. I was surprised to see how quickly the amount had increased. A good sign because I would be needing it once discharged from the Navy. Blanca had been regularly depositing the sum I mailed her.

My temptation to visit Cochise College didn't win out this time. I remained downtown a while longer and then I went to the Naval Reserve Center for old times' sake. I talked with the Station

Master, who for some time had already known about my doings in the regular Navy. That I had been stationed out back in Australia's Northwest Cape. He even described the place, in bleak terms.

We parted, were nice to each other and wished everyone blessings. I thanked him as well.

Pues en este tiempo vacacionando en mi pueblo me di manía de visitar la secundaria por un rato porque mi hermana menor, Clara, atended there and I was curious more than anything about what was taking place there. It had been about four years since I had graduated.

Not too different than before except for the change in students' plans. They now had the option of starting higher education due to the recent establishment of the nearby college. Cochise College, a tremendous, innovative accomplishment for that area of Southeast Arizona. More so for Douglas because the institution was built so close to the International City that it served Mexico as well.

Clara had clearer focus, showed resolve, more of a go-getter and planning wisely. I admired her because she wanted what I had wanted. She had attained junior status and graduated Douglas HS in May 1971. Sears Roebuck hired her, and she did clerical-admin for the credit department her last two years of high school. Getting educated and employed like her brother had done.

My sister continued her schooling and shortly after completing DHS, she enrolled at Cochise and continued with Sears. Did that follow my footsteps?

Clara moved on from Sears and landed in the admissions office of the college where Blanca worked. Both Admin Assistants to the counselors, deans and advisors.

You can see why many are indebted to the college for education and employment, like we were.

I took a leisurely ride to the school to visit my alma mater, an open campus with trees and lawns. More greenery than I previously had seen there. I saw or met a couple of my former instructors.

My intentions were to ensure my transcripts and paperwork were in order. As I would be applying to universities to continue my education for a bachelor's degree upon discharge from the Navy.

By around noon I drove back to Douglas and in time for lunch with my Parents, Clara and her beau, John.

We broached another topic that took them by surprise and yet they knew I had made up my mind.

I expressed my desire to go to Mexico and visit the relatives for about a week, I invited them, but they declined. We talked about this: did I have papers, how would I travel, who to notify if something happened and more.

Impressed they weren't, but I reassured them all would work out and end well. Let me enjoy the time off, my freedom, my vacation in Mexico. A telegram was sent for them to expect me.

With a few things packed and some treats for mis tios y tias, sali al sur en el tren, 'El Caballero', which reminded me of my many trips en el cebollero in my youth. I was even looking forward to some horseback riding.

The long train ride provided ample time to contemplate. I had a plateful. In no particular order; the return to Hawaii and to HEH. Applying and getting excepted to college. The health issues with my eye and Tripler Hospital. Of course, all would require relocating several times even while still in the Navy.

In the meantime, I enjoyed the ride, ate food from the vendors, chatted with the passengers and observed the countryside. How terrific to be able to experience and enjoy the cultures, languages, variety and diversity.

Even in the military, I could observe sub-cultures- the Navy, Army, Air Force had similarities yet many differences and carried on accordingly. In the Navy the sub-groups consisted of the aviation components (aircraft carriers and land-based craft), the submarines, the construction battalions (CBs, aka Sea Bees) and the regular Navy (fleet service).

I also thought now, as I had during this long, solitary chase from Exmouth about my past and how I had grown up on another chase. That of money to get ahead, escape poverty and help the Family. How Clara had begun doing the same.

I seemed to have gained more purpose and learned more from the many earlier lessons of my youth. I wondered about what could have been: such as the loss of my Parents' first born, or if I had younger parents and a more normal upbringing.

Much soul-searching took place during these lonesome trips.

Undoubtedly, poverty did a number on us, the three young siblings who knew this and became accustomed to frugality and work.

At the bend, looking back, I could see the train curving and straining with its heavy rear load of empty box cars, for the cargo it would haul back north- what a marvel of engineering.

Clank, Clank, Clank, Clank, TooooToooo!

Ok, ok!!

I'm not Hemingway.

It's onomatopoeia,

that this peon

will pee on!

Nacozari! Mexico, Here I Am Baby!!

A Jesús García, El Hero, I will salute.

Pronto encontré a mis parientes y fuerte nos abrazamos y con muchos saludos. Juntamos los bultos y luego salimos.

En casa de mis tíos Acosta, a cerca de medio día, ya la mesa puesta para el almuerzo y luego le entramos a un caldo de pollo con verduras y tortillas de maíz y limonada para beber.

Muy bien rato pasamos allí platicando de todo: Clara y Blanca con sus niños; la educación y el colegio; el servicio militar y ni se diga, mi regreso a Hawái.

Sali un largo rato y anduve por Nacozari, un lindo, pequeño y humilde pueblo. Los cerros y alrededor muy verdes como un paisaje decorado a mano.

Regrese con mis tíos que para la tarde ya se sienten cansados debido a su edad y salud. Cenamos lentamente sopa de lentejas y a la hora nos retiramos, yo agusto y feliz.

El día siguiente salí a Cumpas por la mañana en el camión, después de despedirme de mis tíos.

Antes de medio dia estuve en mi pueblo natal, de donde casi todos venimos- mis Padre's, Blanca y yo aquí nacimos.

Un placer que le di a mis tíos y parientes cuando me vieron. Muchos besos, saludos, abrazos y más. Contentísimos y bien alegres al ver a este viajero del mundo, según mi Tio Jesús.

Parecía que había llegado el Papa o otro dignitario con el gentío.

Me dio gusto y me entro tristeza al ver a mis tíos, primos, parientes y conocidos porque los note más avejentados que se veían con el transcurso del tiempo, debido en parte porque life is hard. Very little leisure is afforded and individuals, families must work to survive, even for a meager existence. It's difficult, physical work when few amenities can be found.

Yet, I took in the beauty: the reunion, my Family and many memories from my youth. The gusto in their cheerfulness, closeness and camaraderie.

Having talked with my Tio Jesus, he made a very wise observation, as follows. He felt that God, Family and my conscience brought me back to my roots. Despite my efforts and experiences, I favor my Hispanic identity, culture, language, traditions and more. I was born into this; it cannot be erased.

The Navy Days

I may travel the world, meet many different souls, accept other customs, but I am still a multicultural man. A very Hispanic one at heart, which made me come back to re-energize and renew my ties. As if I needed to be re-baptized because I was away in an Anglo culture and losing touch with my beginnings. I needed my identity back.

It was beautiful the manner in which he expressed himself. His handsome tanned face, his partly toothless smile and his thick gray hair and his gestures helping him. I agreed with some of what he said and left it at that without showing him disagreement or disrespect. Especially with others nearby who showed much interest in my Navy role.

No denying that I sure felt terrific among my folks, eating their food, talking in Spanish, the music, reliving my youth y muchsimo mas.

The days I spent with mis tios, chatting and visiting others in the village. I took a ride to Montezuma y Jamaica with my cousin, being she had business dealings and accounts there.

Horseback riding still seemed fun but not as much as in my youth and the backache afterwards didn't help. A couple of mejoral (aspirins) relieved my pain.

Cumpas had changed. Now it had a better electrical system and roads were better. Much more improvement was still needed.

By the third day I had packed my bags and bid thanks and farewell to my folks, leaving them a nice gratuity. Hermosillo next.

I boarded the camion a Hermosillo en la mañana and by noon or so we were dropped off at the central plaza. We made several stops along the route, picking up and leaving passengers plus delivering some packages.

Lugging my bags while attempting to get my bearings proved awkward. Only after stopping for a snack and soda did I figure my next few steps and where to go.

The city is quite busy with much traffic. It's laid out flat mostly with a minimum of high rises. It has a university, an International airport and professional sports (soccer, basketball, beisbol).

Hermosillo is very important to Mexico, because its central to serving the vast surrounding northern territory. Government at the municipal, state and federal levels provides these services and maintains ties with the United States to the north. Very important links.

After studying the city map and bus system, I was able to locate my destination con mis parientes, who had been expecting my arrival to have been early.

I apologized for my tardiness, but my hosts were very gracious and classy. Whereas before I mostly saw my relatives in Cumpas, Nacozari y Agua Prieta, smaller agrarian communities. Here now was a large urban setting where my Mother's cousins were of means with luxury, big late model cars, palaces, servants and more. Highly successful, very accomplished people (bankers, lawyers, physicians), with strong ties to the business community and various branches of the government.

Totally upper crust, no pretentions. I rarely had dealings with them, maybe in Cumpas a couple of times. Mom and the Tias stayed in touch with them on a regular basis- Christmas cards, letters and such. Very generous by helping las Tias with funds, medical costs, home repairs and more.

They sort of knew I was not one of them but for blood and Family. They even commented that their sons would not be in the military, muchless as enlisted personnel. This would be beneath them. I shrugged my shoulders and said they did not live in America. I hated to be rude to the hosts and benefactors.

A sumptuous dinner was served, and we talked about Family, my Naval Service, career plans, college, etc.

I kid no one, but this thought came across: what the hell was I doing here with wealthy people I hardly knew. I was out of my element and I recalled the time with my San Diego friend Oscar Melendez, and the rich broad he was nailing. I visited her when he took me to dinner at her chanton chingon de lujo. La misma cosa. Soy pelado y pelado siempre seré, al menos en mi modo y carácter, pero con algo de inteligencia y bastante sentido común.

Ya más tarde, al oscurecer, salimos y nos paseamos un rato on the boulevards all over town and then drove up or climbed El Cerro De La Campana. We remained there nearly an hour. This hill near the edge of town provides a panoramic view of the city. The glistening lights and moving traffic presents a spectacle, like gleaming diamonds of a necklace resting on a gorgeous, topless beauty resting peacefully.

We continued sipping our beers and talked, then descending to wind up at a fancy night club, El Camino Real, where we met friends, drank some, talked and listened to music.

Beautiful girlfriends my cousins had, not common but upper crust, well placed in the local society- higher up in the pyramid, probably a few rungs below the apex.

They made me feel welcomed and did not deride my position or situation in the Navy with the ongoing Viet Nam War. They all basically were in opposition to the conflict and killing.

I explained my plight, similar to that of many young American men who faced conscription. We had limited options and realized those called were bottom-feeders, minorities and such.

They asked and I answered that yes, I lucked out by going Navy. That had been my plan to avoid warfare, plus I would be returning to college once discharged.

They heard too that friends and acquaintances of mine in Douglas had died. Killed in action and that perhaps, hopefully not, more would face the same fate.

We discussed California, Hawaii, Australia and spots I had seen, visited and experienced.

The evening fell into flatness, if you've ever heard the term. Probably not, I just invented it. Ni ánimo, ni gusto, y unas platicas algo desabridas y formal.

By near midnight we packed it in and soon, at my relative's place, I dozed like an infant, that's partly due to the liquor and late night.

With daylight came the noise and traffic as I enjoyed at a bistro a delicious breakfast muy Mexicano de tortas con jamon, queso y papas, con salsa al lado. El café bien super.

The time I spent mostly by myself, reading magazines and newspapers in the central district. I saw some government buildings, City Hall, the U.S. Consulate office.

I paid a short visit to the church, offered some prayers and contributed a donation.

People in Hermosillo show much European heritage. The beautiful women have light complexions and appear taller. This contrasts with the dark features seen in people in other regions of Mexico, especially towards Central America.

At the Universidad de Sonora, I did not do much and I was somewhat disappointed. It's much smaller than schools elsewhere and run-down in places. Students did not reveal a deep interest in academics or social aspects of their education. They seemed goal oriented: pay the bills, obtain the skills and expertise, then go to work in your field of study. Many engineers, accountants, medical students (radiology, lab techs, nurses), were graduating.

I returned to my relative's home and cleaned up. Apparently, we were visiting otro Tio who would be hosting a dinner at his Shangri La.

We got into the Crown Vic, Lincoln or vehicle of choice and drove a distance to a Maisson D'Or.

I approached with unease, being I did not feel close to these people nor did care for the ostentation. Be that as it may, I tried to put on a good front and make it through the evening, barely.

Why was I subjecting myself to this? Partly Mom who talked about her relatives, who we never had met but were way overdue.

Ed didn't push it though he did say it'd be good to see how the wealthy, better half of the family lived.

The evening with the stuffed shirts and haughty-taughty talk....... whatever.

I purposely drank to avoid them but tried not to be rude. This was not me. Before, I may have acted mannerly and cordial with meaning, now it was merely an act. This change in me was the result of being older, the college experience, Navy exposure and travel. I acquired a different mindset.

Yet they were my hosts and relatives. I felt like a hypocrite.

So, the next day I excused myself and travelled to Kino Bay, a small place on the coast, the Sea of Cortez, about an hour from Hermosillo.

I did little but lounge, worked on my tan, absorbed nature and its scenic desolate surroundings, empty during the weekdays but full on weekends.

I had seafood for lunch, of course, delicious fish at one of the puestos, which are huts, roughly put together, with thatched roofing. I met a young American couple who were avoiding the crass American commercialism and materialistic lifestyle. The pair weren't flower children but had a free-spirited air about them and probably did pot, peyote, mushrooms and all that.

The two were shocked to hear I was in the U.S. Navy, on leave in Mexico. They wondered if I was AWOL or in trouble with the law, fleeing and hiding south of the border. I assured them they were right. Turn me in and you'll be rewarded! I convinced them I was not one of those, meaning draft-dodgers, but a Bonafede sailor.

We ended our meeting after a couple of beers. I walked some more, enjoying the coast. I couldn't help but think I could sail from that spot and in a month get to Australia, HEH, by boat.

Oh well, time to head back to Hermosillo, Douglas, Hawaii, but another idea had been percolating wanderlust. Maybe after finishing college, find employment in the foreign service of some nation and travel, see the world, learn and find enrichment and personal growth.

El camión me regreso a Hermosillo donde llegue agusto y satisfecho. Pase a la capilla y di unas oraciones.

Ya en casa, platicamos un rato y luego la cena.

Comencé mi despedida y di gracias, explicando que mañana salia para el norte hacia Agua Prieta y allí con mis padres.

Así fue. Nos dimos fuertes abrazos y yo exprese mucho aprecio a mis parientes tan llenos de bondad y cariño.

Los dejes con esta nota: me gustaría muchísimo viajar y ver el resto de México, ambos lados, el caribe y el Pacifico.

Sleeping, dozing and dreaming in the van that's sputtering to the border, the realization returned about my good fortune in many ways displayed before me. Such as travelling half a world from where I am supposed to be, visiting my Parents and Family who are holding up quite well.

My brothers in arms smothering in the jungles of Southeast Asia, at war, killing and getting killed. Yet here I am almost on vacation, in a foreign land, at peace, in good health and high spirits. The Lord I Thank.

I counted my blessings to have some smarts, a bit of pocket change and get along okay in the world. While also being low-downtrodden and misbehaving, such as when I'm in Hawaii in a state of perdition while hanging out in Waikiki and Honolulu.

Or being in San Diego with Oscar, who I will look up and hope to find to go on the prowl.

We arrive at the border and I'm out of my slumber. Forget the balancing of good and evil and concentrate on getting across into Douglas y al chantè de Los Rivera.

Instantaneous change- almost- that's hard to pinpoint. It's partly as described: Douglas/AP is small, isolated lower-class with a hard-working minority which we are not accustomed to high living, luxury and wealth. We tend to reject caviar and champagne tastes and if the B & P Pool Hall serves as an indication, pork rinds and beer do us fine and dandy. Belch, Burppp!

I think that had to be the reason for my unease in Hermosillo con mis parientes de gustos finos.

Home awaited me y mi Panchita contentísima al verme. Me abrazo, beso, acaricio. No me soltaba, incrédula al ver a su hijo en casa, gracias a Dios, al que ella seguido reza para mi protección y bien estar siempre y en donde sea.

Nos reunimos y platicamos de mi visita con mis tíos y contarles de ellos- como están, que han hecho, que hay de nuevo. Les di la mejor noticia que pude. La pura verdad sin necesidad de mortificar a nadie con otros asuntos negativos.

Tristemente a todos se nos pasan los años y llegamos al decanso final.

At this point I don't think anyone from Headquarters knew where I was nor did they very much care, not HEH, Honolulu nor the local Navy Reserve. That's fine.

I'll spend time with my folks before I go back. We started with dinner once I crossed into the USA after returning from Hermosillo.

Mom was telling me that mis Tias had written already, that I made a favorable impression in Cumpas, with the young ladies there willing to settle down with me. Let's put those ideas on hold, just perish the thought.

This sounded like the similar message we heard in the military about young beauties attempting to get passage in one form or another to the USA.

Ed picked up on this and the issue of migration and his harangue about how lucky the Rivera clan had been succeeding with our crossing into this country. You'd swear he'd kneel down often and kiss the ground.

So, the day ended, and we retired.

I visited the Douglas Cemetery I recall, but I cannot pinpoint the time. Probably the following day.

I paid tribute to the very recent Viet Nam War Veterans who perished and came home to be buried in the Veteran's section. All were about my age, around twenty. I still feel the sadness of that moment nearly half a century later and tremble, as I recall these fallen men and my cousin laid to rest there.

Fate awaits me. What will it be? Will I return safely? Will my plans go awry? I had nearly a year and half to serve on active duty and hopefully I'll fulfill that duty. Like I have thus far and safely accomplish this in order to return home in the palm of the hands of the Lord.

At the cemetery a funeral/burial had been completed, I found out the descendant had been an older acquaintance I had known from my paperboy days, I thereby offered my sympathies to the various families paying their respects.

I left because I had to run an errand, rather minor, or else no dinner tonight.

A.J. Bayless and my ties to the store and its employees held strong, after all I gave it four years of my life, pain and equity for which I received little but a paycheck. I quit there approximately eight months ago but it seemed like only yesterday. I still pictured myself in my uniform when I first started my employment there while in high school.

I had left the cemetery and I wound up at AJB, again. After all I had been there last week. I went to get some items for Mom, and I found all of them from the short list she'd given me.

The previous thought of a better life beyond the horizon, of exceeding one's limitation and transcendence entered my mind. I needed to, had to rise above my ordinary being and enjoy newer and/or greater experiences than I was having.

I had already seen too much. The taste of life elsewhere had been rich to settle for the yesterdays of my youth. This hurt because it meant moving on, elsewhere at many costs, principally and consequentially separating myself from my Family.

Sadness and strength were to play a part in doing this and with ease, very kindly and gently to minimize hurting others. This would be a long-term goal and eventuality.

I managed to complete the grocery shopping task with these ideas in mind, but it amazed me that I could even push the grocery cart.

With the bagged groceries in Mom's kitchen, we sat down and talked a few minutes before starting preparations for dinner. I helped by washing some veggies for salad, peeled some potatoes and sliced the tomatoes.

Interestingly in our conversation, Panchita repeated what she had written in her letter to Yeoman Rivera in Exmouth.

Imagine us having similar thoughts. The genie escaped.

She said she'd support my decision if I decided on a military career or left the Navy, adding that she understood. Men seem hard wired to vacate the nest or home and move out on their own. In her mind, I was gone already, something very characteristic of Cumpenos, the men from Cumpas. I would remain far or distant or be close by, but she definitely would feel better if I returned home.

She concluded that it's simply a matter of time.

I was still young, she added and felt I took my steps very carefully, cautiously.

We talked about what she and the Family went through that summer of '69, when I left for San Diego. I just let her roll, hardly saying a thing or interrupting. Her eyes teared and she brought out the white folded Kleenex.

It's never easy having your children leave, she started. Once a parent, always a parent. But it was not as difficult as when she lost her first born, a son.

My leaving brought the Family together and made it stronger. The first weeks and months were the hardest, but at the same time, Lisa had been born and "She took our attention, became our focus", Mom mentioned.

Mom and Dad learned they had a dependable son and the two did a fine job raising me. I wrote weekly, only good reports, sent them money and saved some for college. That made them feel proud, it showed that their dedication and efforts paid off.

She had that Mother's intuition and wondered about my presence in Douglas, asking if I was in trouble. I reassured her I had turned communist, so the Navy discharged me.

I also kidded with her that she was going to be a grandmother again and my sweetheart had a baby in San Diego. I had travelled to see them, then came to Douglas. She joyfully went along with the joke. Boy or girl? Ñame, etc.

Le gustaban mis bromas y seguido la vacilaba con un chisté o otro para disfrazar la verdad. En esta vida nuestra tan dedicada, es un modo para al menos reírnos un poco.

The corker was that I was needed as an interpreter in Hawaii after some Cuban spies had been arrested. I don't remember the whole story but just about everyone had a good laugh with that story.

We also talked about my departure and return to active duty in Hawaii in a few days. I didn't want to mislead anyone about my going back. I wanted it to be a gentle separation upon my leaving.

Yet I held back on the truth. Why worry them with my visit to Tripler Army Hospital, and my very real reason for having been sent to Hawaii.

What is the truth? It lies in many ways.

I felt okay in making their lives more cheerful with my visit than burdening them with worry.

Through happenstance I ran into an individual who helped many people in Douglas. I saw him in the downtown area, and he is one who I have much respected. A large Anglo gentleman I mentioned in my previous books, one who taught at Douglas High School and afterwards at Cochise College when it opened.

The instructor taught distributive education at the school level, plus he had charge of the DECA Club. Perhaps his greatest accomplishment had been the successful job placement of hundreds of students in the community over many years. I participated in DECA and as I recall when and how he visited me at work with A.J. Bayless as well in my classes.

He transferred to CCC in the mid-60's to teach business courses, where we thereby kept our infrequent contact. Factually, I lost track of him after the Navy and my return to Arizona.

Such positive interaction and praise that he had for just about everyone. He knew I had enlisted at a most difficult time of war, but he much encouraged me to return to school.

He pitched the Arizona universities and wisely suggested to get help from the VA followed up with the GI Bill. He felt I had great potential and would easily succeed academically.

What I learned from him and the lessons from DECA I value tremendously to this day, the good and the bad.

One of the key lessons he pushed was what is termed in the business world is 'rotation'. Simply put, it means display the older merchandise first, up front to sell it and the newer goods behind. You keep rotating the items, commonly known as 'change' or 'changing', which what life is about. The most constant thing in life is change. Not nickels or dimes.

You don't stand still but must adjust. The old fashion gives way to the new and this is more obvious with the automobiles. Every year models are replacing last years. Rotate the older cars and replace them with the new.

But anyways, the man was taken by my news to him that I was home from Australia, from my duty station HEH. I described my surroundings, the Navy base and my work. He put on the biggest smile and congratulated me.

Of course, we had to part and shook hands when we saw each other leave and waved goodbye.

We wished each other well.

Flying buzzed over the Pacific I remember best, but the rest has faded. Did I take the bus when I left Douglas? What was that last day like? I partied old-style in AP. I did not reach or find Oscar in San Diego.

Maybe I'm having a senior moment, sitting here by my desk and struggling with these entries.

One thought I had then, dream-like as it comes and goes, is that God has blessed me this far into my Navy days. But how long will this last and I sense envy in others who wished they had my luck, that would rub-off on them so as not be struggling or embittered.

Simply compare. What combat teenage draftee, dirty, tired, sweating and hungry wouldn't trade his plight for a nice clean uniform and be comfortably lounging with a beer on land in cool comfort, with background music. That was me going to Hawaii and for what purpose and to serve what end or outcome. It's an existential question. But I'm thankful that it's worked out quite well for me up to now.

An experience, that's repeated itself too many times follows. It's about envy and maybe pettiness. The U.S. Navy and the Marine Corps go hand in hand. To illustrate, Navy Corpsmen are assigned to the Marines. Many other examples can be found.

I don't know how many times I've seen Marines show their toughness and masculinity by bullying, or trying to, the sailors who are more inclined to a life of ease.

To my face I've had this experience which I ignored and walked away. I'm small, frail and Mexican, not the image of a gun-ho militarized, wanna be Rambo, I don't want harm or to be hurt.

In fact, not often, I've gone as far as calling for Security or the Shore Patrol when my mouth gets the better of me. I've cursed at adversaries and not to intelligently but my instincts for escape are strong. I've taunted the meanest Marines who haven't liked my uniform or to defend myself by edging them on: "Come on jugheads, kill this puny Mexican, and get court-martialed".

The bouncers' step in as does the Security detail when both are inclined to defend or protect the women, the children and the less physically endowed.

The fight does not belong to the victor who realizes that in victory there's more dangerous consequences. For example, two men fight, the winner reigns and the other falls injured, and his family suffers only to be supported forcibly by the victor, so rules the judge, jury and law.

Francisco Rivera

Chapter 17

Hawaii Part II.

"Ladies and gentlemen, please place your seats forward, put your seatbelts on and secure the trays", or at least that sounds like the message on the speakers. We're starting to descend and soon will be touching down in our fiftieth state. Nope. Tricked you. That would be Alaska, not Hawaii. Just testing you, to learn some geography.

The big bird lowers itself through some clouds and below one can view the orange streaks of lava flowing seaward. The active volcanos have been spewing hot rock, steam, fire and the earth's insides.

I'll repeat, if I haven't here stated it already, that Hawaii in a billion years, give or take a few hundred million, will be another New Zealand or Australia with all the volcanic action that fills the coastlines. There may be no one around with all the ash, stench and pollution. See how long you last breathing nature's crap. But this is just an idea and you don't have to listen to this. After all, I won't be around to prove this or any crackpot theory I think of. Call it Franciscan Logic. No, not what Pope Francis claims nor what the church has written about, but my insane input on these pages. Or is it "output on these pages"

We land safely and I bound for my sea bag which I hunt for and try to retrieve. I follow this with a hop on the bus for a ride to the base and report to the barracks to check in on time. Now my leave is officially over and I'm back on duty. Y al Señor le doy gracias y un rosaria.

I'm in time for dinner but not in the mood.

I unpack and put away my clothes and straighten out my locker, with everything in its place.

My body feels the big difference and is running on Arizona time. Being at sea level, the jetlag and humidity are taking a toll on me and feel tired.

My bearings and body are off kilter but it's to be expected, yet I feel between exhilaration and exhaustion. I mean:

Very glad to have seen my parents and relatives but the trip proved quite tiring.

After sleeping it off, I will be re-focused on my Navy job and duty in Hawaii.

Upon reporting to work, I get the usual welcome back, how was the time off, did you have fun, etc. That took place most of the morning, people just being cordial, most not even knowing what I had done or accomplished.

By noon I learned I had a problem. My chief first brought it up and then I met with the officer. The issue had to do with my orders expiring and I was in limbo, not knowing where I would go, whether to HEH, a new duty station or?

The whole mess had to be straightened out, but they asked me what I would prefer. I inquired about my options and no I would not be getting school or Navy training.

I could be assigned to a ship right there in Pearl Harbor and possibly set out to sea. Nice choice to be on a tin-can, like a cork on the water riding the waves. Naahh!!

Returning to Australia had to be worked out and would take some time.

A new set of orders could be cut and accommodate me

The Navy Days

elsewhere, but it would likely be unpleasant duty. A couple of scenarios had me at Adak or Kodiak Alaska, or even Midway.

I likely would be on the Pacific side and not near the states, like California and forget about Europe.

I inquired about Panama or someplace similar being I spoke Spanish. Unlikely, came back the response.

The choice had to be made in a few short days.

My best choice was Hawaii because I had to return to the Ophthalmologist at Tripler in six months, but his was just one of many bargaining chips.

I made a few phone calls to find out where I stood and what would be best.

Again, I was not from there but came from Australia on medical leave, a type of temporary duty. A visitor. Somehow or other my status changed, and I got caught in Alice in Wonderland.

A quagmire or cesspool.

The only two good solid outcomes had to be: I had a medical appointment in six months and the other was remain in Hawaii awaiting orders.

So, I got a new lease on and in Hawaii because I had to wait for new orders from headquarters, blah, blah, blah. I'm good for about six weeks here now. I better get new underwear and some decent civvies, but not the local island style with bright bold colors and big floral prints. Not for me.

The officer in charge liked my idea that wherever I would get assigned, that I must be excused for medical reasons to return to Tripler. It would be a short-term assignment. We just had to wait and see the outcome.

I had written letters and a couple went to HEH, probably Gabe and Andy to update them and let them know what's going on. I'm not sure they ever responded.

In the days ahead after my return to Hawaii I thought more

about going back to HEH for half a year. I could perform a six-month stint in Australia standing on my head, hands tied behind me and naked. I'd save more for college and remain on land, thereby risk very little and not go out to sea.

I talked it over in the personnel office and bounced my idea around to see if it was feasible.

The higher-ups would not comment but I believe they cabled the Pacific Fleet Headquarters or wherever their decisions were made.

I almost went to Jack Lord of Hawaii Five O or Tom Selleck of Magnum P.I. (he was ex-navy), for their intervention and assistance to see if they could clean up this mess. Ooops, forgive me, I'm thinking outside the box here.

Meanwhile, hurry-up and wait a la Catch-22.

I continue my set work schedule: since I lacked a fixed more permanent position and was more of a floater. I would be sent at times as temporary help to the noisy shipyard where I would be in a barrage of loading, welding, pipe fitting and more racket than one could ever imagine.

Even though I was specialized as a Yeoman, there were others (corpsmen, torpedomen, signalmen), like me performing odd jobs and many different tasks. I recall an assignment that required hours of my time to clean some very delicate equipment while assisting a career second class instrument man at his ship on the pier. Not too exciting.

Honorable days were few in Hawaii and in the dorms and work sites sailors would tell tall tales about their escapades and philandering ways. Not all were believable, but some percentage definitely were with numerous babies to prove it and the child support deductions from military paychecks. In admin I could see this with the personnel records at my disposal.

The ladies were after the Airmen, Soldiers, Marines, et al. One could easily check this out at EM Clubs on base and in night clubs in Honolulu and Waikiki.

The airline industry greatly contributed to this by flying in a huge number of tourists and the stewardess at the various hotels and resorts were prime targets.

We all had a few forays and wild nights. This was promoted and encouraged by our government and military by providing R and R to personnel from the war front in Viet Nam.

Hawaii also realized great benefit to its economy that relies heavily on tourism.

As they say in the islands, "Aloha! Welcome to Paradise"!

I don't recall exactly how I may have pulled it off, but sometimes in town, overnight, rather than return to the base I remained in town in the barracks at Hickam, then I would report a.m. to work. I'd call in, tell them I'd be late. No problem. I'd unwind with a date at her hotel or at her apartment or other rendezvous. Cabs were one popular mode of transportation.

The Air Force guys were pretty cool with my situation. They didn't have to know the Navy's business and they appreciated a nice tip.

My second medical leave in Hawaii I again exploited this loophole, only a bit more, I'd say. I even made it look like I lived at the Hickam AFB barracks and had some items there. Plus, they provided some room service.

When asked a couple of times about my affairs, I flashed my military Navy ID and state "Medicals at Tripler". End of query.

Very different than what one sees, reads or hears. Being gun-ho in the military in Hawaii was not what I experienced, though it may be true for others. Part of the reason being that I was in Admin and knew my way around and how to portray the Navy role without too much difficulty. Some mates down in the bilges probably would not be able to pull it off or know the ins-and-outs.

Back to the Klondike! Noooooo! Wrong continent! The Klondike was or is a very distant region in Northwest Canada and Eastern Alaska famous for its gold rush of the late 1890's.

The Northwest Cape reminded me of articles I had read about that cold place, i.e., an isolated area of people settled for the opportunity to make money, i.e., gold diggers actually (not the modern-day Vegas types).

That's where I would be returning to, I had been so informed, but the formal orders had not yet arrived. Once here, the details would be worked on and the trip back to Australia finalized with planning and in conjunction with Hickam. More hurry up and wait- at least ten days, I recall.

I had still a few things to take care of, write home and HEH with the news, get some souvenirs, shop for clothes and more, as well as let some locals know that I'd be leaving.

This shopping refreshes my mind and the blazing images of those days I spent at the PX. Hours on end browsing or gawking without buying, and one of my past times would be to hang around the newsstands to read novels, magazines, newspapers and such.

Another stop was Ala Moana, at that time probably the largest shopping mall maybe in the world. It contained Sears, Penney's, Montgomery Wards and many other outlets.

To this day, Hilo Hathie is still in business and the place wows. It's all about anything Hawaii (HHH). Quite the institution. Since 1963 it has served millions upon millions with its well-known Hawaiian products, fashions and gifts.

The original emporium has expanded and can be found in the other islands and stateside. Fashion attire seems to be the big draw, with colorful prints of the Pacific style.

I repeatedly visited the store because it was very entertaining with the music, dancers, food and thousands of items and knick-knacks locals displayed and sold.

The enterprise also allows people to sell their wares, for example, leis, flowers, food and drinks at reduced prices, however, change: cheap foreign imports from Southeast Asia are now seen and hurting businesses and other commerce- free enterprise and capitalism.

I started thinking about change and my return to HEH and coming back to Tripler in six months.

Like others in my position, we could only wonder about our health and the medical treatment at Tripler Hospital; in the military; outcomes and the like. My situation or case seemed very light weight by comparison, such as men seen on crutches or in wheelchairs, amputees also seen at Tripler.

One bothersome aspect was that these individuals had only themselves to bear the burden and were far removed from family or other support.

The problems of my Military brethren were serious, but those having been injured in the war were in dire need. I don't think Hawaii was the best place for them to be getting medical help. I had heard that some had succumbed, and their deaths had a very demoralizing effect.

I still picture this one gentleman who had lost the fight or his will. I actually pushed him in his wheelchair and met his relatives. He had suffered a spinal cord injury that left him a paraplegic. The injury caused severe swelling and compression of the nerve, but not any fractures.

With rehab and treatment, he recovered sensation, but his limbs had atrophied. He became very dejected and I left him as such, still in therapy, when I was reassigned. I wondered about him and his new life.

We'll see what the future brings him, but I sometimes had a feeling of unease, being off balance, things weren't normal, as if they'll ever be. I'll reflect on this.

For example, a lone Hispanic. A minority, in the American Navy, in Australia- nowhere but quite isolated. A Yeoman no training. Normal?

Another point is my life of struggles in a new country, in which we barely survived the hardships. Normal?

Elderly Parents, indigent and disabled with various

limitations, raising teenage offspring. Normal?

Even the damn Viet Nam War was an anomaly and not in our character!

Perhaps it's a strong will, our moral code and sense of duty and obligation together with upholding our Family that's kept us straight, to hang in there and not stray.

Maybe once out of the military, in or out of college I will have a better idea, something more normal.

"Wild thing, you make my heart sing", so goes the song 'Wild Thing', by The Troggs.

And things were getting wild in Hawaii. Money easy to come by when one worked in Admin- Personnel and bad money begets...., but luckily, I was bailing but what I saw or witnessed needed to be looked at and cleaned up. Me, I wanted no part of the mess. Used leave by sailors was still in the books, plus false ledgers re: travel and per diem and such were routine.

Whatever happened after my departure I never found out? It seemed to me it was criminal, and punishment was due: restitution, demotions, brig time and so forth would be forthcoming.

The way some carried on defied reason. Jewelry, nice cars, fat wallets are hard to come by on the salary of an office worker, yet this one could easily see.

Getting caught and suffering a dishonorable discharge was too great a price to pay, in my view, because down the road benefits, such as the VA G.I. Bill, are lost and employment and jobs can also be adversely affected just about anywhere.

One would hear gossip, rumors and more, not knowing what to believe, but it's quite probable the Navy had serious drug problems in the fleet and in Hawaii. The office of Special Investigations had been looking at some cases, I picked up in the scuttlebutt, and some were with vessels out at sea or on patrol.

This was quite serious because National Security could be

breached, that was the main issue.

This was not on my desk or anyone else's. These sensitive affairs required a great deal of scrutiny, but rumors prevailed.

The Navy saying that 'loose lips sink ships', was very true since centuries past.

I had heard as well that because of its oriental population, spies from China and North Korea infiltrated and plied their trade. They blended really well in Hawaii and would pay handsomely for any information they deemed valuable: weapons, electronics, departure times of ships and their routes and destinations.

To me this was interesting but one I was soon leaving and two I was not interested.

The plans to HEH were a bit more solid, but for certain I kept my ace, a copy of the signed medical orders for my return to Tripler. All the other paperwork could get lost, destroyed, burned, but not the Ophthalmologists reports- my ticket out of Australia in six months.

People wondered about my good mood, smiling and grinning, even whistling at times.

It all pretty much worked out this way thanks to the personnel and others I worked with. Admin people looked after one another and others (Sea Bees, Airedales, ships maintenance men, et al) were not that fortunate, displayed an unpleasant disposition.

I witnessed sailors intentionally getting lousy orders and sent to BFE (Bum Fuck Egypt) or HEH. This is more clearly demonstrated by actor Robin Williams in the movie, 'Good Morning Viet Nam', when his nemesis in Personnel intentionally sends him into the Viet Cong's hands. Luckily Williams is rescued and barely escaped.

Who needs enemies when your own associates are prepared to kill you? I did my bidding. Back to HEH, as bad as it was.

I made my rounds on base at Pearl Harbor para decir adiós

y despedirme, también dando gracias a los camaradas y otras amistades.

Similarly, at Hickam, I stopped by to say goodbye and wish kindness to everyone who helped me.

I sensed a change in peoples' attitudes which may have been due to the lifestyle of Hawaiians, or perhaps the 'revolution' of the sixties with the riots, protests and demonstrations. It was different and now returning to Australia, I was going back knowing a liberation had begun to take hold. The peacemakers contributed to this shift as did the coming events- Watergate.

The women's lib, the Viet Nam disaster, Ellsberg and other events could not be ignored, and people were demanding change, accountability and transparency of our government.

My own outlook left behind the perspective I had when I went on active duty and took off to HEH. My time in Hawaii was well worth it. It freed me from the cocoon and isolation, I had lived in while in Arizona for twenty years.

The time to leave Hawaii at hand, we waited in the lounge for our call. I didn't know who 'we' were other than passengers boarding a gray military aircraft, all very impersonal. Smiling stewardesses greet the flying civilians, but not with the military, which does its business in an uncaring way.

Think about it. One reason is that the profit factor is removed, and Uncle Sam picks up the tab. In the private sector, satisfaction, competition, profit and so forth are part of the equation. Here, it's not a monopoly the military enjoys.

Then you have to consider that the government is transporting its employees and not contracting with private parties to provide a satisfactory delivery.

The missions are different with transportation in conjunction with defending the Homeland and killing to defend it if necessary, plus helping our allies the same.

Civilian aviation serves almost an entirely different purpose,

The Navy Days

but still the bottom line for both is transportation of goods and people.

Time to board and not a bad idea or mental jog with the above thought or daydream while waiting to hop into the big dark plane of the USAF.

A small group I believe hopped into the low-lying beast whose belly almost touched the ground. The inside very familiar, without any luxury, lacking insulation and lots of metal, plus netting to hold the cargo of mostly wooden crates this time. Probably household goods or possibly some delicate machinery.

I started feeling like an old pro being I had taken these MAC Flights a few times for thousands of miles and dozens of hours. Yet, who am I kidding, I still looked like a teenager, a high school student of small build and stature.

Somebody started the conversation and we made the introductory round: name, home, destination, etc. Not many on their way to HEH, but we were soon identified. Then the questions started since I was returning to my base.

I emphasized to enjoy Sydney because after that stop, civilization c'est finis.

After a few hours of sleeping, reading, and snacking, the warning sounded to secure ourselves for landing in America Samoa, also known as Pago Pago, (pronounced like the dance tango; Pangos, (Pango). A small spot of land in the middle of nowhere. A small group of islands in the South Pacific that are a beautiful tropical paradise of unspoiled jungles, beaches and more.

To tell you the truth, I can't tell it to you because I can't handle the truth about Pago Pago. I don't know the place and it has so many different accounts, descriptions, histories and tales- where to begin.

So what, I only stopped there for a couple of days.

The place is also known as American Samoa, but its French as the culture, at least around 1970, did not seem to be

Gringolandia. They have Native customs too.

We disembarked and went to grab a bite, being told to hurry, to get going cause of bad weather, to make up time, to get into Sydney on time for fun and some action. Whatever.

Keep in mind, however, that in Samoa the people are huge, giants and do what they want, and many want to play in the NFL, and they do. Time is a difficult concept over there, like a minute is eighty-nine seconds long, not a second less.

Vagueness strikes me but I think a cab materialized to get us to a restaurant, but don't ask who, what, how, when or where. They accepted American money. We paid, tipped and left……….. and left behind we were, because the cab was late.

We missed the plane by a couple of minutes, but it could've been hours. We hung around the terminal lobby and soon agents took us to a compound of sorts where many stayed in such similar situations. The whole matter seemed insignificant.

And so, began our taste of Polynesia where people were polite, quiet and willing to help. The girls were pretty, cordial and interesting but we kept it cool. We didn't want any more trouble nor some three-hundred-pound, six foot-six Samoan pounding us to a pulp.

The stay in Samoa is sketchy, such as what clothes we wore and where did we get this (Goodwill?), because I remember Polynesian apparel.

What arrangement was there for meals? I don't recall getting updated about our flight out of there. At the same time, not to worry.

Some things are fresh, like going into town, which had a backward style, but was very clean. Cobblestone streets, thatched roofs on buildings and few vehicles.

We caught Gilligan's Island filming, with the crews and actors very friendly. That's all BS.

The whole place was way different, with entire greenery,

moist, damp air and misting. From the sight-seeing we did when walking, the beaches were pristine, isolated, as if they had just been swept. Scenic beyond description. Not even National Geographic could paint it so perfectly. Nature at its purest, brushed by God's hand.

A vast difference from the last island I saw hours ago with so much congestion, traffic and noise. Eat your heart out Hawaii, this was paradise.

This brief stop in Samoa brought sadness, nostalgia, melancholy and here's why. A short, serious, metaphorical poem by Alfred Lord Tennyson, a British Poet, was written in the mid 1850's. It's "Crossing the Bar", about a drunk staggering into the cantina for another shot and the saloon keeper telling him "No mas". He staggers, crosses the bar, then to another establishment for more drinks.

Noooo! That's not the one. It's about a law student who has repeatedly failed the bar exam. He laments his anxiety and efforts at passing/crossing the bar (exam) to become an attorney.

Pendejo!! Try again because that's not it either.

Anyway, this is but my poor, weak effort at humor to keep you alert and your attention here. Hey, I don't have too many tools and I do what I can for you my dear reader to entertain you.

But actually, the poem "Crossing the Bar" is about our finality and coming to terms with our life and legacy, our peaceful march, voyage, travel and odyssey from infancy to death. Some of my favorite lines, as I recall them from my British literature class at Cochise College are:

"Sunset and evening star

And one clear call for me....

Twilight and evening bell

And after that the dark

Maybe there be no sadness of farewell

When I embark....

I hope to see my Pilot face to face

When I have crossed the bar."

Do yourself a favor and read or study this great poem, that touches me, a sailor attached to the sea, such as I found myself en la playa in Samoa en 1970.

For whatever its worth, to me it's genius, but others may feel differently and that's okay too.

I too hope to meet my Pilot face to face....

When I have crossed the bar.

It's my Odyssey.

The day went by fast and I fail to piece things together fairly well for those forty-eight or so hours in Samoa. Other than to enjoy the natural splendor of the island.

After we cleaned up, we went to a park once the sun fell. Open to the public with a bar and later some local music and dancers.

Food was available that was Polynesian, no hotdogs, chips or burgers, but a great amount of fruit, much variety and very tasty.

The crowd started rolling in, young people to middle age folks. Very quiet and cordial and I could see how well elders were respected.

Some came by and introduced themselves. Their curiosity got the best of them as they approached us then asked questions.

Very innocent conversations are we French, Americans, what. Where are we going? Our names, what we did, where do we reside or come from? Enjoyable.

Some girls got the nerve, probably after drinking the spiked punch.

Yes, we danced or pretended to, whatever the jumping and

swinging and hopping is called. A pleasant evening.

Soon enough orders came with the name, time, date and place for us to meet and be at for our flight out of Pago Pago and onto New Zealand and Australia. The particulars are not essential here and don't ask about the airline, day of the week or plane itself.

I feel I'm still on that aircraft up in the sky because initially the weather rocked us while it lurched and rolled and dipped, raining cats and dogs. Outside was a thick broth coming down in thick sheets. It didn't last though, and the plane again flew smoothly.

Yet the bigger worry for us was not the bad weather or the flight. We wondered about the trouble we'd be in after missing our plane.

Somebody mentioned AWOL and this fit our situation because we were absent without permission.

We agreed that we were given the okay to get some chow, which we did, and the cab took us there, but the cab brought us back late when the bird was up in the clouds, gone.

Later I found out, when I got to HEH, that the flight itinerary excluded us, however, the tele-communiques to Exmouth read that 'passengers missed flight: transportation irregularities'.

The last line cleared us. It did not say we were bad actors, misbehaving, nor that we became sick or ill, nor were we detained or jailed or locked up.

We touched down in Christchurch, New Zealand, but not before I had a chance to sit in the cockpit to chat with the navigator, pilot and crew. I listened mostly or tried to because the noise drowned the conversations.

Very intelligent men these fly boys. The entire group as well was highly trained, and most were career men in their second or third enlistment. They especially liked the travel throughout the world and experiencing different cultures and much more. It seemed foreign travel was preferred more than flying the

Continental United States, with Europe at the top.

I'd enjoy that too very well but career wise it's not too appealing.

Once having been processed and checked in, (with our few belongings) we found a watering hole with decent grub and the action just starting, not too late.

I find it amazing, how cliques go. The Air Force guys, and the Navy Sailors stayed apart, with the Air Force Officer's refusing to mingle with their enlisted men. Plain as day and that's just how it was.

We ordered fish and chips to go with our beers, which seemed to be standard fare. It didn't take long before some 'Kiwis' showed up and the introductions were made. Great conversationalists.

One point that popped up was the station in Antarctica, ooops, that's Antarctica, which had many international types. Such as scientists or university intellectuals going to the South Pole to study, do research and perform different experiments for months at a time.

The gals said they loved those guys because on their way back, on their stop-over in Christchurch they would get royally screwed silly by these men who were all hot and horny after being isolated for so long. "Best sex ever", the ladies claimed, with wicked smiles to get their points across quite clearly.

What an education?! I never read or studied that in books or the classroom.

I guess the point was were we returning from the South Pole, because they wanted to get laid royally and though we were honest and truthful, we could still accommodate them and did.

But did so only after we went off to another party at a private residence that had quite tasteful decor. The whole neighborhood appeared upper-middle class, but so does all of New Zealand for that matter, compared to the USA.

Really a wonderful get together, nothing raunchy, loud, etc., but there was weed, and a few joints being passed around. Absolutely nobody inhaled. Guaranteed.

The mood was fantastic with plenty of large trays of snacks, too much liquor, soft music, talk and do not forget the S.E.X, aka, South pole expeditionary force.

Upstairs the loving went on and the floorboards creaked. Oohh mama!

How safe was climbing into that government plane the next morning? We were all so polluted and wasted, a disgrace to the US of A and its military, that it could be dangerous to fly.

Of course, we didn't say anything. We were on the hush-hush, but the blood shot eyes said it all y gracias a Dios por tan rico y fuerte café que hasta el muerto lo pide para despertar.

We got on board and that sucker took-off then flew on automatic pilot while we gobbled Tylenol, aspirins or whatever we could get our hands on.

Getting into Sydney proved a breeze and a welcoming crowd waited for us, but not a long wait.

But I'm trying. I can't figure out the details because we were not on the regular scheduled weekly USAF MAC Flight, which we missed days ago.

Maybe all the celebrating the night before killed all the memory cells to erase the incident, though sometimes HEH would receive two flights in a week.

We flew out of Sydney and I may be wrong, but we sailed over South Australia, landed to take care of some matter then turned to the Northeast. It seemed that way, but my bearings could have been way off. Have another drink.

CHAPTER 18.

Returning to The Cape.

Some light boxed meal was handed to us and we joked that it consisted of sheep or kangaroo that not even the dingos (the wild dogs of Australia's outback) would eat!

We ate it anyway.

Staring into the strong daylight, I could see that the Northwest Cape stood like before, unchanged, reddish earth with lots of brush and beautiful beaches, untouched for millennia in this desolate, unmanned desert of the world.

I had a thought and as far as I could imagine, astronaut Neil Armstrong successfully took to the moon at about this time.

Then I thought if maybe the Australian outback in the Northwest would be a suitable site for his training.

Just floating thoughts and crazy ideas upon returning to the Cape, HEH and Exmouth.

The heat hit us hard as we exited the plane and the shimmering wave could be seen dancing on the runway. A sight I've been accustomed to just about all my life- live in southern Arizona and you become used to this.

The various operators jumped into action to secure the aircraft, open it, move the equipment like forklifts in place to unload the cargo, put this on the trucks and reload the bay, quite efficiently, smooth and with precision.

Some of the same old gang greeted me and mostly welcomed me back with handshakes and pats on the back. It was great to be back, wasn't it? Flip a coin. Was I getting a chewing-out for being AWOL??

Heads I win and tails you lose. But it was only for six months or so, with lots to accomplish in this short time.

I had to concentrate on getting into college among other things and ease myself back into work. This time there was no welcoming parade ceremony or orientation. I grabbed my luggage, got on the bus and went to the base. I checked in, then to the barracks- the same space, bed and locker.

I unpacked while talking with my curious mates about everything, anything and nothing. It seemed little had changed.

They seemed glad or okay to have me back and queried me about Hawaii; what I did; how come it took so long to get back; did the doctors treat me well and more questions.

After an hour or so of this I visited personnel to find out about my status, duty and assignment. I also picked up my mail and met with Gabe and Andy.

The chief instructed me to report tomorrow a.m. per the usual and I'd get additional info., adding that the officer wanted to meet me, and we met.

It appeared to me they were treating me with kid gloves, as if fearing me because I may know more than I let on, and I used this to my advantage. My having been on leave to Arizona, missing the MAC Flight in Samoa, having orders to return to Tripler, etc. All alarmed the staff to wonder about how I pulled this off without any repercussions whatsoever- Mr. Untouchable.

I left them wondering and silence proved powerful and enigmatic, so I found out.

Allow me to back-pedal a few hours, to the arrival of the

The Navy Days

MAC Flight. I've described before that the plane is met by working parties to help loading, unloading, cleaning and what not.

On this day, Carl from my admin group had the duty and worked on the big bird so when I got off, we met, and he welcomed me back.

HEH received him a couple of months thereabouts after Andy and I arrived that summer.

Carl was an attitude on feet. Nothing pleased him it seemed, and he was a walking bad conduct discharge possibly. He skirted the rules repeatedly, hated the uniform, the food, missed the women and loving, and on and on. About the only thing he enjoyed was running around naked in his speedos, with his tape player to his ear. Of course, this was at the pool and the barracks.

Most of the sailors enjoyed his company because he was funny, a laugh a minute, he was rich, intelligent, whip smart, and college educated. I think he was a reservist going for discharge. I heard he wound up with us to avoid the draft, Nam and the war. What else is new? Like many of us.

The SOB liked me and tried to take me under his wing, but I refused and had nothing to do with it and told him so. He had checked my personnel record like I did his and he admired my spunk and background. We weren't enemies nor friends but got along.

I kidded him as being not too smart to avoid conscription or the Navy, being he could have bribed his way out of serving and he agreed with me- bone spurs like Trump. For him, money was nothing because they sent it to him from home, more than he earned here. He was carefree. Covered happy hour for us and paid for some of the girls that came up from Perth.

But I and others could not shake him off being he wanted us all to rise above our station in life and I was a good mark saying I was returning to college. That impressed him.

He too would be returning, I think to his Texas roots, and pursue a PHD, be a psychologist. Carl offered some good advice and helped several men, counseling them about the GI Bill, vocational training, school, etc.,- all post Navy.

Carl got a big kick out of me- a Mexican sailor in Australia- Bum Fuck Egypt- who should be in college, but he knew my Family and I were indigent.

He gave me a big hug when I got off that MAC Flight and welcomed me back with that great big, teasing smile of his. He knew I was up to something.

I just got inspired. While I was stepping out of the plane, I also saw the twin on the working party, we waved at each other and they were wow when they were around together. So funny the two were- fighting, joking or doing whatever.

Don't ask, I don't know who was younger, but I could tell them apart by their haircuts.

So only one of them was working the MAC Flight, but their story becomes interesting. They joined the Navy under the buddy-system and made it to Exmouth together as Seamen.

They bunked, ate and smoked together, but by now no longer worked together being they went into separate divisions. I think they were from Pennsylvania, steel mill country, either Pittsburgh or Phillie.

Terrific athletes the two and everybody wanted them on their team for softball, basketball, bowling, etc. They weren't very big, five-ten or so but light and swift. Plus, this macho pair would kill anyone, they were so protective of each other. One other point, they had Stalin-like brown mustaches.

For some reason they included me in their company like when the two visited the library.

Competition and gambling were in their blood and would clean up at the E-M Club at darts, ping pong, billiards (snooker, nine ball) and so on.

But I think everybody's favorite was their card game, especially on Friday night, payday. Poker.

They'd play straight through, twenty-four hours in their barracks cubicle, with the Filipinos being keen opposition.

There'd be tons of snacks (chips, nuts, candy), beverages, beer and liquor with plenty of sweet background music. It was our casino, our Vegas. I usually lost, just small change.

Believe it when I say that my two mates here and I actually made it to Catholic mass a few times, more so on special days, like Christmas.

The two left together and at the door of the plane they turned around and- (you probably thought they mooned everyone), no- they gave everybody the bird, the Middle Finger Salute!

In life, society and the world over, one sees classes and the status of people and the British Commonwealth presents this, and Australia belongs there. Their snobbery is ever so present that they treat others as such. They spread this to the Americans and when we, I, stand up to them they are embarrassed. We are not Australian nor part of the Commonwealth.

The US of A is without classes, unlike England for example, that has commoners, royals and all sorts of protocols. It subjugates people.

I bring this up because the American Military, the Navy too, has numerous enlisted career men essential to the service, its purpose and mission. These sailors provide important support, but in ratings or areas of less significance, cooks, boatswain mates come to mind, unlike corpsmen, those in the nuclear subs, or aircraft techies who are more skilled.

And me, being a yeoman in educational services could see this, by reviewing records or talking with my fellow men. In leading up to this, there is an observation, if HEH is a microcosm of the entire Navy, it then carries too many, a high portion of sailors getting fleet promotions, which were explained as being awarded for re-enlistment or because men had plateaued. This meant men could not advance anymore nor passed the exams for the next higher grade. They repeatedly took the test but did not succeed to move up in rank.

These men are very important and perform proudly, loyally and know their role and jobs well, but are stuck in rank but for field promotions.

I could identify several on base performing grunt work, usually in security. They usually had a much larger role with the MAC Flights, as did some of the Australian civilian personnel.

The Aussies ragged these sailors who bristled but held back. I'd seen flights with civilians losing their jobs, because you can't easily fire an enlisted man. Which brings me to my first thought about how Australians suffer and feel inferior, by not being in a higher class that they take out their rancor on others. Like I watched them on the job at the airfield when I arrived from Samoa via New Zealand.

The Aussies would cuss

and make a fuss.

They'd heavily drink

not bother to think.

They had no plan, just play

time slipped, passed to another day.

Some clarification here. Changes started not only with the Navy, but with other branches of the military, though I cannot tell exactly when, but such is how these huge bureaucracies operate and manage.

One of the biggest had been previous outcomes: changing the draft to the lottery system based on birthdays. But that's another story.

What I am referring to pertained to cutbacks, starting in 1970. I may be off a few months though. But anyway, by this I mean that the services were winnowing personnel and the war winding down.

Three-month reductions implemented meant soldiers' discharges or separations came about ninety days earlier.

Mine was still far away.

This meant for many that plans for civilian life had to be expedited, such as housing, transportation, funds, etc.

In my case, I had to step on the gas while also getting busier with more sailors inquiring about education, training and benefits once they became civilians.

Some of my mates started seeing the light, while we in the educational services office had counseled and advised many to think ahead: save, prepare and make arrangements for post military days.

I had as explained already. My two-year Navy stint over early meant I'd regroup and figure out or plan my moves for about the summer of 1971, still more than a year away.

Foresight or foreseeability favored me yet were lacking in many young men at HEH.

Gabe, Vic and others who knew me better could see that my aggressive preparations would put me ahead, but many did not do likewise.

Because of the job I had and the position I held, I had access to much valuable information and people who gave keen or sharp advice. This advantage proved fruitful to us in the admin division as we did both, work and also honed up our future with better planning.

The general consensus ended up being 'Hurray' for the early out program regardless of whatever took place, once no longer a sailor. Freedom has a cost.

Actually, some men fretted and feared leaving the service for one reason or another and enjoyed the security, the three hots, a cot and a pot. Plus, the regular paycheck.

I'll be the first to admit that these blokes were fine men, most with families (on or off base), who put their life on the line to protect their ship mates and our Homeland and nothing wrong if they made the military their career. Many chose not to and left happily for other pursuits.

Fun and enjoyment were had when we'd play cards, ping pong, darts or billiards in the barracks, sharing a pitcher at the E-M Club, or sitting on the bleachers watching a softball game.

These guys were tough, guts and glory. Amazing what they had experienced, seen or been through.

Such as a nuclear sub on a secret mission trailing a Soviet sub along the Northern Russian Coast. There'd be no hesitation by Moscow to sink it, because they're daring. They hide their subs on our eastern seaboard to spy and patrol the British Isles and the English Channel.

I'd sit there enthralled with their tales, like the Airedale blown off the flight deck, but managed to get recued and survived the ordeal. The shock was too much, did him in and he had to be reassigned to shore duty.

Viet Cong snipers picked-off American sailors on the river boats. As if killing weren't enough, they'd blow up the vessels and wait in ambush for the rescuers.

Hours we'd spend, late into the night with many accounts about the episodes and adventures of Navy life all over the world at any time.

Roto Spain was described as a favorite spot to be stationed because the duty provided easy access to Europe for travel, booze, history, sites and beautiful women. Many sailors extended or re-enlisted as long as they were guaranteed a tour there. I have a friend who also did this and loved it.

But probably some of the best duty these lifers described was a State Department assignment- Embassy duty. Many described it as comparable to living like a king, in splendor.

A plush life, mostly not being shot at, regular hours, clean uniforms and seeing world leaders, with the preferred locations again in Europe. Terrific conversations that we had.

By the following week and after a meeting or two, I was back to my old routine and at my old desk. The first day, rather morning, was a bit unusual in that my co-workers in the building stopped by to chat, say welcome, etc. Others called and did the same by phone. This made me feel appreciative.

I made my rounds as well and checked in at the health clinic to get on the duty for ambulance driver.

Vickie and I met. She's just gorgeous as ever. I got back my job in the library. Ever the flirt, she wanted the juicy details and she liked the few I provided. Just looking at her, that gaze and lovely expression, she wanted more. I mean more information.

In the corner desk we talked, and she inquired about my health, was I okay, what treatment did I receive, that sort of thing. I didn't say much. I knew, like she mentioned, that people were talking, and I agreed, there are many gossip mongers and I expected it with me. It's been like that since I first arrived.

I live with it I explained. I have good sense and I'm Mexican. I quickly made Yeoman and I have an attitude. I'm not gung-ho Navy. I work in Special Services, having money and more.

She reached for my hand and patted it.

When I informed her, I took leave to the states, saw my Family and went to Mexico, she smiled, then laughed. In disbelief she giggles wholesomely, almost orgasmic.

Wanting details, she asked how I managed to do that because it's forbidden per policy. I have a top-secret clearance I told her and left it at that.

I clued her about Hawaii, Samoa, New Zealand, Sydney and such, she took it all in and couldn't get enough, especially Sydney and the pride of Australia, the gem and the fabulous Opera House.

Like I've heard before, it's difficult to get off the rock to go see other parts of the world. Australia is quite isolated and very far, plus expensive to travel from there.

She got serious and put on her counselor's thinking cap to advise me I had to put solid effort in my remaining months at HEH: earn the money I needed for civilian life. Nail down the college I'd be attending and get everything in order. She very strongly, motherly-like, emphasized a college education.

Oh Geez! My best Gomer Pyle, "Gollyyy Geee, Sarge! What to do?" The days will be awfully boring, worse than before, much worse. Six months or more. How can it be much different when compared to my adventure for weeks away from HEH, in Hawaii especially?

And to think so selfishly, when my brothers-in-arms are dying in the rice paddies and jungles of Viet Nam in combat, while I've got my cushy job and only have to fight the boredom.

The adjustment was hard mentally though and I hid it well and carried on like before. But I avoided displays of any other problems and did not lapse, though perhaps my daydreaming increased. Gabe and Vic embraced me.

I questioned my sanity, my decision in returning to the Cape. I showed stoicism, but inwardly felt otherwise.

Still much later I saw that I had reached the right decision for various reasons. HEH was better and more familiar to me than being out at sea, a likely scenario. I had a much easier job. I'd avoid the war. I could save more for college.

Once I buckled down, I wrote some letters and caught up on my mail.

I also dedicated myself to the correspondence courses I took from USAFI and the University of Texas in El Paso (UTEP).

Further, I knocked out a ton of paper re: college and received in return catalogs, financial aid forms, applications and much more from Cal, USC, Washington, Oregon, Colorado and other schools in western U.S.

This was still in 1970 and I considered that now would be the time to improve myself by picking up a hobby or learn a new

The Navy Days

skill that would benefit me later. I thought about auto mechanics and have the Sea Bees help with this, but it did not happen.

I checked out the Navy's training manual for electricians out of our library and did pick up some rudimentary knowledge, but I did not follow through. Funny however, how I was connecting this to my experiences in those days when Ralph and I messed around in his dad's shop- EMS en Douglas, en el barrio.

You're not going to believe I also tried music and studied somewhat. The piano which I practiced at the chapel, but I didn't advance beyond 'chopsticks', and the trumpet too. I even purchased one and gave it to Clara.

Luck was really on my side and I was truly blessed, along with Andy being that we had a close friend who lived the Navy life. Allow me to explain.

Months after landing in HEH, Andy worked his way into a position with the base post office, not a big operation but with much responsibility. The Base P.O. came under the Admin Division and had the same officer in charge. Therefore Andy and I did admin stuff, except he did his part-licking stamps, selling money orders, registering mail, etc.- in a small, clean, storage area or room with a couple of desks, shelves, chairs, telephone and little else, eight hours per day. We saw each other daily.

Andy became a Third-Class Petty Officer- postal clerk. That's E-4 and a better paycheck.

He became well known with the constant flow in and out of the postal center. People- civilians and sailors, Australians and American, young and old, you get the picture. In and out picking up the mail, sending packages, restocking supplies, custodial duties and more kept Andy busy.

When there was a crowd, such as around Christmas, enlistees were pulled in to help. Present company included.

So, each workday at morning muster we'd meet and shoot the breeze, i.e. Andy, his staff and me. Guys were jiving, tobacco, smoking, sipping coffee, chewing gum, whatever.

We became close and the P.O. Nut Jobs took me under their wings simply because we were admin buddies and because Andy and I hit HEH together. We'd kid that their brains where shot from licking and inhaling stamp glue.

The dude that ran the postal unit was a First Class (E-6) Petty Officer. He was a lifer with about twelve years in and eight more to complete his career and retire. A very likeable fellow with a family: an oriental wife, kid or kids, base housing, a car and more. The family had it made with more than enough it seemed.

The family often had us over, very informal, for cookouts, card games, work on the car or a number of things. I remember babysitting while the mom and dad took in a base movie or even running errands to the PX or the store for items- napkins, pickles and the like.

The Mrs. was a great cook, especially when preparing delicious elaborate Japanese dishes that went just super, oh just swell with sake wine. Other Filipinos hosted parties and we went.

We'd celebrate and congratulate estos buenos amigos de la postal. Los cuatro y yo fuimos una pequeña pandilla. Como puede ser que en el militar y con el gobierno fuéramos unos desbalagados. Si así fuera, pronto nos corren o nos avientan a la chingada.

El jefe, pues como no sería el de más señoria, a great fellow sea man. Our lifer led us.

He had a very good heart and love for his family, comrades and humanity. I don't remember that he'd been cross, loud, angry nor insulting. Though I was the fifth member of the gang, I didn't belong because I was a yeoman and the four were postal clerks. Nevertheless, they said I belonged with them, no qualms about it, because of Andy.

Probably what they liked most about me was the Mexican meals I'd prepare from items my Mom sent. Tortillas, carne seca and chile. They called it a feast y se chupaban los dedos, but I couldn't convince them it was nothing, and that they should try delicious south of the border cooking when they visit Arizona.

My God! ¡Dios Mio! Se encantaban con mis tacos. I'd take over the kitchen and give everybody a rest, including the Mrs. This would be a Sunday dinner, perhaps.

The prepared shells would be stuffed with hamburger from the commissary and I'd spice it up the manner in which I knew from the barrio just common ingredients. A dash of tabasco, a bit of garlic, a pinch of salt a tablespoon of fresh lemon or lime juice. Shredded lettuce add picadillo (diced tomatoes, onions, bell pepper all mixed con poquito vinaigrette Blanco). They all scarfed it like manna, and it seemed quite genuine enough to pass for Mexican tacos.

The corn tortillas were packaged shells, not fried and no fresh salsa but everything went down just swell.

The downer may have been that the stuffing was lamb or even kangaroo, but who knows.

The rice the Mrs. prepared, and I took care of the canned Rosarita fried beans- con chile y tantita Manteca. Sabrosisimos!!!

My correspondence home would be read by my entire Family, I gathered, and maybe the barrio as well. This included letters, post cards, cassettes and such and the replies many times were comical in addition to being very encouraging.

I would relate how I was being adopted over here, such as by Gabe (as a father), and Vic the mom, plus the 'Postals' as my new siblings. I'd express jokingly how Andy and his crew would go postal, like putting dead fish in the outgoing mail bags to stink up the mail, even canned farts were included.

Just about anything to make them laugh and lift their spirits, to not worry about me. But in return they loved it and my Panchita started caring for Andy, who was more serious and looked after the four of us. She carried him in her heart, because Andy and I together went to active duty in San Diego and out of NTC flew to Australia. She felt he was my guardian or good omen.

My take is that moms are way different in their very strong, natural attachments to their children and families compared to fathers who are more standoffish, detached or stoic.

My Parents appreciated that I was in good hands at the Cape and we were living healthily, staying out of trouble and serving America.

They appreciated the good sense Gabe and Vic were pounding into my head, like working hard to save for college and to not delay in finding that school.

But you got to believe this. As much as my Douglas and barrio people wanted me to play it safe and not take unnecessary risks, they also mentioned that I should see Australia and visit other sites. Get more exposure and learn about the world. They said I'd probably never return to the island country or continent in my life.

I was further told to avoid marriage or having kids at this stage in my young life.

I would not be at all surprised if my Parents did write confidentiality to my bosses and higher-ups, like the base commander, to get a report about me, what I was up to and how I was doing, but I will never know.

Parents did this out of worry or concern, as parents do, and at times the Chaplain's office handled these queries.

Well, I asked around and I received 211% rejections, but no offense taken. What's this about? I followed up on the suggestions of seeing more of Australia.

Some sailors did this, but most didn't, and I figured I had better hurry, because it's there and I'm not sticking around here for a long duration.

To be truthful I don't remember the sequence of four or five items worth writing about that took place but exactly when?

CHAPTER 19.
Leave in Perth

One of these was a leave of absence I took, call it a vacation, of about ten days. I didn't find anyone else to go so by bus I travelled by myself about straight south from Exmouth and HEH to Perth, Western Australia.

I did this for kicks, just to get away and learn more about the continent. Many Aussies from Northwest Cape went to Perth, on the Southwest Coast, as did Gabe. He had told me about the city and encouraged me to go visit there and provided a list of sites to view.

He even said who to contact if any problem or trouble arose, but that I shouldn't have any being with the American Military, a U.S. Navy Sailor at that. They loved the Americans. Gabe assured me I'd find a girlfriend and probably come back married, all worn out and simply completely wasted and drained of body fluids. He wasn't too far off the mark.

Before taking off, I took care of things at the base, such as the drivers' duty, the library job, rounding up money and so on.

With my leave request approved, my duffle bag well packed and cash in my wallet I set off to Southwestern Australia on a late afternoon, probably a Thursday afternoon, once I left work.

This trip would be long, nearly fifteen hours and about eight hundred miles or more. Not a bad ride because we'd be sleeping in the bus while travelling by night.

In Exmouth I sat on my bag in a shady spot para esperar el camion, asi Como lo haciamos en Mexico. Luego llego y salio el conductor who instructed us about this, that, tickets, costs and more.

This was the driver, a short, fat Czech out of uniform and a heavy accent and poor English. Not a confidence booster, third worldish.

I understood, perhaps incorrectly, that's because of the long-haul and the heat, night travel was preferred. Yep! Just an easier way to have an accident. A dozing driver loses control, rolls over a few times and kills us all.

Here we go. The bus with a small crowd pulled out of Exmouth pointing south. I didn't know anybody, but a few cursory introductions were in order. The passengers that stood out were the Aborigine couple- young, in love, different attire and dark. Most of the others were plain White folk.

We stopped after a couple of hours at a small town to do some business, like bathroom break, get snacks, drop off a passenger and pick up some more. Very light traffic passed by- fuel haulers, semis, truckers with rigs.

Soon we were rolling again. People slept, played cards, read, simply anything to kill time or put it to better use, until our next stop in the Outback.

The place seemed like a settlement in the middle of nowhere that I heard was the center for small outlying mining, agriculture and ranching communities.

We were warned to take care of matters, because with darkness the box on wheels would move till daylight near Perth. The chauffer suggested, besides some food, that some booze or pills help one sleep better on the bus.

By now we had mas pasajeros y entre ellos more Aborigines had boarded, then we were on the road again, going places I ain't seen before, oh sweet Lord, please just show me more.

Needless to say, after a small bite of fish and chips plus beer I crawled into a long, deep slumber made deeper by the motion of the vehicle and sound of the road.

We must have stopped, I don't recall, yet we added and discarded passengers because by the morning light this had become quite obvious, Pero asi es la Vida en el Camino real.

Perth appeared on the horizon and further out and beyond the magnificent blue Indian Ocean.

We were all awake and I could hear the chatter of a couple of children with their mother tending to them and feeding them.

For whatever it's worth, I think Perth needs to be spelled PEARL= a lovely city. A gem! Maybe it was the euphoria that made me feel this way. Being on my own, out of uniform, rested and breathing crisp cool air.

Everyone had quickly vacated the bus, and all seemed famished. After grabbing our luggage, we headed for breakfast to a spot not far at all.

The simple meal of eggs, toast and sausage links hit the spot perfectly and with strong coffee I felt rejuvenated. Now to find my hotel.

Truthfully, I don't have much of a clue as to how that went. I believe I may have had reservations or maybe I found boarding through a phone directory. It didn't take long at all to find clean lodging reasonably priced.

I washed up, put on fresh clothes, stored some items and I went out to experience the city. Soon enough I was on the Waterfront where I found dining al fresco and I also found out how friendly the people were, quite cordial.

Not knowing where I was and darkness settling in, I took in a bar and grill, drawn there by the live music with the Basa nova sounds of Brazil.

We chatted. That would be the bartender and the lady assisting him. A nice, clean-cut pair. With two gin tonics in me, I then decided to return to the hotel. For the life of me, I cannot remember the name.

I hailed a cab and the driver quickly got me there.

With the strong drinks, I felt just fine and mellow, I then decided to turn in for the night but not too soon.

I wrote a few post cards I had bought during my walk and I would mail them the next day.

To this day, before I travel, I jot down some addresses and mail post cards to Family and friends. I also pick up a few souvenirs, just trinkets; now, for the grandkids who get a big kick out of the items old Tata brings them.

People tell me the joy they get from such mail and point out the foreign postage, quite colorful and interesting.

A short description of Perth is in order, and more will follow when I write about areas and tourist spots I visited. I'll just highlight a few points as I move along.

Perth is a very old center of civilization from what history has recorded. That's nearly 35,000 years ago or more that the first Aborigines inhabited the region even though the large metropolis, (now in or around 2015) has two million inhabitants. It is very isolated with nary a neighbor nearby (you like that alliteration, amigo Americano) and Melbourne, Sydney, Canberra thousands of miles away to the Nation's Southeast.

The fourth largest city in Australia is Perth and it's the capital of the state of western Australia, with terrific weather, mostly sunny.

It's teaming with foreigners, with a great influx from Southeast Asia, more recently Malaysia and from India now. It's becoming a 'boom town', I've read. New Zealanders, south Africans and Europeans continue to move there, as do also the British migrating to Perth or its surrounding suburbs.

I was surprised that it is so Catholic, with even a university, Notre Dame, with about a quarter of the city's population claiming this affiliation. But ok for the Catholic Europeans.

Anyway, I'm on vacation, not getting too serious and in doing so I stop at a music store. Lots of music, tapes, records as well as instruments: string, wind and more.

Simon and Garfunkel's 'Bridge Over Troubled Water' is playing. One of my all-time favorite English songs. A terrific album, I love 'The Boxer.

This is the time that I bought the trumpet which I wanted to learn to play. I eventually gave it to Clara. At this point I fell in love or lust. Here's why, how, etc.

An elegant, forty-ish, blond blue-eyed Swede- a pretty woman without a flaw, almost angelic, we struck up a conversation about S & G's music album and soft rock and so on. She was there to pick up an order and evidently me as well.

We paid our bills and walked out to a nearby joint for tea and talk. She seemed interested in my story- college, the draft, Navy, immigration, as we started to put the moves on each other. I noticed she had removed her rings and offered drinks at her residence. MILF!(i.e., Mexican ILF)!

Next, I'm in her dark BMW getting driven to her home in the luxury end of Perth. Simply astounding neighborhoods. Through the gate and up the long cobblestone driveway, into the garage and to the bar, but briefly.

Well, couldn't believe it but there we were, disrobed, intimate on her bed, in love with her wedding portraits, kids and family pictures and more gazing at us. She described herself as wealthy, alone (divorced, widow, single ??) and ...... Smart lady, educated, probably in banking or business, but we had fun and wow, was she ever experienced.

She liked me more Mexican than American, she claimed.

Never saw her again after dinner at one of Perth's finer establishments by the coast. Very generously she took the tab and gave me thanks for a fun time. She boasted being thoroughly pleasured and dropped me off near my hotel. We hugged, kissed and said goodbye as we wished each other well.

She'd marry me she added but the age difference, that I could easily be her son........ the usual farewell, but oh, that feeling and the rush.

Well, up to now I hadn't any need to be calling Gabe's friends to rescue me, but maybe, who knows, someone at the beach.

I had lost track of the time but by now it was probably Monday(?!?) I started with the trumpet- reading the instructions, checking the case, etc., and fell asleep.

The next day I emerged from the hotel late morning and by the afternoon I wound up at the beach, which had a large crowd watching a surfing competition or other activities.

No doubt, to me at least, all of Australia's long coastline was nothing but beautiful, pristine beaches and here in Perth was the evidence and the absolute truth.

I returned late and picked a bag lunch to eat at the hotel.

The following morning, I made it to brunch and went to Hyde Park and the Zoo with both holding some interest. Both needed more variety and larger displays.

One very interesting highlight that I recall was that I was introduced to the Spanish club at this restaurant I dined at donde la paella me llama la atencion. The staff and some customers spoke Spanish, as I did. We introduced ourselves and one thing led to another and I was treated like royalty, being from Mexico and a U.S. Navy man.

We went to this hall, officially lettered en español y una celebración se acontecía con comida (mucho marisco), bebidas, música y baile. Nos pusimos bien alegres y me hallé una novia,

Sarah, muy simpática, alegré, preciosa y animada who I woke up within my room.

I remembered my boss and friend Gabe who said I'd fall in love and marry.

We both were hungover, our eyes bloodshot, our mouths dry, well you know the feeling, but feeling great!

We talked, apologized and learned more about each other over breakfast, thanks to room service. And the happiness continued until about dinner.

Again, I thought how prophetic, what a sage Gabe proved himself. But he knew Perth and knew me.

She and I had a short and wonderful companionship. She said her beau was elsewhere, Adelaide, I think. Not serious but between boyfriends, she latched onto me, claiming being smitten by my independence, quite different: a lone foreign traveler, military and Spanish speaking. Rare.

We got along great and I felt lucky, charmed by this beauty studying medicine as far as she could, maybe beyond nursing, while employed as a phlebotomist or lab technician. She liked pharmacy too.

She loved conversing in Spanish and tickled by our distinct language styles and my accent. She liked que en Español le llama "Sara', 'Sarita'.

Daytime she worked while I toured, and I avoided her family. I didn't want to get too involved, be in too deep and she knew I would leave and return to HEH and the states. We were honest to a fault perhaps. Let's just enjoy ourselves in the here and now.

Funny though how one develops similar behaviors in life through its different stages. I was reminded of my days at Cochise and coeds I had known well.

I think I met her sister or cousin, but I don't know, women can be tricky. It's sort of meeting for a coffee and then her friends supposedly bump into us and hang around briefly. It turns out they are relatives not friends. You know the games people play.

It seemed amusing to me how carefree and liberal the crowds of young people were, like in the sixties, the Beatles, television had blown the doors wide open so that people could enjoy more freedoms.

This reminded me about what I saw in Sydney at the King's Cross, but in Perth, more restraint was present. Except at the beach where one sensed the drugs, the toplessness and such. Sarita and I discussed this, and she felt it had not yet become a troublesome public issue but may be sooner than later.

She and I hung around together, did some light shopping, got ice cream, visited the library and museum. I was impressed how comfortable she felt and made no bones about sleeping over. She'd go to work by morning of course.

And through the years, I've wondered about her and them, how briefly they entered my life and how had their lives turned out. Where are they now and not just them but others, in or out of the Navy, such as some high schoolers, college buddies and co-workers. I just don't dwell on it. It's been such a solitary ride, quite long.

Back in Perth, Sara didn't want to lose time but wanting attention. She admitted enjoyment and satisfaction, regretting the coming separation and departure.

Our adventure would put a damper with her beau, she said, for reasons of her own. Mostly though she liked the casualness of our affair and a style she got to like, however short.

Long term though, she wanted stability, a job and career, family- most normal people's desire.

I didn't fit into that equation. We knew it. From the very beginning, when we started.

I was a passing fling, a momentary thing- with love, fun and leisure and pleasure.

She believed my story and history and most of all, that she met an American Navy man from HEH. She had heard about the Cape, Exmouth and the servicemen.

That I smartly avoided the war impressed her, and that I'd return to college and get my degree even more.

Several times delving, inquiring what I'd like, perhaps a military career, business, a family man.

Sara had dreams that could become real, with better planning and she had youth on her side. Her ambition, energy, youth and smarts could take her far, especially with help, such as her parents helping and pitching in (room and board and other essentials).

I encouraged her, especially when she was more positive and vivacious.

One time at the beach or the park she explored or expressed some ideas about foreign travel, being she viewed Australia's offerings quite limited. With an education and skills in medicine she could almost go anywhere, find employment and live comfortably, especially in the Commonwealth. Canadá came to mind.

In Sara I saw a partner who was well grounded y una que hablaba o pensaba más de cosas serias que de estupidez como de Hollywood, peinados, revistas y por el estilo. Cosas más practicas es lo que contemplaba.

Hermosa, mente fija y una sensualidad- bonitas cualidades ella las poesía. Lindas platicas en español o Ingles nos entretenían.

Pero también teníamos que marcar el alto siendo que los días marchaban, el fin de vacación llega, así como mi regreso en el largo viaje a HEH.

We had a lovely and loving farewell with a stroll, a fine dinner and a final night at my place. We hated to see it end, but such it was, ending.

She had left quietly before I woke but later rang to bid goodbye, wish me well and say thank you. She claimed the week was entertaining with a real and polite young gentleman and would gladly love to do it all over again.

I too said thanks, enjoyed her company and Perth and offered blessings, adding that I hope she and her beau could work things out. We said we'd correspond. An everlasting memory.

I sensed she became melancholic when we disconnected. The phone immediately again rang, and my thoughts were still on her. Thump went my heart, but....

Room service called to inquire about breakfast and I simply declined ordering.

Unsettling was my departure from Perth. In more ways than one. Simply that I took off by myself made a statement such as being a risk taker in a foreign land.

Similar to when I travelled from HEH to Hawaii then to America, plus Mexico. Was I in search of something? Was this partly how man matures and develops while breaking from his clan.

And then Sarah and our swell time together. She'd be okay.

I see myself then near the crashing sea, the sound of the waves rolling in topped by white caps and she very adoringly stands there.

Southwest Australia adios.

The city noise subsides, the bus shoots north as we make ourselves comfortable on the thickly padded reclining seats.

My mind pictures Sarita, and I only wish her well and much success. I see her in a doctor's coat, seeing patients and I start mentally writing her a letter of thanks, encouragement and goodbye. Awkward I felt but I must move on, go forward and meet my future. Live in the imagination.

The Navy Days

In doing so I think of my return to HEH and what awaits there for me. I have to deal with Carl, who is becoming a bit of a pest and knows I have information he wants.

Let's move along faster: further north we stop a Caravan. I had visited the town before. It's on the coast with beautiful beaches and full of nature's wonder. Big mining companies doing exploration in the region.

Truly surprising were the cactus and such specimen that I saw and wondered if I'd experienced a flashback to the Southern Arizona and Sonoran Desert. Barrel cactus, prickly pear, saguaro and variety.

But the damn lizards took first place. Ugliest reptile you'll ever see, similar to what roamed the Cape, HEH and Exmouth. People say its part devil. You need to see it live, but a photo will do. They may be related to the Komodo dragon. These massive seven-foot beasts have coordination and agility plus superb strength. They are grayish-green, spotted with yellow, black, white, etc., markings. Their tongue must be a mile long. They symbolize pure evil and meanness. I'm shocked that some pro team, like football, does not have them as a mascot because they'll give you more if you're weak and meek, so catch them at Caravan. Terrifying!

Once back on the bus and bound more and more into the Northwest Cape, the isolation, nature and barren landscape, became more obvious whereas before it hadn't. My mind was playing tricks with me, like how quickly I reverted to Arizona upon seeing the cactus, which instantly recalled other images.

Mental tricks are part of the brain's automatic function, autonomous controls and I push myself to think of something else. Such as planning ahead, not necessarily fore thought or foreseeability.

In the distance, the tall red antennas began to appear, and I started sensing relief, oddly, as if returning home. Yuck to the barracks as home.

More like at ease, with acquaintances now and security and stability. I'll emphasize though that I felt safe in my travels by myself to Perth, the entire trip. Not even a sneeze, bug or gas.

In Exmouth, after tipping the bus driver, one way or the other I reached the base. Did I have to check in? I don't recall but probably.

Getting back offered one consolation: one less week to serve and much sooner to Hawaii.

And Hawaii was the subject Carl was interested in.

Yes, I had unpacked, settled in and returned to work performing the usual office/clerical duties during which Carl called or he'd stop at the library.

His approach and intent, rather underhanded, was to obtain information about leaving HEH, getting to Hawaii and so on. Maybe go AWOL. I jokingly told him to go to Perth and fly away from there.

He used various tactics like trying to bribe me or by praising me. My truth he did not believe nor my advice. "Brown man does not speak with forked tongue", I told him. His retort was, we laughed, "Rivera, you're whiter than me, you pale faced Mexican, if you're that, you're probably a spy or undercover"!

"Is that like underwear", I'd respond, stretching the joke as much as possible.

Carl felt that I had somehow changed in the Navy or the system to get to Hawaii, because I worked with the Personnel Office and had familiarity with the regs.

Another angle was that he believed I fooled the medics and doctors with my position and connections as an ambulance driver.

I told him this wacho or greaser was not that slippery, and again we joked.

He was just envious and that I'd be leaving for Tripler irked him even more. He wanted out.

My hypothetical to him was that I had seen Navy sailors leave due to hardships (death in the family); promotions (an enlisted man is offered OCS and goes to Officer Candidate School); medical.

Medical can succeed if one has powers of persuasion (money). Think of Klinger the cross-dresser in MASH, trying to get a section 8 discharge. All Klinger had to do was fire his rifle a few times to get out and be home.

Carl was smart. I never told him to leave the Navy, get out, go AWOL. He had to figure it out.

Carl's smirk time and again when we met or ran into each other said it all. He was up to something but quietly and he said little besides the usual greeting and such, small talk.

He and I had no animosity, would chat at our section or division meetings while drinking coffee. He had his own ideas but deep down he probably thought I was with Naval Intelligence.

I don't believe I even blew my cover(?), and not even the doctors who are highly trained and educated figured this out.

Did I actually come across as an undercover?

You can fool some of the folks some of the time, but you can't fool all of the folks all of the time, who said that? Groucho Marks. Karl Marx, Karl Malden. Don't know.

And on to other happenings at our Looney-Bin, I mean Naval Base. Not a whole lot to bring up or talk about. The flicks, no. The wildlife like sharks, snakes, seabirds, nope, (but notice the 'S' sound, more alliteration). How about the Aborigines? No, leave them alone and show some respect.

I didn't have too much time left at HEH. Something like prisoners waiting to be released.

By now I had pretty well completed the process of my college application to head to the University of Arizona in Tucson, Arizona for the fall semester of 1971. My two sisters helped me with this and I'm grateful.

I almost forgot. I don't think I mentioned it and I apologize if I'm repeating myself. I acquired my U.S. Passport, and this entailed a great deal of crap- forms, birth certificate, translations, proof of my American citizenship (naturalization) y mas Mierda.

People became curious and loved my green, red and tan Mexican documento de declaration de Nacimiento the antique crinkled paper with official government stamp. Todo escrito en Español. Guys wanted me to interpret it for them. I did.

I turned all these papers, forms, application and cashier's check to whoever- the US State Department, the American Consulate, the White House, the Vatican, God.... who knows, whatever. They refused it. Marked 'Return to Sender'- moi.

The refusal: due to language. My birth certificate had to be translated 'Officially' to English and they would not accept this wetback's interpretation. No, Nope, Never.

Some illustrious professor in the Languages Department at the University in Perth School of Health, Industry and Technology, did the job that was acceptable to the powers that be. You know, more time, more mail, more money, da, da, da, da, da, da, Just BS.... bureaucratic stuff, but I got my new shiny American Passport with my pretty face in it.

So, what else can I add to this discourse, other than to tell you I put on some weight and my uniform fit too tightly. The same for my civilian clothes, but in Hawaii I had picked up some new threads, mostly Ala Moana Shopping Center and I purchased a tailored dark blue blazer. Made me look totally handsome.

What in blazes does weight gain, a blue coat, etc., have to do with the story?

Silencio por favor, frog lips. It's called transition or continuation, smoothly. Going from A to B to C...........to Z, and not A to L to J then R.

No. Tratamos de cambiar los párrafos y seguir lógicamente, con un punto o idea continuar con el tema principal en la

The Navy Days

comunicación. Did you get all that? It's hard to absorb all of it. A mouthful.

So, I bought a blue blazer in Hawaii and when I returned to Australia, I wore it to a big gala, Exmouth's annual elegant ball. A huge extravagant affair. Note how the blazer ties in connection.

Now then, before I was interrupted, I'll describe the town's celebration. Any more questions?? Can I proceed?

The Northwest Cape where the Navy had me stationed had tons and tons of roughnecks. An absence of niceties and decorum existed.

See, here's my linguistic jewel- the existence of absence.

I wouldn't call the Cape completely uncivilized, some.

The community yearly planned the ball and Gabe was in the planning committee. As Gabe's sidekick, I helped him, just don't tell the Navy we were performing unofficial duties on company time.

The lists were long and the committees various. The food and beverage group. Those handling the entertainment. The money bunch. The hall and cleanup crew. Ticket salespeople. You get the idea.

DON'T forget the bouncers.

People get excited. Very. They loved the whole idea and for me a great learning experience and fun. We had Navy personnel pitching in. A lot of spirit and camaraderie during the entire time- about four months- before the big show and final performance. The night or nights. Una extravaganza!

Practically the entire Northwest came. I exaggerate, but the entire region was well represented. There they were: law enforcement, teachers, military and nurses. Locals, foreigners, Aborigines and one Mexican, me. All dressed in their Sundays best, as if going to church. Maybe a couple of tuxedoes and a few fancy gowns, but many clean descent outfits. Guys combed, clean shaved, in coats and ties. The dames in splendid outfits, just radiant.

The Navy was well represented, with some in their dress blue uniforms. Others wore formal civvies.

The place rocked for about six hours. I think it was the school auditorium nicely decorated, with al fresco seating also available.

The bars served wine, liquor and beer and made a killing- a bunch of money, with bar tenders, waiters and bus boys cleaning up with large tips y una cena gratis. Fabulosa comida!

The dinner consisted of appetizers and rolls, followed by fresh salads and an entre of lobster with fettuccine- out of this world.

There was the richest coffee in the universe to keep everyone up and awake in the electrifying atmosphere. Un gran ambiente social como nunca se había visto en esos rumbos.

A small orchestra, all in matching suits, played and entertained for over four hours. From Perth they came and played mambos, cha-chas, jazz, Sinatra and much more. The couples adored the music and each other with dancing, kissing, twisting and more. Una noche de amor.

And there I was, getting drunk with Gabe, his family and company at the head table. My postal guys a no show.

During intermission the MC- Master of Ceremonies- would speak. Welcoming everyone and thanking them for contributing to a worthy cause, blah, blah, blah! So did the HEH Base Commander, "Thank you for supporting our mission....... fighting communism, blah, blah, blah"!

They gave away prizes too; like a free weekend getaway to Adelaide or Perth; a tea set; free oil change. That sort of thing.

I got shoved up on the stage during one intermission to help out.

"My name is Jose Jimenez", I used as an introduction and got a big laugh. The audience roared. I think I awarded the winner of the drawing candy, sweets, " A box of chocolates and the cavities that go with it", and more laughter.

People liked me, knew me and my easy-going manner y el Unico Mexicano working with Gabe, probably the most popular guy in Exmouth and surroundings.

We all left bombed out of our minds, just loud, obnoxious, laughing, throwing things. Terrific fun and an unforgettable night and my blazer, not ruined but a stain or two and some lipstick. One Humongous Blast!

Except for the two drunk blokes arrested for fighting.

Whenever the following day was, could have even been Mayday, that's how bad everyone felt after the fiesta and all hungover, we had work to do to put the gala behind us. All the cleanup, bills to pay, equipment to return. The various committees reported for duty and a meeting.

Afterwards, being responsible citizens, the entire matter was pretty much taken care of but for a few loose ends, and until next year, another celebration.

Such civic participation impressed many by seeing the dedication and contribution made to the community, that almost wasn't even on the world map. That existed practically nowhere. That was labelled 'Bum Fuck Egypt'. Yet people showed their love for the place, for this tiny speck of human existence.

Not too much wear and tear on the school's building or the grounds where children played. Exmouth appeared very much like before the ball, if not better with the streets cleaner after we picked up the litter.

I felt good, with pride in being with the people and doing my share. By participating in improving this itty-bitty piece of humanity and leaving a positive impression of America and myself.

And leaving I was or would be but not before I suffered another pair of cyclones that wrecked, if not destroyed our beloved Northwest Cape.

I'd venture that the second season of cyclones that I suffered was worse than the previous one. It seemed to me, though I didn't check the gauges for the amount of rainfall nor the wind velocity and so forth.

More debris was scattered, windows broken, fences down and such. Thank God though that there was no loss of human life nor serious injuries.

I checked my shorts- clean.

The scuttlebutt was that these storms could or had toppled an antenna or two, but again I don't know if it was true or not. I imagine it could happen.

I'm just glad that I never had to be on duty driving the ambulance on such stormy days.

CHAPTER 20.
Farewell H.E.H.

The medical orders were now effective. "I'm leaving on a jet plane, don't know if I'll be back again", so goes the song by Peter, Paul and Mary. That's me as I pack, get my things ready and squared away, my bunk, locker and space in the barracks. I'm leaving items behind and Andy has been informed.

What develops remains to be seen, because I may return, and I want to depart on good terms. Leaving things in good order with my job at Educational Services, the library and the Ambulance Corps. I realize that if I return it will be for a short stint, because my tour of eighteen months in Australia expires in early 1971.

I've talked with numerous friends, mates and acquaintances and said farewell in case I don't come back.

Gabe, Vic and the other Aussies were kind, warm and generous with their goodbyes. They are used to this being so many sailors come and go.

The postal crew put together a small dinner and were very gracious in bidding me adios.

Fellow seamen who I worked with or got to know, like those in the dorms, acknowledged my departure.

One last round at the EM Club with the crowd, toasting and hollering, " Hip, Hip, Hooray, Anchors Aweigh"!

The last morning per the usual routine; wake up, make the bed, hit the showers, dress and head to the mess hall for breakfast, I would not be reporting to the office except for a few minutes y adios.

I hung around the barracks until noon and had lunch. By about one, the bus picked up the passengers. We boarded and not long afterwards were at the airfield.

The best I can do is call it early December 1970, the last time I saw Exmouth, HEH and the Cape.

The MAC Flight experienced a delay due to the large cargo that had to be rearranged. Therefore, they had us waiting on the bus, we took off about three and we're soon kissing the clouds up in the spectacular wild blue yonder.

I get choked up. A flood of feelings overwhelms me when I think of the Pot Shot Inn, Perth and Sara, the fishing and more.

Sara never answered my correspondence.

Whhrrrrrrrrr revved the aircraft taking us away from HEH, and I contemplated what would happen if it ceased whhrrrrrring. We were still in the direction of Sydney and what happens? Going in for a landing, perhaps an airstrip or road can be found, that is if the plane doesn't explode in mid-air. Are parachutes an option?

Maybe a water landing once we're over the ocean. Are we gonna be found if we all sink? The vests, the life raft, water markers (dye), and all that plus more. Does the radar work or track us? What about the radios?

I was making conversation with the pilot and navigator and it wasn't going too well, perhaps I made them uneasy as we sat in the cockpit. Was it appropriate to ask these questions or talk about something else?

We broke it up when we were served our brown bag lunches. More like dinner of the usual stuff. Mutton on buns, chips, veggies (cherry tomatoes, carrots, etc.) and tea/soda or fresh coffee from the pot on-board the plane. The food broke our hunger, but it tasted like nothing to brag about.

The Navy Days

I got drowsy then passed out for what seemed eternity, but no. The Air Force Sarge woke me up and ordered me to strap on my seatbelt being we were experiencing turbulence.

We all had obeyed and took our places until the shaking subsided and the flight calmed down. At which point we each checked our shorts. No need to visit the restroom.

I'm in a fog, unable to place ourselves. It may have been that we flew to Christchurch without stopping in Sydney, either way, we landed safely and remained there overnight.

Quickly we made it to our lodging, registered, then to a bar and grill where two of my mates quickly met, and each easily picked up a beauty (a nickname given to New Zealanders is kiwi) and returned to their rooms to get their plumbing serviced (screwed). All night! The moaning, groaning, shrieks and laughter could be heard into the early morn.

One can imagine just how hard-up those two poor fellows were after a year and a half at the Cape without female companionship. Like long incarcerated prisoners. Desperate that they'd nail a cow, kangaroo, and I've heard sheep was a close second.

Even an ostrich, I've heard.

The rain came down hard and harder still the closer we got to Hawaii and Hickam Air Force Base.

During the flight, our two friends who were in such a celebratory mood last night felt like death warmed over. All that loving, the booze and no rest or sleep means a sad or bad combination for air travel on a noisy military cargo plane in foul windy and stormy weather.

We all laughed, getting some kicks and wondering out loud if their fun was now worth the price, sexually speaking. Not only were they affirmative, but emphatically hollered, "Hell Yes"!! Repeatedly, holding their arms high in victory, like Rocky.

The two didn't last. They rolled over, covered themselves in blankets, after putting in earplugs and passed out, happy to be free, happy to leave HEH, and happier to have been screwed all night long by two really fine, attractive ladies. Or it could've been six.

Me, well, I was saving myself for Hawaii. Like that old sheep herder's joke. His son says, "Hey old man, let's run to the meadow and do some sheep". The elder replies, "Let's walk and bang them all day"!

Si, era casi fin de año, the month of Noel with love, peace and joy. Even the plane had some of the Navidad spirit, like a wreath, Xmas coffee cups/mugs and a short string of lights.

We would look out the windows to catch the Xmas glitter below, but no, we saw Santa instead, with a loaded sleigh and reindeer. What the heck, we wondered, asking each other what's going on with the big fat red elf. We could even hear him, Yes!!! Unbelievable!

Nick kept pace with us though our plane was travelling at over, I'd say, 400 mph. He laughed, waved and hollered at the reindeer, Rudolph had the lead and his nose was lit really bright, and it appeared like the reindeer smiled and talked to each other.

Part of what we heard was that Santa and the herd were having a practice run in preparation for Christmas morning, when the millions of presents would be delivered World-wide.

Santa even told us a few jokes, like the Cincinnati Reds of pro baseball had a player named Rudy, a pitcher with a strong but arthritic arm that hurt in bad weather, cold, hail, etc.

The whole club house would laugh when the pitcher yelled, "I, Rudolph the red knows rain, dear friends", holding his arm while massaging it.

So, we passengers were playing tag with the North Pole gang and Sir Nick chewed out the herd because he was catching wind, the smelly kind from the herd passing gas.

The Navy Days

One of his favorite tales took place up north, Minnesota, I think. He landed on the roof and down the chimney he went, only to find a tall, voluptuous lass in a negligée waiting for him. He sang loudly to her.

Ho ho ho,

Santa won't go

to play in the snow,

He's gonna stay

and take care of his lay.

All on board our plane were just ripping in uncontrollable laughter.

Then, next, the lights instructing us to sit and buckle-up came on being we were much nearer to Hickam. We stared out the window, and saw Santa waving at us, as he headed into the misty darkness of this beautiful night. We were all in awe because of the miracle we had just witnessed.

¡Ay! ¡Ay! ¡Ay! ¡Qué maravilla! Entre vida y sueño. sonámbulo estaba siendo que me quede dormido, imaginando a San Nicholas y su trineo bien aluzado.

Bonita es la vida, pero alivianando por la imaginación y los sueños, que también dan vida a muestras aspiraciones y si no lo comprenden, les explico. Por ejemplo.

Padres con hijos aspiran a algo mejor para ellos. Luchan para tener un futuro donde disfruten. Y ese sueño se vuelve realidad cuando logran ver al hijo o hija graduarse del colegio con un título de médico, ingeniero, profesor.

Serán los sueños para vivirlos? Que significa esta freso, esta pregunta. Piense lo bien, es tema muy filosófico y profundo, que no tiene fin.

Ya stamnos bajando y pronto the wheels are touching earth, screeching to a halt as the fumes penetrate the cabin, but it doesn't matter. We're ecstatic!

Happy, actually overjoyed, to touch American soil. God bless the USA.

We're off the plane, a long MAC Flight that seemed to have lasted an eternity, but successful and we're safe. A few of us passengers thanked the crew and wished them happy holidays. They will rest some and after fly to the mainland.

To me it seems like a repeat performance having done this only about six months ago. In fact, I noticed a couple of familiar faces, USAF personnel working the planes, driving fork-lifts, fueling, delivering luggage, all in a very efficient manner.

I say farewell to my mates from HEH who go on to other destinations, some separating and going home, others to their next assignment, be that a ship, school, etc., yet others on leave or R&R.

Me, I'm sticking around Hawaii and will be settling in at the Hickam dorms, bunking in for a few days till they kick me out, knowing full well that I have to check-in with the eye clinic at Tripler Army Hospital. My orders are open, meaning set time or appointment has yet been scheduled.

So, I'm free in paradise, again. Should I have guilt, shame, what? Or feel just fortunate and thankful that a year and a half in the active duty of the U.S. Navy, it has worked out fairly well and have been treated quite decently, which in surprising because I didn't expect it, this cold war warrior.

After some snacks I am done, and it's lights out. Sleep and wait for morning.

If I check in with Naval Operations at Pearl Harbor it will be quite different than if I remain at HAFB, which gives greater liberty being they don't have command of me per my orders from HEH in Exmouth, Australia.

The result of a typo or two from friends in personnel at the Cape. What are friends for. A few favors here and there, schmoozing and greasing some palms makes life much easier.

The Navy Days

Innocence lost. Those days were lost or gone for most of us who no longer believed in Uncle Sam and his goodness. No longer naive were we whose eyes were opened by the War, My Lai, Nixon/Watergate, the protests, riots. The ethics were there but not always followed. Just read the Uniform Code of Military Conduct (UCMJ).

But all this aside, and not by coincidence, I did find myself thinking about December 7th, a date that will live in infamy, when the Japanese attacked Pearl Harbor.

The event spurred the Americans into World War II and it has significance for me as you will read later, but for now a few brief notes about December Seventh.

In 1941, on a Sunday morning, a beautiful sunny day for worship and Church, a surprise attack by the Japanese occurred and caused tremendous devastation upon the American Naval Fleet in the Pacific.

At the time when war and hostilities took place in Europe and other parts of the World, Americans wanted to remain neutral, stay out of the war.

The next day, December 8th, President Roosevelt declared War on Japan and by doing so turned our isolation and country into a strong, dynamic, International powerhouse after we entered WWII.

The attack had the opposite effect on Japan which aspired to overtake and control swaths of the western Pacific for economics, shipping and materialistic reasons.

The Japanese had planned on the attack to cripple America and force it to its knees.

America rallied and wave after wave of volunteers swelled the Military ranks ready to fight. Our Country was transformed.

In the long aftermath of the war, years later Japan fell to its knees, humiliated and greatly devastated with the two atomic bombs America dropped on Hiroshima and Nagasaki.

Back to December 07, 1941. The USS Arizona sank in Pearl Harbor where it was anchored and to this day is a Memorial seen by millions. It commemorates the men of this battleship who died and are entombed there since the Second World War.

I recall sitting in bars that December 1971, after arriving from Australia and listening to accounts about the Japanese attack on Pearl Harbor, Ford Island, Hickam.

CHAPTER 21.
Hawaii- Part III.

It definitely was a different type of Christmas that I would be spending in Hawaii.

Mele Kalikimaka or Merry Christmas in Hawaiian. A popular song also with the same meaning. When in Rome, do what the Romans do. In Hawaii, do like the Hawaiians. But do we have to overdo it X a million! Everywhere! Over kill.

Maybe not. Think about locking yourself in a soundproof room or in a padded cell, tranquilized.

Let's get on with business at hand and the reason and purpose for being in Hawaii, as well as the fun and entertainment.

I'm certain the reader is familiar with the island's flowery necklaces, the Hawaiian leis and to the second type of Hawaiian lay, also very famous! Simply ask servicemen stationed there for an explanation.

The first couple of days were seen as decompression: being away from Exmouth, back in civilization, some time for relaxation, get over the slog and jet lag.

I had however, a pressing issue. Remember, I had written that servicemen were being granted an early-out of about three months. I would be due one as well, meaning that I'd be serving less time.

My active duty term was for twenty-four months, from July 1969 through July 1971. Minus ninety-days means I'd leave, April 1971, and I had to plan accordingly as if I would get out early. No chance I'd be re-enlisting or beg for an extension. It could happen but it's not even close, not likely.

By now my Parents and Family knew I was heading stateside with a stay in Hawaii and they had my new address. It didn't seem I would return to Australia. But nothing was set in concrete, nothing very firm. I would simply do the best I could with the situation, while trying to dig more and better information and keeping abreast, because decisions could be sudden that would affect me.

And then again, I contemplated what I'd be doing once I returned to civilian life. I knew college had my main attention for the Fall semester, 1971, in Tucson, Arizona at the U of A. I had made progress there and preparations include dorm selection and roommate, but more had to be completed.

I also mulled the acquisition of a vehicle once I returned to civilian life and all that such a purchase entailed: the title, registration, insurance and more.

My driver's license had expired, but I had an Australian one. Another matter to take care of.

The to-do list was becoming lengthy, with everyday more additions and me writing more letters.

One thought I had was the high school graduation of my sister Clara, who I'd write to along with Ed y Panchita. Would I be able to attend the late May 1971, ceremony and see her in her cap and gown?

Clara had already made plans. These were laid out for the World to know. She would continue working at Sears and enroll at Cochise Community College in general studies, liberal arts sort of, for two years. She'd reside at home with our Parents.

She would follow with attendance for another two years in Northern Arizona University and study in the field of education, probably finish as an Elementary School Teacher.

I knew at that time that nothing was going to prevent her from accomplishing her goal. Dicho y hecho.

At least Clara had a good job and some firm plans. I couldn't say the same for me.

I couldn't dismiss government work. Recently discharged Vets received preferential treatment in order to help them adjust when returning to civilian life. I had ninety days to claim a job or find employment after leaving active duty.

The post office was a possibility. Work there while attending the University of Arizona. I started the process by researching this at the library, calling the USPS and even writing a letter or two to the Douglas Postmaster.

Becoming a civilian was becoming a real bitch with all that I had to do. It could be discouraging and even overwhelm some one less inspired or dedicated. Add to this the war protesters who were truly very demoralizing for the troops who, against their wishes for many, were putting their lives on the frontlines.

What a mess. No two ways about it. No matter how rosy the picture was painted, the media, more so television, presented darkness, pessimism, negativity on a daily basis. Still, though, I had my own concerns to deal with.

I felt and saw it this way now due to more exposure. In Douglas, an isolated, sheltered border town and in Exmouth, I was not too aware or as aware as being in Hawaii. Perhaps getting away from it all was best.

Now that I came to American soil, I had a serious matter to take care of at Tripler Army Hospital. Soon, after a few phone calls, I had my appointment scheduled.

Which pace is faster, the turtle's or the snails? Doesn't matter. That's how quickly things got done in December, with the holidays, the pace dragged even more.

I had heard about priority patients being seen first and the less serious one's next year. Therefore, I'd have to wait till 1971. More of the military's catch 22 of 'hurry up and wait'.

Specifics evade me although I did meet with the ophthalmologist and also, I had a physical exam. All this was completely alien to me being I had enjoyed good health, though I was underweight. I never had been a hospital patient or seen a physician on a regular basis, nor a specialist that I thought was a sniper who knocked-off people or perhaps a helicopter pilot of a Huey. That's how naive I was.

Thus, I had weeks to kill, and not that much to do for about a month, un mez de Descanso. Pues como decía mi Abuelo, "Como bien, duermo agosto, me peo fuerte y me escape de la muerta". También, así dicen en Costa Rica, "Pura Vida"! vacación y más vacación en Hawái en Navidad.

Maybe I could have again taken leave and flown to the mainland y ver a mi Familia. I took care of all that was unnecessary. I had cash, meals and lodging with plenty of time to go sight-seeing like Diamond Head, Punch Bowl Cemetery, the volcanos and more.

One can see Hawaii in a few days unless one visits the other islands, and then be stuck, no escape afterwards. Consider too that the places are on the pricey side. Military discounts help quite a bit as do some subsidies, such as for housing.

Troops in the lower ranks economized with the abundance of nature fruits and vegetables I scarfed, bananas, coconuts, cumquats, avocados and much more. An actual cornucopia.

Noel time put almost everyone in a festive mood and unbounded generosity that meant the GIs, sailors, marines and such troops were looked after. The patriotism and benevolence of Americans, Hawaiians and others was on, treating us with such kindness and pride.

The Navy Days

Who were we to say 'No' to this bacchanalia? I wanna go to Sydney's King Cross.

Such was Hawaii-Waikiki, Honolulu, Hickam, Pearl Harbor and other spots- my second time on the island in late 1970 when the Heavens opened up to a deluge of rain. I don't recall ever having been in so much rain over a period of a month or two. But then again, the annual rainfall there is one of the highest in the world if not the highest except perhaps the Philippines. Who knows?

Even so, and without a vehicle, I met some locals and other acquaintances. Trusts developed and the ladies were friendly, yet I only got so close with any long-term compromising because of my circumstances.

Situations were like with Sara of Perth. I was honest: an itinerant sailor destined for the mainland after a short stop in Pearl Harbor. College awaits. They liked my story that led to fun and pleasures.

I even went as far as disclosing that I, like thousands of other young American men, were the unfortunate victims of the draft and the war. Our lives were interrupted and our appointments with our destiny altered, sometimes horribly.

America lost well over fifty thousand individuals in the war with the results and consequences awful. How many future nurses, doctors, engineers, brilliant minds, were lost? If in that number we lost one Jonas Salk, it's a significant, tremendous tragedy. A huge loss.

And yet we did, as another tragic example or account follows.

Admiral Elmo Zumwalt had a thirty-plus year career in the U.S. Navy with service and command in Viet Nam, where he ordered the spraying of agent orange defoliant in those jungles. It was his honest and sincere belief that his son, Elmo Zumwalt Jr., who also had served in those jungles, died of cancer due to his exposure to the chemical. In short or in other words, it's like the father killed his very own son, who was Elmo Zumwalt III, 42 years of age when he died of cancer on August 14, 1988.

Extremely sad, in my view. A parent never wants to be at the funeral of his very own children. I can only sense or feel the despair, horrible anguish and uncomfort of such a parent whose actions led to the demise of his very own child. God, please bless them and spare me.

Oh my! My heart aches and my conscience hurt after putting together the last couple of paragraphs. Please allow me to move on. Let's go.

When young, one has vim, vigor, vitality, testosterone, ego to spare and a don't-much-care-attitude with defiance towards authority. If there exists one place where this occurs, try the military. I was not much different, but I subdued this with respect and control of my demeanor and behavior, for years, a decade or more.

I could have told Ed, Panchita, Blanca y a otros más que se larguen y me dejen en Pas, pero ha sido 99.9%, para mi mejor aguantarme y seguir luchando. Es honorando a la Familia y religion.

In the military you obey and follow orders, like them or not, such as being told to clean up the barracks and bathrooms or get the mess hall shaped up for chow.

Trust me, there are far more examples, much worse, than I described here that I witnessed. To illustrate, look at videos of the Navy Seals in training- pure brutal torture. It's honor, one serves.

So, I was under orders from up Top to report to Tripler Army Hospital, but why should I, I felt fine, no health issues, nothing but me, no fractures or bone spurs in my ankles. Maybe a burning implement raw from carnal pleasure.

Orders were orders, so I performed as I had been instructed by having checked in, then scheduling an appointment. Don't ask for times, dates, etc., late 1970 into 1971.

I kept going in and out of the hospital, mostly the eye clinic for check-ups, exams, cancelled appointments and such. I had been informed my situation was not high priority being the Ophthalmologist stayed busy and had serious cases, very.

A ton of optical fractures, blindness, missing eyeballs with blown eye sockets is what I viewed at times on my long trips to Tripler Hospital, where I visited the eye and ENT Clinics. Not very pleasant at all watching my brothers who fought in Nam.

My circumstances were far less, such as a picnic by comparison, a walk on the beach.

I also ran into retired Veterans, those from WWII or Korea as well as some dependents, such as wives' being examined or treated by the various doctors.

I passed many hours in the lobby, at times into evening, not to be examined, yet trekking it to the barracks late, in darkness. Such is the cause to serve.

I lucked-out at times when someone would offer a lift to Pearl Harbor and I'd hoof it a short distance to the barracks. One way or the other I would always safely make it back.

In Hawaii there is quite an influence of the Hispanic culture from early explorers and settlers from Spain, Portugal and other nations. One sees this in the many different family names, such as in the telephone directory and the name Rivera in various spellings is well represented: Rivero, Riveiro, etc. You get the picture.

At Tripler I met an ex-Navy sailor who became an acquaintance due to our similar surnames. When he saw me, he pushed himself over in his wheelchair, greeted me, offered Feliz Navidad then introduced himself. He too had taxied me to Pearl. He spoke poorly in Spanish, but at least he made the effort and was saddened when I informed not being local but from stateside, a real Mexican from Sonora, on the border.

He laughed. Me too. His take was how low Uncle Sam and the military stooped to find men to fight the war. He was right in many and in several ways. We'll call him Iggy, like others did. Ignatius or Ignacio.

Ours became a semi-casual, informal companionship. He'd call me infrequently at the barracks and picked me up to party with his girlfriends, sisters and other ladies. We had a good time, but I did not like or trust his driving being he was paraplegic and a recovered quad, but hell, he had a van and that really was all good, great even, with the dating at some cozy Lovers' Lane and the couples enjoying themselves all out. He had a lust for life and did not entirely give up in-spite of his disability.

His rehab was slow, taking time and he was not the most cooperative patient. He described his accident and injuries, but memory fails me. He had spinal compression but no fractures. Fortunately, he'd recover in months or years, doctors said, but he needed better participation and less social life. I selfishly helped him with the ladder and his many gorgeous girlfriends he willingly shared.

His everything- popularity, charisma, mouth- got him almost all that he wanted.

Maybe not a diaper change.

Enigmatic described Iggy. He'd walk if he dedicated himself to rebuilding his atrophied limbs and gained strength, build himself up to what he once was. Not necessarily herculean, but enough muscle mass to leave the wheelchair behind.

His therapists, nurses, doctors and friends all agreed it came from the mind, which he needed to convince and motivate in order to become independent. Examples were offered to him. Testimonials, videos and literature. Iggy made progress but not enough.

He seemed to use his injury or disability to get attention, get pity, not applying himself but have others do things for him or handle matters. Also, he was receiving all types of benefits without question, which was bound to stop once he regained his health.

Hearing this and watching him was depressing, hard, a bummer and difficult to accept as he manipulated the medical system, the public assistance, his friends and family.

I would not be shocked or surprised if he clandestinely walked, such as himself only locked in his bedroom and moving about freely without assistive devices and such. But I don't think that was the case. He'd come around and become his former self eventually.

I recall that I spent part of Christmas Eve and the early afternoon hours of the twenty-fourth, at his chante con su Familia y parientes. Como un rey me trataron, pero fui yo más por el respeto y ser cordial porque después de una o dos bebidas me fui. Creo que les lleve chocolates como regalo de Navidad.

That Christmas Eve we (some sailors-mates from the barracks), spent it first in Honolulu getting ripped and then proceeded to Waikiki to finish off. What else to do when there is no family, do the best you can.

I think it was raining (or was it New Year's Eve) and being plastered and poor didn't help. Someone had rented a cheap motel room and the taxis got us there. We all pitched in for snacks, booze and some girls joined us. Some Christmas music and dancing followed into the early morning. Just beautiful, at daybreak with the early rays hitting the beach and the surf, and God to thank.

Christmas in Hawaii in the Navy became unforgettable, but some details fade, more rapidly now.

Still, total strangers honoring Jesus birth simply.............and no, I did not attend mass.

Sometime near the end of 1971 and I hope my Military Medical Records reflect I'm right, at least somewhat accurate, I was ready as I was being prepared to be admitted into TAH, subject to postponements and some delays. The ophthalmologist recommended being patient.

I had a chance to see where I'd would be, the surgery, recovery and the patient ward.

Not too surprisingly, I met a mate from HEH who was there, probably the fourth floor, recuperating from TMJ surgery.

His jaw had been wired shut and would remain as such for approximately six weeks. He couldn't talk much.

He was just pissed about the whole situation, confinement to the hospital and all. Further he was on a liquid diet and losing weight, plus his teeth just about rotting from lack of oral hygiene. He drank malts and milk shakes constantly that we kidded him- he should have his own cow.

Funnier was how he would almost choke because barfing could kill him. I don't know how to explain it too well, but others in similar straights had to be revived after the wires in the mouth and around the teeth had to be cut, otherwise the person dies from the blocked airways and no oxygen to the brain. Talk about having to deal with the emergency and clean up the mess. No gracias.

Anyway, I vaguely recall, that this bloke somehow got kicked in the face during a baseball game by the runner stealing second base. The pick off didn't work as the runner went in feet first. Ouch! His face had swelled like a fat stuffed hog.

Stuff, stories, tales and more that I'll carry the rest of my life from Australia, Hawaii and the Navy. No one to share them with other than you, lucky reader and companion.

The cutting took place on a late morning I think, even though I had been admitted the night before, told to clean up and prepped at dawn. No food or breakfast, but hunger.

This was all foreign to me except from what I saw and learned reading, watching Ben Casey, Marcus Welby, etc.

One humorous flick I saw that made me laugh was MASH. Do I need to explain? Starring Elliot Gould and Donald Sutherland with Hot Lips. The movie, not the tv series.

Should I have been alarmed, scared, laughing, what? MASH, both movie and tv versions, were a huge success by ridiculing Military/Army life in the medical corps, up in the battle fields, the front lines.

And here I was a Navy sailor in an Army hospital ready to be operated on, then get more post-op treatment. Should I run while I still could and had the chance, or maybe just take it in stride with hopes all will turn out well. Escape was possible.

What started my thinking was that I could go blind for whatever reason. Others had similar thoughts. There were instances where surgeons goofed, like operating on the wrong limb or removing the wrong organ, even leaving instruments in the body.

We soldiers/patients laughed with MASH, but just wished to God all went well with us and that our doctors and surgeons were sober and serious, unlike the drunks and skirt-chasers from the films.

I had said my prayers all along since leaving HEH and had even visited a church or chapel for mass.

I had not confided in my Family, no one back home because I did not want them to be worried or panicking. Additionally, we were not used to dealing with serious medical issues, such as surgery.

The operation proved successful. Only the left eye was treated, with the right one left alone pretty much. They left one eye alone. Heh, heh. The doctor ordered at least an annual checkup for vigilance and be certain my vision did not deteriorate. Keep checking the right eye, be attentive and stay awake. Did I slip a double redundancy by you? Didn't notice it.

After the sedative wore off and out of recovery, the orderly wheeled me to the ward. My eyes were covered, and I was blind for some hours, I think until morning when my physician returned and uncovered my right eye.

He instructed me about this, that, and the other. Careful walking as I could fall. Bathe but keep the head and face dry. Don't leave the hospital and remain seated or in bed. Simple instructions.

The good doctor saw me daily for, I'd say, two weeks straight. I'm fuzzy on this detail. He'd add eye drops, check the swelling, removed and replaced the white gauze until final removal on the fourth day post-surgery. It itched like a bitch but healed.

News comes to me that I'd remain in TAH, probably for a total of about two weeks from the day of surgery. Details still sketchy, but what follows was state of the art or even advanced science, the future of medicine I read and heard, and I was a candidate for it.

Radiation. More of the same stuff I had been listening to back in HEH. Heh. Heh! Over there, it was the antennas; here in Hawaii it was beamed laser lit into my left eyeball. They explained that the remaining cells that may have been missed were burned away without damaging the healthy tissue. Who knows? I believed the doctors gathered around me when they zapped me.

I'd lay on a table in a certain room. I'd be stopped and told not to move, then a mild tingle or burning sensation on the left side of my face for a few seconds. That was it for about six to eight treatments.

And it really worked, not that I was ever bothered by the growth in that eye, but I suppose the physicians felt the need to remove it. I felt no different after the entire treatment was completed. Clear white tissue, though the right eye had a speck not sufficiently mature yet to be removed. My vision was not affected and I to this day do fine, but near-sighted and I wear glasses, like before. Now eye doctors comment poorly about my left eye.

Up to the present, physicians admire the terrific surgery/work the TAH Ophthalmology Clinic performed on me. (Thank you and thank God) not to cut the right one.

While in the hospital those two weeks. I was ambulatory and given simple work assignments, such as helping feed patients, literally spoon-feeding the badly injured soldiers; running specimens to the labs; changing bandages, hauling trash; changing linen; pushing patients to the x ray labs or to the cafeteria and sometimes the library; turning the televisions; bringing magazines, tape decks, escorting visitors, you name it I did it.

I'd knock off about three-thirty and head to town. Weekends I had free.

It turned out I would be having a second surgery, which had to be scheduled. In the interim, they sent me to Pearl Harbor, Ford Island, where I had to bunk, but I still escaped to Hickam. I was on light duty per written medical orders from the Ophthalmologist.

My well-worn path to TAH: leave Ford Island by ferry, catch a bus, usually to downtown, take a transfer to the hospital and be checked over, either at the eye clinic or at ENT. Once in a while I'd catch a direct ride.

The round trip took almost the entire day, and at times I'd reach Ford Island at sunset.

I just followed orders.

Estas discusiones son de uno, junto con la historia y experiencias, y muy bien, buenas e intimas con amigos que sufrieron lo mismo, no con esos hipócritas que evitaron servir a la patria.

We cannot refute the danger of War and how men mostly senselessly join it, there exposing themselves to great harm and death in addition to causing immense grief to their loved ones.

At eighteen I had an inkling, instinct, self-preservation, but not sufficient maturity or intelligence that I gained in later years to understand with better sense that which we young men were getting into, or rather exposed to or thrown into.

I'll admit without lying, but some forgetfulness that once upon a time, many decades ago, maybe in high school or college, as required, we read Stephan Crane's <u>Red Badge of Courage.</u> Quite profound and philosophical after the numerous rounds of class discussion tearing this book apart. Check it out. It almost fit my bill: the young man of about eighteen enlisting in the military, seeking glory and crapping his shorts once he realized what War was like a century and a half ago. A lot of it applies even today.

But I return, even if for a moment to TAH, those wards, halls, rooms and bemoan the poor damaged souls therein never to regain their former selves, as Iggy and I watched and talked. Very pensively we conversed, about the lives, our lives, of young adult American males involved in the Viet Nam War, and how they have been affected.

We noted the long trip ahead of them, perhaps years, in rehab, therapy, etc., upon leaving TAH, which was mainly temporary for them before returning stateside for extensive recovery, in hospitals or centers like Bethesda, New York or Boston. Many times, much closer to home.

I took leave of TAH, no longer an in-patient but checking in per my appointments. This went on for the remainder of my days in Hawaii, I recall, but I'm not sure when I quit visiting the medical center.

My duty station became Pearl Harbor with boarding at Fort Island, still holding my 'light duty' status.

Very oddly, getting off the ferry, just like it was yesterday, I clearly saw Carl, from HEH, in the crowd. He approached me, greeted each other, embraced and laughed. He seemed embarrassed. We talked a good while, sitting on a bench in the shade, with many people passing, going in many different directions.

I would be seeing or meeting Carl a few more times on base, the E-M Club, the Exchange and the like.

He was hard to figure out and to determine his reason or reasons for being in Hawaii other than he was in the U.S. Navy. He was hedging, guarding the truth. My interests lay elsewhere.

Carl inquired about what and how I had been doing, which I answered that it seemed to me that I enjoyed a vacation in Hawaii and that I probably would not visit the other islands. I was having the time of my life almost. I'd be leaving Hawaii and the Navy, returning to school, etc.

My job was easy, mostly working in an office with civilian and military personnel didn't bust my chops. Many females where I worked.

He asked, then I told him to mind his own business but that positively all went well medically with me.

And no, I did not know if I'd return to Australia, which to me, in retrospect, had not been all that bad and in fact I did quite well saving funds for college.

He felt I was putting him on with my light, positive spin on my duties and Navy life. But we were different. He was college educated and came from wealth. I was a survivor, an immigrant. A working stiff with hardly a life or background.

It came out of Carl that he worked an angle to get out of Australia, probably using connections, like calling a Senator. He may have even bribed someone, like a physician or shrink, to find him 'unfit for duty' or 'unsuitable for duty in present status' (such as climate, working environment) or even a priest, rabbi or chaplain doing a 'conscientious objector' thing for him.

I didn't demonstrate much interest, but noticed the change was good for him by not being in isolated duty in the outback of the Cape. Put him in Adak, Alaska, and he would go bonkers there as well if he didn't freeze first in the speedos he liked to wear so openly.

Life seemed okay to good in Hawaii which required a hefty paycheck. The Navy pay didn't cut it. I managed though. For Carl, money was not an issue.

With time, it seemed Carl became a figment of my imagination, because life goes on and new developments take front and center, with Family many times doing just that.

My circumstances now centered in Hawaii at Pearl Harbor for a number of reasons. Primarily I had been under medical orders and remained under observation or follow-up for several weeks. During which time I learned, I, like many in the military, have received a ninety day early out or reprieve.

Rather than serve in active duty for two years and be released in July 1971, I would be out in April or three months earlier than I had planned or expected.

CHAPTER 22.

Remain in Hawaii.

The Navy decided I serve my remaining active duty in Hawaii, because I would return home soon, I believe, in about six to eight weeks, by April, which seemed much sooner, almost like tomorrow. I had to put my time to good use and make the necessary preparations for my return to civilian life.

I promptly notified my Family, that in April I would be leaving active duty and return to the mainland. I would keep them informed as things went along.

Navy personnel in Australia- principally Andy- had been contacted and I requested that my belongings be forwarded to me. That took a while because of the MAC Flights, but I did get these, which I went to pick up at Hickam. I am fairly certain that's how it happened, not too complicated by any means whatsoever.

I wondered still though, if I had made the best of my period in the Navy. I never went to school, I stayed out of trouble, I didn't learn much of a trade, but I did have some fun. Maybe it was best this way.

Consider that at about this time, in the sixties, the Navy had lost a submarine, not the first time. The Scorpion, a new, quite advanced nuclear sub disappeared with about ten dozen men on board. In a watery grave for eternity. Buried at sea, but where? These men live very dangerous lives, without a doubt.

This would not be my fate. Hell, I was very grateful, beyond anything, at not having been at sea.

A risk taker I was not. Not a sky diver. Not a Mt. Everest climber. Nor a race car driver.

I usually used common sense, my preferred way or approach and a much safer M.O.

The race does not belong to the swiftest or the strongest, but the one who wants it the most, I had read in the Bible or church missal. Endure baby, you'll win.

We can agree or disagree.

At this point, I'll wrap up my medical surgery, treatment and recovery, then proceed to life in TAH, Ford Island and Pearl Harbor.

My re-admission to TAH occurred maybe two weeks later, if it took place then. I may have been on medical hold, but I most certainly wound-up back in TAH for a second operation performed by an ENT specialist, a young mild-mannered Oriental surgeon, with excellent skills and professional demeanor.

I took it quite easy for a week, and again all went well at that time and recovered after about ten days of hospitalization, but I was ambulatory.

While there I performed these tasks previously disclosed, during which I helped staff and patients. I was discharged and returned to Ford Island, though weekly for about two months I returned to TAH for follow-up visits.

I still had light duty status.

Again, nearly fifty years later, this is how my TAH medical experience took place, however, there is another side to this story.

Having mentioned that I was in TAH as an in-patient for about three weeks, I witnessed firsthand some of the trauma and suffering soldiers had while in the hospital, getting medical treatment for wounds and injuries suffered in the war while fighting or in accidents.

The Navy Days

If ecstasy existed entering TAH, it went AWOL, as agony and anger prevailed. This was Dante's purgatory before descending into the inferno. The suffering could be seen, heard, smelled.......non-stop when the soldiers or Veterans moaned or yelled for help while in excruciating pain. My all went out to them.

We, the staff, visitors and others were driven to tears from the experience and witnessing the ravages of war. Aiding them as we tried, provided little relief to their physical pain and mental anguish.

Some patients openly welcomed death, rather than fight for life to continue.

Unbelievable! Very Traumatic! Insane!

Yet, I could be one of these men, knowing and seeing them now, but I had foreseen this years ago. Not only in my own mind but in the news from the radio, television, newspapers, magazines and conversations. The carnage, the burnings, the waste of human life.

Despite my innocence and naivete as a very young adult, I thank the Lord for his guidance and protection in helping me play the better cards I was dealt.

Recuerdo mi muy buen amigo, Ralph, y las pláticas sobre este tema y como nos salvamos. At the bars over the years we'd recount experiences and the barbarism we heard and witnessed.

Having been in TAH as a patient and a sub-orderly- I was very mobile- I moved throughout the hospital. In the evenings I'd run to the cantinas or snack bars for liquor, sodas, candy, cigarettes, etc., for the injured, bedridden men with missing limbs, maimed and disfigured.

Once upstairs we'd snack, play cards, shoot the breeze and many times we'd be listening to the horrors of the war, read, watch tv and hear music.

Awful tales about inhumane acts involving the killings and torture of people by the hundreds were reported.

One Veteran described watching a partner die. The platoon walked cautiously in the jungles, when the scout suddenly, quickly vanished into a hole, impaled by punji sticks, which punctured his body clean through and died instantly. No chance of saving him.

Flame throwers were another means of destroying the enemy by burning the tall grass and vegetation. The Viet Nam Cong were slaughtered as they fled the flames. In the process, villages, huts and animals were also torched.

A gunner described the incident that led to his present hospitalization. His helicopter was on an evacuation mission, which was actually a trap set-up by the enemy who would injure the American men. They'd call for cover and rescue. Upon arriving, the Viet Cong bazookaed the airships that would explode. The enemy would then kill them all.

Hearing and listening to this history was heart rending, gut wrenching and at the same time magnetizing in the sense that it held you, you wouldn't leave, it grabbed your attention.

Like the incident of the head or heads bobbling in the water. The river boats were blown up by the Viet Cong and bodies exploded with the boat and arms, guts, feet floated in the river.

Repeatedly the word was that the enemy was intelligent and used many schemes. The Viet Cong would blend into the population, and with this type of integration could not be easily seen or discovered while creating havoc with explosives in urban settings.

Wow! Hell! Damn! The meetings and card games became enthralling.

Like Ed back home used to say, "Life is the best teacher"!

No book, class, film or tape taught me what I saw, did, smelled, heard and touched at Tripler.

¡AMEN! ¡Gracias a Dios que me escape de semejantes horrores!

The Navy Days

Yes, I vacated TAH for the barracks at Pearl Harbor and nearby Ford Island, my principal accommodation. I'd escape though to Tripler, Hickam, the YMCA and such, on weekends especially.

At Ford Island though, the commander there ruled over me. He was a tall, tanned, slender career officer, probably washed up and on his final assignment. Hard to get along with this frustrated soul of about age fifty. We didn't like each other much and however figured why the Navy signed me up. "Draft avoidance", was my response, that made him grit his teeth.

What angered him more: my ninety day early out likely popped his hemorrhoids. Then again, he knew young reservists preferred civilian life, not the military nor the war. He hated this attitude about them, which he said I epitomized and that I exemplified simply by never pursuing a promotion. "My next promotion is to college, the U of A", I answered, which I was certain, quietly, inwardly unnerved him, " As Uncle Sam and the VA will pay the costs with the G.I. Bill"! Sinking daggers in him and twisting them.

No estoy para dejarme ni pendejo soy para que me maltraten. Debemos defendernos.

It wasn't that bad. We'd hardly see or meet each other, and he damn well knew of my record: medical orders demanded light duty for me.

At times there was work for others when men were needed and working parties were formed, but not for the ones designated as having light duty status. Moi!

It all worked out. I never got written up and other mates behaved much worse, like smoking and starting fires when they tossed lit Camels into trash bins. The base fire department put these out, investigated, found the culprit, blah, blah, blah, then court martial the poor, dumb bastards.

The set routine that I had elsewhere, like in Australia was hard to come by in Hawaii.

Chaos in some forms existed, such as watching the war protestors, but such were the times and then the many naked women on the beaches.

Nevertheless, I had to adjust so that I would not fail, have problems or get into trouble.

Having said or written about the little I know of, Ford Island, allow me now to add some personnel experiences regarding my staying on Ford Island. My barracks was near the dock for the ferry and the library plus a couple of tall, older buildings. This was in the early seventies. When I revisited in 1989, I noted some improvements. Now in 2019, nearly fifty years since my Navy days there, much refurbishing, remodeling and construction has taken place.

But I will say this, one of the biggest tourist attractions has not been altered much. Videos and photos from our 2015 vacation there will reveal the sameness I encountered in 1971, when I regularly saw the Arizona Memorial.

The old rusting battleship and its rusting metal underwater rests somberly, a reminder of the Japanese attack: the American call to arms in WWII, and a grave to the many individuals who perished there.

My memory fades, details blurry and age takes its toll, but by being on Ford Island in 1971, with the ‚Memorial almost across the street, I carry that military honor and service with me until my last day, for you see, I served the Arizona, please let me explain.

Part of our duty as sailors on Ford Island required us to be the color guards to raise and lower the flag. Usually I had the evening call. At times I have felt it was the height of my Navy service and very brief military duty, but what a terrific honor. And for me to be from Arizona and to go the distance, to board the ship and Memorial was what I valued and cherished at the time, at age twenty-three. It touched my heart and I felt the presence of those who fell there and are entombed, as if angels were present and floated in the air, guarding and protecting the watery grave.

We did not have to be ordered or yelled at. The plan of the day indicated the squad or group for color guard duty. No one balked and we were in unison, gun-ho even to serve. An act of service and duty we truly revered, no matter what, such as bad weather, illness, etc. We would not slouch, wear soiled uniforms or joked around. We performed with pride, clean, crisp sharp men marched and brought about silence and respect to the surroundings, only the bugler was heard.

Somewhere in the world there probably may still exist a tourist's photo or two of me performing the color guard duty at the Arizona Memorial in 1971.

Life on Ford Island in 1971 to me seemed idyllic, quiet and peaceful mostly. The landscape very green throughout with tall trees. The buildings were old but not in bad shape.

There were a few residences with vehicular traffic discouraged. The calm was disrupted by noise from flights- jets, helicopters, boats, off the island.

The place provided a movie theater, library, dispensary, chapel and the like. The people by and large preferred to shop and do their business away, either off base or in Pearl Harbor.

I would conclude that the Navy encouraged people to shop and perform this by utilizing the launches, ferries and a few instances by speed boat.

One would see much outdoor activity like walking, skating, bicycling and groups or small families meeting or having picnics in the parks or on the beach. The weather seemed perfect for these ten out of twelve months.

Ford Island was a male domain, with not much female companionship neither civilian nor military.

The main event was Pearl Harbor which offered much more than Ford Island, and sailors went there for better entertainment with larger crowds, live entertainment and more activities not found on FI.

What I recall was that the Marines had a large presence and their attachment was separate. They did their own thing, but I think held amphibious training with Navy landing craft or nearby beaches and lagoons.

I believe it was here that I saw some helicopter training where men, probably Marines, slid down ropes onto the ground or the water. It seemed very dangerous, especially weighted down with all the gear they carried.

No thanks. It just seemed too crazy for me to risk serious injury.

Was it ego, testosterone, low IQ that made grown-up men commit such stunts. Too many Rambos.

What I saw turned me off no matter how you describe the activity. I'd stick to my desk duty and seek the light, avoid the darkness.

The games we played. Ford Island was prime, ideal ground for women in search of companionship. I believe I've heard this activity called 'Hub Hunting' or looking for a husband or a hubby.

They could be seen volunteering at the Red Cross, library, dispensary and such, and some succeeded but most men avoided the trap while enjoying the girls.

I belonged in the latter and in admin/personnel where I worked, the clerical staff consisted mostly of women and the pickings were not slim but lovely.

This added to the "bevy of beauties" in Honolulu and Waikiki. We sailors shouldn't be so chauvinistic but there it is. We've had great mentors, mostly female and friends like 'Playboy, the Navy's GQ, Hustler, the Mexican brothels like in Tijuana and more. Not much women's lib or bra burning yet.

Plus, the guys came up with a million excuses to avoid the guiles, tricks and tactics of these love interests. The favorite of these, not very original, was, "My ship is heading out on an eight-month west Pac tour". "Gotta Go"!

Others used were, "I'm here temporarily and must return stateside".

"Guam did it to me, I gave up and masturbate now".

"I overdid it in Subic Bay (Philippines) and am totally burned out".

"Hawaii is too damn expensive that I can't even take care of myself, much less afford a girlfriend".

"I'm pure, a virgin, I'm saving myself for sacrifice to the Gods of Kilauea volcano".

Take your pick, "Why me when there are hundreds of better suited studs out there for you".

"I'm just a low-ranking enlisted man. You deserve an officer".

"Can't you find a better ticket to the mainland"?

The draft board classified me 4-F: find them, feed, feel, fun?!, then forget them.

We sat around at bars, the EM Club or wherever, chatting and coming up with these dumb lines to get us out of trouble and entertain ourselves.

Oh, the sweetness! The great times and memories of island life in the South Pacific.

Many topics were covered- cars, women, movies, sports, women, home, the Navy and did I mention the women?

Emphasis lately was about getting away, leaving the base.

America seems closer, four hours away by air, as I wait for my days to pass in order to return there, say adios to being a sailor and to our tropical fiftieth state. I refer to the continental USA, because America is many things besides a huge piece of land and fifty states. It's also a state of mind because recognizable to me, which I had not considered or thought about these before.

One would be our leadership, like we're at the forefront in space exploration. Americans take the lion's share of Nobel Prizes. It's a cornucopia. Great opportunity

The peace corps is another fine example. Not many other nations have provided similar services or aid to another country.

The past twenty months or so have made me cognizant of this, unlike before, and I'm not sure if this resulted from my active Navy experience or maturity, but I'm grateful for a more developed analytical mind and perspective.

I appreciate also that I acquired much independence and confidence and feel I can solo in many ways or with the best of them but will do better once I've obtained a college degree or two.

I've spread my wings and have flown far, safely and with great steerage, mostly on my own, but with great assistance in the past from those who were there, especially my Family.

Sincerely stated is that merely breaking away and sticking with my decision is huge, and to give service to my country has none equal. I didn't shun the call of duty, claiming bone spurs, college, leave the country or seek special favors. I couldn't become a U.S. Citizen and a draft-dodger.

Tuve los huevos de cumplir como es debido, a Dios gracias le doy por ayudarme en esta acción.

These sentiments I expressed to mates and to my sisters, as well as to Rafael when we corresponded.

Upon reflection, after years gone by and checking those significant points or highlights in my journey, the Navy days and college years were a period of transformation. To explore and learn, to better prepare for an adulthood that can be prosperous and fruitful.

One very significant, truly defining change was that I practically never returned to a job in the private sector but found my calling in government employment that was quite beneficial.

The Navy Days

Rare is the person who has led a life in a straight path because of the variety we see, find as well as experience. The many variations I have had and presented in this work are daunting, so much that I wonder if I could repeat it. I doubt I could again pull it off.

So fortunate to reach each juncture without a scrape, almost unscathed. There are some regrets.

In my days in Hawaii, with almost all of my Naval service behind me, I could see that I had balance, an internal gyroscope that kept me on an even keel. I don't know why, but it has happened, integral to my being.

Several have told me this, such as Andy and Gabe, who got to know me well in Australia. That is my gift, they stated, maybe not brilliance or genius but plenty of smarts and savvy to stay ahead.

The time to head east was fast approaching. I sent goodbyes, farewells and thank you to friends and folks in Australia, the place that gave me a great ride and opened my eyes even more.

Initially I tried communicating without much chance of maintaining the connection. I'd say the distance, our returning home, just the separation proved too much, and loss of contact occurred.

Yet the many memories are vivid, remain fresh in my mind, especially those with the postal crew, at work and after hours.

Not to be outdone were the Educational Services Building staff, the officers, the enlisted guys in the legal offices, the journalism people and let's not forget the friendly custodians, whose immigrant status I could relate to as we whiled the hours away.

The corpsmen, nurses and doctors were terrific, dedicated professionals I gladly chauffeured around.

Then there were/are nature's friends- I mean kangaroos, sharks, snakes and the other creatures.

The opportunity, the challenge, and duty were presented and I, like others, made the most and best that we could out of the situation. They say you get lemons, then make lemonade.

Those servicemen who as civilians worked after hours in special services, (for example, I worked in the library, others were lifeguards, umpires, etc.) were grateful for the extra cash.

By dint of character, ambition, hustle, imagination or whatever else, others like myself came out better individuals after our 'Outback' experiences.

Opportunity comes knocking, grab it by the horns, especially if it's the positive type, where it's honest, gratifying, rewarding and legit. Employment is a good illustration. Then again, one must exercise caution because opportunity may be disguised and result negatively, such as when there may be a requirement of payola.

The time I spent in the Navy may not have been put to the best use, however, pros or cons, I'd say I came out ahead and did well.

Actually, in the years since my days as a sailor, I've returned to those locales where I served. California foremost, San Diego I've visited many times. San Francisco, L.A., Seattle, Hawaii, as well. To relive the past, those military times. Perhaps but also travel, vacation and Family fun.

So, the papers to move to California. LIFE Baby- San Francisco and the bay area were handed to me in the latter part of March 1971. Indicating I was to be separated from active duty with the Navy in early April.

I must take care of a number of things, because of my position as a Yeoman, I had the inside track. Many sailors did not know or care about this, they just wanted their discharge and be home.

I on the other hand, knew about travel reimbursements, per diem, leave, mileage rates and more. I wanted to be certain I received my fair share, what funds I was due by the Navy upon being separated and returned to Douglas, Arizona.

My tabulations indicated a few thousand, but, per personnel and disbursing departments, I had to keep this confidential. It seemed to me that in the rush of hundreds of men being processed and released, payola was occurring: the possibility that these men were not receiving the correct payment due. I would move on.

Anyway, still in Hawaii with my to-do list.

One, Iggy, had to be seen or visited one last time to thank him and wish him well, plus say adios. His situation remained status quo though he expressed optimism. I bid farewell to him, his Family and many friends gathered around.

At Hilo Hetty's I purchased some trinkets and souvenirs for my significant others.

I stopped by at Tripler being they had called me back for my signature on a couple of forms of which I received a copy. I saw some staff who had attended to me while I was a patient there for a few weeks.

Honor. Now there's a ubiquitous term. It exists beaucoup in the military. It's found in the UCMJ. At the academics and other documents.

So, I honored my military contract though not entirely in an honorable manner, but close enough to receive an honorable discharge soon from active duty. I think its form DD-214.

As such, one is released from active duty because of positive and acceptable conduct, behavior and actions. Piece of cake, que no chico?!

With me, this was easy as my entire active duty to me seemed like normal civilian life, except for the uniforms. Believe me, I thought life in Douglas-AP, the college, AJB were tougher and rougher. A worse grind. Come April, I'm gone, out of San Francisco. But then what?

Short term is five months at home and Douglas, then aim for Tucson and the U of A by September for the fall semester.

I'll take my Navy separation pass and go. Follow the Pacific Coast south riding the bus going through the many towns, view a few sites, then hang out in San Diego. I may take a trip to Mexico and visit los Parientes.

I have much to take care of in the coming months and I hope the change to again being civilian goes well. I hope the transition back to school I do not screw up.

I'm thinking wheels, which I'll need to get around and to go to school, work, back and forth to Douglas. That's another big item on the to-do list.

I need to read up on the San Francisco/Oakland area because soon I'll be there for a few days. So, I might as well experience it and get a good taste of it.

Especially of interest is that great feat of modern engineering, the beautiful Golden Gate Bridge. Let's hope the place is quiet, peaceful and without any tremors.

Overall, I took care of all matters. Some individuals gave me warm hugs, kisses and handshakes. All had been previously informed I would be leaving Hawaii. Mine was a brief temporary stint on the island, like with many servicemen. Forewarning was the best policy so that people wouldn't expect too much and know I'd leave.

I even saw my commanding officer and thanked him. He wished me well and strongly endorsed my plan to return to college in Arizona.

He even asked how my jaw was, because I had a wisdom tooth extracted. As I had requested time-off, medical leave, R&R or whatever it's called. He gave me the thumbs up and to take pain medication as well as prevent infection.

I, or we, left Hawaii behind. Pearl Harbor, Honolulu, Hickam AFB, Waikiki, Tripler, Ford Island, Arizona Memorial,

The Navy Days

Diamond Head, Hilo Hatty, Ala Moana, Punch Bowl Cemetery y muchísimo más se han establecido como parte de mi identidad y carácter, dándome lindos recuerdos que me siguen por el resto de mi vida.

A day does not pass, I assure you without flashbacks of my time in Hawaii. And, for whatever perverted reason or pleasure, I recall and treasure how I was able to convince those in the military into granting me leave to fly from Hawaii to Douglas. The return trip, all the way back to Australia, was legendary, according to friends, staff and those in the know. It went against all rules. A major feat per the HEH personnel, Gabe and others. Perfect! No consequences! Nothing! Or maybe they all know, had prior knowledge.

The same with overstaying in Samoa/Pago, Pago, and ditto in Sydney at King's Cross where we had the night of nights. What a riot! What a partyyyeeeee!!

Perth was very lame by comparison, mostly because I went solo, but throw in a couple of mates and we coulda, woulda had a wild, wholesome, obnoxious time, one helluva celebration!

Time to board. Dear reader, please don't ask when and where, but I think we flew out of Hickam on a chartered flight, maybe United Air or American Airlines. The plane seemed overloaded with so many servicemen in very high spirits and returning home. We were high or drunk, boisterous, noisy and all that you can imagine.

All lucky cause we made it back home safely. 'After one helluva job very well done'!

USS ARIZONA March 1922

CHAPTER 23.
Hola San Francisco.

They were the heroes. The keepers of the flame. I learned we supposedly were under security to prevent clashes with was protestors and flag burners.

It was raining hard in Frisco. The relentless rain drowned the Bay area, as best as this ancient mariner's brain puts it. Can't say where we touched down, maybe Travis Air Force Base, then we took buses to Treasure Island (TI)? I'll go with that, but I can't swear by it. The whole thing does not ring true, or does it?

The cold, wet night was not friendly at all, as I'm seeing protesters and anti-war demonstrators carrying signs, emblazoned with meanness and really nasty messages. That night is a jumble, however, we landed in the Bay area somewhere.

I was in a stupor when my head landed on the pillow. Somehow or other I got through the night, dead even though I, we, loaded our gear, made it onto the base, registered, entered the barracks and found our assigned spaces, then a group death soon followed.

The next morning, fresh. Rise and shine. Showered, dressed in clean dungarees, I readied myself, but oh was it cold. Even the dark, thick heavy wool CPO jackets did not help, and the wind and drizzle made it worse, unbearable, at least for a sailor used to Southern Arizona weather.

They called muster and we were formed into a company, sort of boot-camp style. The squadron(s) each had about three dozen men. Each day new arrivals had to be processed for separation or discharge. I'd guess several hundred were constantly on hand during my stay at TI.

We went through a brief orientation, given meal passes and instructed to be patient (hurry up and wait routine). Not much was expected of us. We'd be given a physical exam and met with Operation Specialists and be out and on our way shortly, three to four days.

Except for me and similarly situated mates, because we were Yeomen and Personnel Men. Our specialization in clerical matters meant we'd be held back a few days to help the paperwork and administration.

We admin types soon acquired the knack or got the hang of how things were supposed to run.

The supervisors reviewed our work and generally all worked well with a few 'atta boys' and a good pat on the back.

San Francisco, my namesake. City of fame and beauty yet so much danger. Reminds me of Joe Montana and the Forty Niners. The Giants more recently with three World Series titles. Now Steph Curry and the Warrior's under Steve Kerr, so well loved by U of A fans.

Leaving one's heart in San Francisco can be easy, the way Tony Bennett sings it.

Before proceeding, allow me to step back somewhat to catch up on some minor developments, such that alter my course or direction in the coming days.

I mentioned I would not be leaving right away. I had to stick around to process the long lines of servicemen who were leaving the Navy on the 'Ninety day early out' program. I too was doing this.

Another point was that mistakenly I would not be separated because of medical orders. A hold on my paperwork had to be straightened out, which was within a day or two.

The Navy Days

Thirdly, we were celebrating too much and arriving late on base. Our rowdiness sure got us in some trouble with security (Shore Patrol). Seriously initially but then lightly after we apologized and stated we were being discharged, hence the reason to party.

I can't say when my group landed in the Bay area, probably late in March, but every night we went into the city. We were the ones-disbursing clerks, corpsmen, personnel men and yeomen- who were held back about two weeks to help with the processing of personnel leaving the military.

We even established our favorite watering hole. This was Ghirardelli Square. For too many of us, this was our first and only time in San Francisco or even California. Some sailors were dropped off as their ships from other ports or bases went elsewhere.

For Corn Huskers from Nebraska or Hawkeyes from Iowa, this was the life because they'd never left their farm country. A terrific eye-opening experience.

And San Francisco, being such a liberal city, offered way too much- the drug scene, sex, topless or all nude dancers, Castro Street, you name it that these young impressionable men, some still in their teens, acted out with relish and gusto.

Going home added to their emotions and joy.

I felt likewise and didn't want the partying and celebrating to end. And I was unlike them, just ready to head home and start working. What to do? I had a new life to begin.

Anyway, to work on base was for the daytime. Six or seven hours then liberty. It was on such a day or days that I encountered two or three seamen who took advantage of the 'Ninety day early out' program. They were from, that's correct; NAVCOMMSTA H.E. HOLT!

I recognized them without the paperwork, but there they were.

We broke out laughing and couldn't say enough! A lot of catching up to do. I had been in Administration Educational Services, while they came from Communications Division. They were antennae boys, thumb injuneer's.

They were the daring ones leaving the military behind and the fat reenlistment bonuses. These men expressed displeasure: the stifling heat, the rotating shifts, plus isolation and much worse out at sea.

The Navy attempted to retain them with more schooling, promotions and better pay, because of their critical ratings (computer technicians, instrument men and radiomen). The clincher was the hefty reenlistment award, in three days at ten thousand Simolean's. That's a high number of Ben Franklins, Jacksons and Jeffersons.

Many, many young men in their twenties grabbed the money. It was too much to leave on the table, plus some liked the travel, the security, camaraderie and fun. Some sailors changed their minds there in our offices and stayed in the Navy.

'Freedom is just another word, nothing else to lose', sings Miss Janis Joplin in that raspy voice.

The military had invested tremendously in its forces and up to the last day tried to keep these servicemen on board in any way possible. Like stationing them near their home or family, no sea duty, cross training (switch ratings) or even reassignment that meant transferring, for example, from the Navy to the Coast Guard or even to the Air Force. Some took to Officer Training School with a college education thrown in for good measure.

Yet in TI, processing people out of the Navy, mostly young men age twenty-five and under, I felt my conundrum build up. Like comics use the technique called 'pregnant pause', when the joke is told but the punchline is held back for buildup, delivery then the laughter.

Like my duty was complete, I served, I'll be out, but then what, when, where and/or how? At times I even felt the whole time the approximate two years being active seemed comical.

The Navy Days

I'd even say this to my doctors now. The whole affair of living is quite comical, and we joke about the inevitability, somewhat morbidly. It all ends.

Saner words could never be said, yet we prolong living with treatments, pills, surgeries and transplants.

My active duty would be history and I had thought, even before Hawaii (the first trip), how leaving the Navy would be like, the freedom gained after avoiding the war, with all that behind me.

I thought I had a good plan initially. I left college in May of sixty-nine, went active July that summer, return two years later in July, seventy-one, then enroll in the U of A in August.

The best laid plans may go awry, and now I was thinking of new ideas, hatching a different plan. Was I insane, having a breakdown?!

When we were on liberty my comrades and I would think things through. Most of them approved of my return to school. One guy even had serious thoughts that rather than go home to the Bayou, he'd head north to Alaska, taking his sweet time doing so.

The cold, the wilderness, the long nights, did not faze him. Like living on the Frontier. He'd later hook up with Alaska pipeline. The end to this would be his return home if a bear didn't eat him alive. He'd meander on his long trip home and visit Yosemite, Yellow Stone, Mt. Rushmore, the Mississippi, etc. He felt strongly that it's better to try and to take a risk, than never to have tried at all. The 'what ifs', the risks not taken and regrets that follow. My Dad's very words.

Ed left Mexico with his Family, risked it all and never looked back. He greatly succeeded beyond just dreaming.

Anyway you describe it, a swell time had by these mariner's exiting the Navy and celebrating, happy to have opted out, at bistros and bars like the Buena Vista, where we swelled on the wonderful, pure manna-Irish Whiskey coffee.

A confession from me a must. May be out of ignorance. True, I've indicated in these pages (volume one), that the musician in our small Family was Dad. Quite talented or gifted that Ed, considering our background. He loved his piano, the songs of many (Augustin Lara, Pedro Infantè y Javier Solis) as well as those he himself wrote and composed. He tried corridoes, waltzes, cumbias and much more.

He even played in those years the Art of Herb Alpert (Lonely Bull album), Nat King Cole (Cole Español album) and Sergio Mendez. He also did some vibrant Cuban pieces, as he explained historically of the popular Buena Vista Social Club, which I think arose in the 1940's.

And in San Francisco, in my confusion, I thought the Buena Vista Bar had a connection a los musicos del Caribe.

How dumb of me that I went there thinking of the Latin music. It turned out to be an endearing mistake.

I've been to that beautiful city by the Bay on several trips and each time I visit the Buena Vista, loving it simply much more, but no Hispanic melodies.

Excuse my diatribe, just another interesting foot note.

Returning to that time, in my last days as an active duty sailor, I recollected the pleasure I had when I had returned to Douglas and the days in Mexico, then back to Australia.

I also redid my leave, a week in Perth. The joy I experienced in Pago, Pago and New Zealand.

Did I have just what it took to do it again, a similar voyage, or simply be satisfied with wanderlust and miss out the opportunity and forever regret it.

I questioned myself. Was I thinking clearly? It didn't seem rational. These discordant thoughts had not been my nature, but then I now had developed a different outlook.

The Navy Days

Similarly, I had previously, years ago, fleetingly considered college but that certainly changed that now I had hoarded my money for practically that sole purpose.

In working hours at TI Admin., this Yeoman started calling travel agencies, the state department about my passport, the Mexican council for permission.

Travel, so I called bus lines, airlines and more.

Next up, the weekend with things to see, spots to visit, lots to get done. Pronto!

One crazy night was Friday, though it could have been Saturday and I was filing my income taxes- to meet the April Fifteenth deadline, in order to not get slapped with the late fee by mailing beyond its due date. WHAT A LIE!

Did I get you? Wake up! Stay on your feet. Don't go to sleep on me. Heh, Heh, heh!

Hell no!!! That Friday, early afternoon, the four or five of us took off to get into more trouble and one was waiting for us in the Castro District.

We were not gay bashers, but like many tourists we wanted to check out this part of the city. It didn't go well.

First of all, us five were mostly of good moral character, law abiding, etc., and Castro is just the opposite and when its residents looked at us (shined shoes, short haircuts) figuring out who we were- military- we had it coming with verbal attacks hurled at us. No assaults but many arm gestures and middle finger salutes. We were not wearing uniforms. Hissed, pissed and dismissed for our loyalty and patriotism.

In the 70's, the District started forming and it was transcending, becoming a force. People were curious and so were we to check it out.

Today it is very colorful, vibrant rainbows, tremendous artwork and terrific entertainment that now has been, I'd say more acceptable and not as much of the counterculture phenomena that it became forty years ago.

Anyway, we made it and got out alive. We were their antithesis being that, in all the services gays couldn't enlist in the military or were kicked out, if exposed as homosexual. This was the case until the late nineties.

Were servicemen (public employees, priests, et al) hypocrites for wandering into the Castro District.

It's debatable.

All over the place we continued with our cold weekend adventure. I report it here without any particular or logical order, but just what we saw and did those days.

I know I marveled at terrific feats of engineering illustrated by the Golden Gate and Oakland Bay Bridges, dazzling tall skyscrapers and BART (Bay Area Rapid Transit), just getting started.

I think I possess a latent gene in me that drives me towards architecture, engineering, building and construction.

Onto Oakland, which in retrospect to me at that time showed blight and signs of decline, a rather sad picture and I've noticed some improvement, change on the trips back. But oh, those great Raiders of Al Davis. Just win baby! Now they are to relocate in 2020 to Las Vegas. Great memories of Blanda, Blunkett, Allen, Stabler (the Snake), Madden and Flores.

I've been to Alcatraz- no, not as an inmate, though I've been told I belong there, if you even heard some of my Douglas High School Instructors. That crowd, very loving. Heh, Heh, Heh.

I do not believe I went on the island; tours were not available back then, however, ferries gave us a good close-up. I've got to contact Clint Eastwood or Burt Lancaster (Birdman) to learn more.

In later years I tripped out at Alcatraz, must have been in 2010 or so, or when my wife Gloria and I went to a hairdressers' convention. Wow! I loved it: the cell for solitary confinement, the dark hallways, the chains and restraints. How long has it been vacant, maybe since the Ninety's? I can't explain it but movies/stories I enjoy are 'Escape from Alcatraz', 'The Great Escape', 'Shawshank Redemption' etc. Actually, being in Alcatraz, sitting on those benches, walking the yard. Oh man, I can't explain it but what fun. I'll put it in my bucket list to go back and toss feed to the seagulls.

Too bad though what the famous island prison has been through lately, wasting and decaying.

What's next? I don't recall exactly but a few more tourist sites to catch, but we'll call it a day.

Our return to TI was on the trolley and the bus, then the barracks, bed and zzzzzzzzzz. Work and afterhours.

Even while sight-seeing, your Seaman here could not rid the mind of the ideas re post Navy, with the one about not returning to Arizona gaining. Should I follow through, what are the repercussions?

Less money with which to enroll at the U of A, where I could start in June rather than September.

Different scenarios. What if this, then that? Too many hypotheticals. Yet, again and again, I thought about Ed y Panchita que ya sabien de mi gusto y deseo de viajar y al mismo tiempo separarme, volar muy solo, como se los explique.

Cuando en el colegio les dije que quería mi propio apartamento, pero me quede con ellos, soportándolos con mi empleo en AJB.

Just then, POW! BAM! Interrupted enough to lose my train of thought by the huge shark caught earlier and now on the hooks, on display, ready to be weighed. Something like that. A fat beast like I saw in the sea off Australia's Northwest Cape.

You guessed correctly, if you called it Fisherman's Wharf which we were cruising. A large crowd had gathered to view the scene, taking pictures and kids shrieking. The shark kept attracting people who were in awe. Indeed, it was a sea monster, terrifying.

We four or five moved on by the souvenir stands, the bars, apparel stores and other nooks and crannies. Entertainers wowed the big crowds with many tricks- the stilt walkers, magicians, jugglers, fire eaters and more. Very amazing and amusing.

We finally dropped into a fish and shrimp pub on one of the piers. Looking down through the planks, sea life was swimming about, nibbling on crumbs kids and parents were tossing down.

The sound of the seals could be heard and the seagulls flying around, making noise proved interesting, a great ambiance.

One tidbit about San Francisco, it's famous for having or baking delicious breads and here we would be treating ourselves to fondue with fresh warm sourdough, along with wine. Heavenly.

We must have gained ten pounds each. A meal like no other, being it's my very first fondue, unlike Mom's.

Pity the cows that make the milk, that makes the cheese, that makes fondue, and the bovines don't get to taste the delicacy they create.

Tomorrow's another day. We depart back to base.

You'll have to excuse me, but I lost the sequence of events and days, nevertheless we continued our forays into town. I do still feel the hangover after indulging the wine and fondue the following morning, with barely enough umph to shower and dress. Breakfast, dynamite coffee and aspirin provided rejuvenation.

We again took-off and found Chinatown, which seemed seedy, somewhat lacking in civic pride. The buildings needed painting and remodeling. Things just seemed older compared to downtown.

Gangas could be had though, because prices were very modest and haggling and bargaining welcomed. The owners and sales people very friendly and smiling. Recent arrivals from the Orient had difficulty with English, but I tried to break the ice, warm up with my usual dumb jokes about the FBI, being we're new in America. They loved it and loved that no we're not law enforcement agents but FBI, Foreign Born Individuals! Duhhh. People to this day still get a kick with my trick, joke about the FBI. An Irish priest related that joke to me.

After walking a couple of hours, we took lundin (lunch/dinner) at the Dragon Buffet or some such restaurant and piled our plates. It was an 'all you can eat', smorgasbord, and eat we did. The place likely did not make a profit that day because we cleared out the food bars we ate so much, stuffing ourselves with all sorts of oriental delights, desserts and sake. A feast.

A very hearty meal-royally. But it's to be expected when five young men drop in and see the ambrosia. Yeah! Ya wanna taste everything twice.

That means we each probably gained twenty pounds. Ten from the night before at Fisherman's Wharf with the fondue, and now another ten at the Chinese buffet.

Living it up, I figure is what we were calling it, doing it.

We paid and crawled out of there, barely, holding up our guts and looking for a taxi. Onto our next destination after picking up ourselves and sticking to the plan. No, we had no itinerary, but we had good entertainment in mind, and it was still early, not even evening. Eventually we left.

You like that, right or did you notice? Three 'evens. It's another of my masterful literary tools. I should have added 'Evan'.

Probably about six more days before we are released and free to leave, fly away from TI and the Navy. I was firming up a plan and a loose itinerary for that day of departure which would likely be Friday, the end of the week.

I considered taking the Greyhound that evening and see San Diego the following morning, then stay on base a night or two to avoid the costs for lodging. Easy enough to do.

My presence, with my other companions was now at the popular Filmore West and I thought about next week's departure. We had the tickets, obtained by one in our group from a scalper.

The place was jammed packed like sardines and the girls just loving it and giggling from all the fondling. Remember the saying or slogan 'free love'. This was it in practice. Many had no shoes, bras or panties and lots of perfumes, colognes and nature's best scents. For sure, stand up intercourse big time, among many other activities all night long. I wonder how many babies were conceived there that night.

Grass, LSD, meth, etc., could easily be obtained quite openly, being cops were almost absent. The event or gathering was not just about the music. People of all types were there- one humungous potpourri unlike I had ever seen, in many kinds of attire. The African American's really stood out beautifully with their huge afros.

I did not know who was playing but lyrics from the Grateful Dead, Jimi Hendricks, Santana and others could be heard, loudly enough being it had been piped throughout the auditorium.

My limited knowledge about music, in all areas (female/male; vocal/instrumental; rock/country, etc.), didn't help nor could I add much to the conversation. I was tagging along with the guys, but I did enjoy certain pieces, such as 'Black Magic Woman', by Santana. Aretha Franklin always superb as well as Stevie Wonder, and let's not forget the Motown sounds with Diana Ross and the Supremes are always a pleasure.

A couple of points about the Filmore West. It closed in July 1971, and the Filmore East in New York I believe lasted longer. Or was it the other way around? Better ask Bill Graham who was in charge of both venues.

The mob kept getting bigger, and it seemed it would become uncontrollable, so we left and returned to TI.

That last week in TI, I ran some numbers and took an accounting of my funds, plus my pay, separation allowance and travel reimbursement. A pricey sum that could last me six months

The Navy Days

at the rate of twenty-five dollars per day. I doubt I'd spend it all. I'd split it into mostly traveler's checks and a smaller amount in cash, that's dollars and pesos.

Now we were a foursome, considering a disbursing clerk received his orders and went home. He couldn't be happier and told us he'd call while waving good-bye.

In those last days, Sausalito became one of our destinations after hours. Whatever you are up to in the Bay area, do not miss beautiful Sausalito. Though small, it offers art, scenery, galleries and great food. It's a bit expensive for one especially, but much less in groups.

We went there twice, once we took a ferry- another time we walked across the Golden Gate Bridge.

The outstanding scenery of sail boats in the Bay, the many floating house boats and the views of the city as San Francisco lights up the night and much more. You can't or shouldn't miss it.

All these neat experiences of Northern California in the last days of my Navy active duty I will treasure forever. I greatly enjoy visiting the region.

I almost forgot about El Presidio, a gorgeous recreation area that belonged to the military. It allows for viewing the bay and skyline.

Knob Hill is very ritzy with much history and a neighborhood of old 1800's buildings and architecture.

The last item would be Lombard Street, otherwise known as the 'Crookedest Street', in the world. It zigzags at a steep incline and can be difficult to maneuver. Don't try it, you may get sick and spill your cookies.

There simply was too much to do and see in San Francisco, with so many nearby communities one can visit, including the wine country, like Napa Valley.

I said to myself that I would be returning to this cold, windy city by the Bay. It's such a lovely place that brings back great memories.

My namesake, a saint, San Francisco means sainthood.

The Grand Finale! Hold it, not just yet, maybe another forty-eight hours. I'm about the last one left from the admin group held over. New men are replacing us, and additional ones selected for those to be discharged in May.

In keeping with my faith, I visited a chapel to pray around Holy Week, to give thanks to the Lord for His primo guidance. Wow! What a performance, great job that He did for me and I just pray and ask that he continue this for me in the days, weeks, months to come.

At confession the priest heard about my wicked ways and I felt rather hypocritical.

Besides to the ten Hail Marys and a rosary as penance, the conversation turned to my future. He said many men come to the chapel upon leaving the military for thanksgiving and returning home safely after their service.

These men talk about their plans and days ahead. I was asked about mine and I responded "college", but first a long rest and vacation, with some travel.

The priest reassured me it was well deserved after our service to our country. Encouraging words. Men with free-will choose and do as one pleases within reason and not breaking the law.

He also stressed to walk in the ways of the Lord, obey the Ten Commandments and contribute to the church, be charitable. Lastly, he thanked me for serving and that the nation appreciated my service in the Navy.

He added that I was a good man. Simply by stopping by to express such gratitude indicates a man's positive and moral character.

The Navy Days

In the end I left, said a prayer and dropped some change in the basket or box marked 'For the Poor'.

I strolled outside for some time, went back to the base mess hall for the evening meal.

Sitting there I noticed a couple of seamen I had earlier processed for discharge. We greeted each other and bid farewell. Sitting there for their last meal, courtesy of the Navy, in their civvies, packed duffle bags at the ready.

Soon a bus or cab would take them away to likely return home safely. 'Home Is the Sailor, Home from The Sea'.

Me too!

Group hugs, kisses, handshakes y luego adiós, amigos y amistades. Hasta aqui nada mas llegamos. We had our folders, pouches and envelopes stuffed with our military papers. Probably the DD-214 being the most valuable.

Only two of us five were the last to go. Emotional enough, with lumps in our throats, a final good-bye. We knew what we'd been through, feeling lucky and thankful that the whole experience hadn't turned out worse.

He asked, "Still heading to Mexico"?

"For sure, first San Diego, then Tijuana, then south to follow the Pacific Coast", I responded.

We parted. We could have become good friends, but we went our separate ways. We remembered the fun. Ghirardelli, the Wharf, the gals, Chinatown, Golden Gate, the women, Filmore West, Sausalito and much more. some wild times. Heh. Heh. Heh.

Cuídate. Buena suerte. Dios te bendiga. adiós.

That's the last I saw of them, of him. Our last detail had been us, a team of five, spitting out paperwork and sending men out of the Navy to their next destination, likely home.

I did that to myself as well, subject to review of my own forms by the higher-ups.

I had mailed stuff home with my duffle bag, Douglas could wait, had to wait.

With my light suitcase, a brown Samsonite, and a wallet full of Benjamins, I waited at the bus depot for the Greyhound south. My confidence ebbing at times or like Samson at others.

It was raining hard in Frisco; darkness had settled in when we boarded. Large crowd, hopefully not a loud one nor a noisy bunch. Need some Z's.

I enjoyed quiet decent sleep riding the bus, waking to catch a glimpse of lights here and there, like Santa Barbara, when just passing through this beautiful city.

Was it Easter weekend, now that I'm thinking about it, a flashback. It may have been.

What a day! First day of freedom, without uniforms, the silly white sailor hat. Amen!

The ride seemed so quick, yet it was ten hours or more with the stops, until San Diego, which by now I had become quite familiar especially around the Naval Base.

I left the bus terminal and went hunting for Oscar who I had contacted already. He had seemed eager in welcoming me back with hearing I had completed my active duty tour.

The stop in San Diego did not last, maybe a half day thereabouts, but I sensed that I moved on rather soon, then I took to National City and Chula Vista.

CHAPTER 24.
Bien Venido A México.

In a relative short time, I crossed into Mexico through Tijuana and blended right in. I wanted to mix in well, as a Mexican to avoid problems and not draw attention. Customs checked my visa and passport, then allowed me to proceed sin problemas. They like que decía mi pasaporte, 'Cumpas, Sonora'. Hasta me recibieron con 'bien venido' al darse cuenta ellos de mi servicio mexicano en Australia, desde allá.

Me espere un rato para bordar el camión 'Estrella' or 'Star'. It's a very well recognized bus line throughout Mexico, from the larger metro centers to the small locales.

I hung around, bought a dozen post cards I'd be mailing home often, to keep my Family abreast and up to date about my travels and whereabouts. My meal consisted of tortas y sodas right before they called us to hop on the bus.

Muy simpatico el conductor who called his camion 'El Cometa', not 'Estrella'. He joked that 'Estella' was too sissy but that 'Cometa' was forceful y mas chignon. Then he added a gesture that made us laugh even harder.

The shuttle seemed full and we rolled with pleasant tunes from the speakers, the passengers talking and the wheels humming entertaining us.

Outside the beaches and the sea soon appeared and we could see bathers, taco vendors, food stands and boats, until we went further south and all disappeared.

Now only the surf and the seagulls seemed to be keeping us company.

Evening was approaching.

El camión sequia muy solitario siendo que no se veía tráfico, la carretera casi vacía. Lo contrario de América donde a toda hora es un trafiquin bárbaro. así es porque muchísima gente tiene su propio vehículo mientras que en países hispanos no es así. Y los que tienen auto, estos son con muchos kilómetros y años.

The stop at Hermosillo at around God knows what hour saw travelers leave and new ones board.

We waited longer there being the bus was serviced, just routine maintenance during which some of us stretched our legs, potty breaks, bought snacks and such. Still others couldn't be bothered and remained asleep, snoozing soundly.

The vehicle continued south to the shore, coasting into Guaymas to quickly drop and pick up passengers in this older town. Its livelihood comes from fishing and diving and is a major port that well serves Mexico and the United States in trade with nations from the orient.

Our travel follows the shores of the Gulf of Mexico, not the Pacific Ocean, which is much colder and rough, just on the west side of the peninsula of Baja California. The Gulf has more of a serene sea and is much warmer.

From Guaymas, and Puerta Penasco too, ships sail from the mainland to points on Baja, its eastern coast. Two very well-known cities are La Paz and Cabo San Lucas. The latter being very popular internationally as a mecca for tourists, especially the Hollywood types and jetsetters.

My destination, is Mazatlán for a couple of days of R&R for now, because I intend to come back on my return north.

Having mentioned Cabo and Mazatlán, the two seem to face each other across the Gulf. Directly across but for the ocean. Where the waters of the Gulf and the Pacific Ocean meet is extremely treacherous, right at the southern tip of peninsula of Baja California. I've never seen anything like that. It appears like the two bodies of water are battling one another. And on the beach, you will see seals, sea birds, lizards and other animals that hang out basking in the sun or hiding in many of the holes on the cliffs.

I've diverged a bit here to Baja, which my Family and I saw in the 80's and 90's.

A most interesting or peculiar feature one encounters. Again, at the most southern tip of this land mass, the peninsula; is the huge Arco de Cabo (which people at times refer to as the 'donut') the waves, wind and elements have carved into the cliff. Surgically almost.

A very amazing site! Unbelievable! Hard to describe. It must be seen because photos do not do justice to this wonderful creation of nature. The sheer size of the huge hole is simply overwhelming, and to be sitting on the beach underneath the arc when the tide is out is a big attraction.

This spectacular display of nature is a venue for weddings and other types of celebrations. Indescribably beautiful ceremonies.

I've heard rumors, gossip and such, that it's a matter of time and the entire cliff will collapse, with man contributing to its demise because of recklessness (graffiti, carvings, trash, etc.).

Before I forget, when the tide is in, the water has been seen covering the entire donut, which then disappears.

I'm just very glad or thrilled to have witnessed such natural beauty, especially at sunset when the sky turns orange and the light gleams off the water, the waves lapping the beach.

Again, in these pages regarding my stay in Mexico I'll refer to places I visited, and those others that exist. For example, I saw pyramids, but not all of them and I will point this out quite clearly. Be forewarned.

So, we've been on a stop in Guaymas, heading to Mazatlán but proceeded to tell you, tangentially, about Baja and Cabo San Lucas.

Let me just briefly touch on San Carlos, which is a gorgeous seaside town near Guaymas, just a few kilometers. San Carlos offers some exclusivity. Yachts at the marina can be seen and people display their wealth and well-to-do status.

I like it because it's small, very clean and isolated. No crowds, no vendors, no pachangas. Also, a footnote, Hollywood has filmed there, with Catch-22 having been produced (at Catch-22 Beach) nearby in the eighties.

Ay! I failed to mention La Paz, a smaller city close to Cabo, on the eastside of Baja. It's very tranquil and more tropical than Cabo with more desert like surroundings. Kindly excuse my forgetfulness. Thank you.

Both La Paz and Cabo are worth visiting and do-able on one trip.

La Estrella salió de Guaymas a buen paso después de recoger pasajeros, más damas que caballeros y unas como gallinas cluecas, las damas ruidosas como quien sabe qué. As it was, the cacophonous commadres took over. Non-stop chatter from the gaggle.

During this time, like other times, one chats with the travelers or hears ongoing conversations about families, work, school, etc. Uno tambien observa those praying rosaries, reading, studying or sleeping. Myself included.

The svelte, brunette, thirty-ish lady next to me did some needle work, embroidery and talked with her teenager. She turned her attention to me, however, and we brought up different topics. She seemed amused by my story and background, somewhat fictionalized.

Not wanting to be overheard nor be a target of pickpockets, I presented myself as a struggling engineer student, here, now and at other times. Travelling alone presents dangers.

I made up the account of attending the Universidad de Sonora en Hermosillo, on my way to Guadalajara, blah, blah, blah. Thus far I had not been the target of petty-criminals and thieves who failed, like in Tijuana, when I went there with Oscar years ago such was one occasion.

What did I have to lose lying? These passengers would be lost, gone, never to see me again. The aim was to be decent and civil with folks, but not be too open or expose oneself to harm. Exercise caution. Grifters, scammers, rogues, rascals and con artists abound.

In fact, here's an interesting tidbit. Several years ago my wife and I went abroad for our fortieth anniversary and several professionals, from travel agents, hotel security, bank tellers, law enforcement and others cautioned us regarding assaults and becoming victims of thieves: watch the luggage, lock the room, secure wallets and purses. Italy and Vatican seemed the worst, but life and enjoyment are a must, one cannot live in perpetual fear. Sorry about my digression on a depressing subject.

Where were we? 'On the road again, going places where I've never been, seeing things I may never see again.... like a gypsy down the highway'. Thank you, Mr. Willie Nelson.

Continuaba, platicando con la Dona, ella que no le paraba y yo con poco entusiasmo le daba oído.

Pero ganas sí que desperté cuando ella abrió su costal de harina conteniendo abarrotes. 'Gracias a Dios' dijeron mis intestinos, que llego alivio.' Ahora sí que me puse más atento y cordial con esta dama.

Pronto saco del paquete: pan, verduras, latas, frutas, queso, bebidas, etc., y repario o la comida. El caso fue que nos Atacamos de salchichas en french rolls with fresh carrots and some cucumbers that she sliced, downed with cokes and other drinks. Galletas y naranjas served as dessert. A decent meal and free. Gracias.

Just as efficiently as she served us, she cleaned everything, packed it and put it away, all the while maintaining her story telling and joking, for a while.

I had to excuse myself, and she understood, because the meal made me drowsy, gave me heavy eyelids. I apologized but she said to get some shut eye.

She returned to her embroidery.

I finally woke up, not knowing how long I had travelled though I quickly learned Mazatlán appeared closer.

We picked up our conversation. I figured I'd inquire at the bus depot about a hotel or boarding house. Something reasonable, practical, not the Taj Mahal, Ritz nor Hilton. I had to make my wallet stretch.

She offered that she stayed at the casa de huespedes y explico como, donde y cuanto. Muy bien situados y bien limpio todo, ella dijo.

Le di las gracias, porque no. Her teenager also pitched in, adding she too had been there.

En Mazatlán we grabbed un pesero y fuimos a ese lugar, esa casa. Bien dijeron las dos damas, bonito y limpio los apartamentos y buen precio.

Pagué por mi cuarto y salí, dando las gracias a las dos, así como a los Dueños, reservando dos noches.

Después de mi aseo personal fui a cenar y luego al regresar vi a la Doña en el patio y platicamos un rato: 'noté' que se había cambiado y muy bien arreglada.

Prefirió pasar a mi recamara que ir por una bebida.

Una linda noche inolvidable. La mejor bien venida a México imaginable. Duramos muy buen tiempo unidos, hasta el despertar con la mañana. Sequimos otros ratos con el placer al amanecer.

Bañados y vestidos, los tres salimos por un desayuno en un restaurante cercano, donde ordenamos, pero primero un café industrial, bien fuerte.

Muy a gusto y felices, con gusto platicando y saboreando el exquisito menudo. Paque la cuenta y a ella le di buena propina que ella bien la recibió, dando gracias.

Pasamos a la casa. Le ayude con sus maletas y las subimos al taxi que la llevaba a la central para salir en La Estrella a un sitio en Sinaloa, to resume her teaching Elementary school.

We hugged and embraced for a long moment before we said goodbye and blessings. Never for us to be seen together again, even if fate wanted it.

What awaits me? I was free the rest of the day, half of it gone after a delightful morning. She had told me I was quite chivalrous and a fine gentleman. I guess this comes from custom, being in Mexico and the culture.

I responded to her compliments by thanking her and her beauty plus allowing us such pleasure. We both knew it as a passing-fling, un breve amor o cariño, un momento largo, para siempre, en la mente.

Me encontré uno o dos camiones municipales que viajan por toda la ciudad. Me subí en uno, pero al sentirme incomodo, me baje.

Me aconsejaron algunos que, en estas situaciones, más en la juventud, no hay que ponerse serio, pero ver las relaciones como placer y recreo.

Recuerdo Oscar en San Diego. That was his moto. Find them and have fun.

Somewhere, sometime, much later, I found a lively spot with cantantes, marimbas and dancers. I took a chair and table, then ordered dinner.

Uno's camarones estilo scampi with rice, salad, veggies, rolls and cafè muy mexicano, industrial strength.

In the course of my travels, here, now and later, but at least while in Mazatlán, I saw and met many foreigners, mostly the Americans, also some Canadians, Europeans and some Orientals.

Practically all spoke English and little Spanish. At times I'd help out as an interpreter and admitting I am from the U.S.

For example, over a brew at a bar or on the beach, chatting, people would become quite curious. Which most disagreed with my position of enjoying a long over-due vacation in the place of my birth, which I much wanted to visit and learn more.

Los americanos piensan que lo que más vale es el trabajo o empleo y esas ganancias- el dinero. En realidad, México les gusta más para vacación porque los norteños no demuestran mucho empeño, más gustan rebajar al mexicano y aprovecharse de él y regresarse a su país y seguir una vida materialista y de gran consumo.

Dos naciones muy juntas (fronterizas) pero muy aparte y distintas. Rico el norte, probé el sur y principalmente católico. Son más diferentes que similares.

Me fui de vago por Mazatlán hasta el atardecer, vi mucha playa y muchas lindas casi denudes on the beaches, in the water, with guys, like me, dripping in testosterone and wanting to just suckle all those large, voluptuous, full and gorgeous........(STOP, wait, hold on a minute, I was getting a little carried away with my description). Almost X-rated, I must simply regain my composure.

I'm strictly PG-13. Family reading only.

Okay. Alright, I'll change the subject. I checked out the museum which really did not hold my interest too much, because of the mood I was in. Nothing against the curators and all those folks. But come on dear reader, I am however on vacation. Right?

La catedral muy bonita. Pasé y dije unos Padre Nuestros, Ave Marías, etc. Lástima que seguido o siempre pida limosna para una cosa u otra como obras de construcción, fondos para el Papa o Roma, el catecismo católico, etc. Esto es al frente, al aire libre.

Por favor, sean más discretos.

Lo que tambien note en Mazatlán during my touring was the industriousness at the Port.

International shipping in many forms. Ships from China and the Orient. Yachts, Ocean Liners cruising, packed with tourists. Don't forget the fishing crafts of all types.

Like I stated, había, y supongo que todavía es lo mismo y hay muchos americanos en Mazatlán y otros lugares en México. Una tarde en un bar and grill bien alegre cenaba a solas. Bonito el puesto sobre la playa, admiraba el mar, las olas, el bello anochecer y las bellísimas damas.

Una música estilo basa nova y el ambiente ATM (no, not the bank machine- ATM or 'a toda madre') y empezó la plática con dos del norte, algo filosófico, más con unos cuantos tragos.

Californianos estos dos cuates muy machos.

Side tracking here. Bear in mind what I've written before, que no? It's 'califernia' because they sure know how to live it up, have a great time and enjoy it to the fullest.

As I was saying about these two men, non-Spanish speaking Viet Nam War Veterans drinking to the high-life, luck and good fortune. Both Army, Infantry and recently discharged. Just happy as all hell to get out alive.

They promised themselves a rollicking vacation upon leaving the military, into which they had been drafted. And if tonight was any indication, they were honoring their pledge. Tonight, being only one night of many, with money to burn and the Good Lord to thank.

The two still did not know how they got out alive or how many times they escaped death after so many, many close encounters, even hand to hand combat.

Bodies disappeared before their eyes when bombs exploded. Many friends and buddies were lost. Others became severely burned yet survived only to be maimed for the remainder of their existence.

The more que estos tomaban, lo más triste que se ponían, al punto de llorar, lágrimas y penas. Muy doloroso su sufrimiento debido a la quera. Demasiadísimo, muy salvaje, requeté perro el pleito con las guerrillas que se disponen a entregar sus vidas, su todo, por su patria y por Ho Chi Min.

Mostly I just listened and sipped my drink.

I tried to be positive and offered encouragement.

The two in turn felt, stated, that they should have gone to Canada. They even said that avoiding the draft and getting into the Coast Guard, National Guard, Air Force- anything beats the damn Army- was far better.

The glistening sea, with the stars reflecting, seemed similar to the glistening eyes of the two drunks with PTSD, the two mates next to me. Not that I was much better off. We had a good time of swearing, cussing and bitching about our military experience. The more we imbibed, the better we felt, but the two were way over me being they had drinks, shots and beer chasers. I went lite.

We separated. They left their trackers behind because they couldn't drive back to their hotel. The bartender called taxis for us. We hugged and said adios.

I returned to my room feeling already like the morning after, but I safely found my way. Knowing full well I better locate my senses because I'd be leaving Mazatlán in a number of hours, noon probably, when I'd get La Estrella going south.

With some strong coffee y dos mejorales me compuse, más con el dichoso pan, jamón y queso para curarme de la cruda.

Solo llevaba poca mochila y la acomode fácilmente. Paque la cuenta y me fui en un pesero a la estación para llegar a buena hora y comprar los boletos de pasaje.

I hung around the bus terminal waiting for the hour of departure. I browsed around, read some magazines, newspapers and low and behold on the front page, headline news, was a picture of me, just my face. WANTED! It read.

The Navy was after me because after my discharge I had to report to the Naval Reserve Center ASAP in Douglas.

Do you believe that?! I didn't either. I was fooling with you to keep you alert, awake and alarmed. Don't fall asleep on me or get bored. Keep reading, it gets better.

But I can always claim I was hallucinating or having delusional thoughts, especially after getting drunk last night with those two blokes.

The announcement from the speakers clearly called for us "All aboard", for points south, with the carriage heading a la Cuidad de Mexico, Districts Federal- CMDF. La capital de la nación, de todo el país y gente, pueblos y estados. It's commonly called DF.

Iba repleto el mentado camión que hasta parados viajábamos, unos, y hasta en el piso se sentaban. Las damas sentadas y los caballeros ni modo. Women and children first.

'El Camino'. I like it. It means 'the road'. It connotes strength. Very mucho that's probably why a truck carried that name. And here I am en El Camino hacia el sur. Very likely to Puerto Vallarta, but it's quite a way down. In the meantime, some pasajeros have been dropped off here and there, it's less crowded and seats are empty.

Many are asleep and snoring. For a while I was one of those individuals, but now awake I feel fresh and reenergized. Some kids invited me to join them at their games- old maid, checkers, hangman and that sort of stuff- and I do but not too long. I lose but win by letting the youngsters feel victorious. I open my bag with snacks and offer them some which they gladly accepted.

I step back to relax some more, snuggling on the bench and get lost in some thoughts, college for one.

Clara comes to mind. My younger sister will be graduating from high school in a month and I intend to be there in Douglas at the end of May. She indicates she'll continue working at Sears as a clerical and enroll in the community college for the fall semester.

Rafael, who is still in the Navy, I remember next. He will be discharged this summer. His plans included starting classes at the U of A in Tucson in September.

My brother-in-law, Raul, will be transferring from Cochise College to the U of A, as well.

Unheard of. There will be four of us in college in a few months. As for three of us in the Rivera clan, college a few years ago would have been an impossibility, but lucky we are in several ways to have had Cochise Community College open its doors to us, and thousands more.

Do you want me to rehash this or did you get enough of it in my second volume, 'The College Years'? I will be lazy, not repeat myself here and suggest you read Volume II.

Come on Willie Nelson, strum your guitar and sing it, 'On the road again, going places where I've never been.........

Actually, some would say the travelling conditions are brutal, like the well-off have chauffeurs and private jets. The travelling in Mexico no me lo mencionen.

I've mailed a couple of post cards to Douglas, letting my folks know I travelled well and doing fine, in order to minimize their worrying about me, the wanderer en La Familia.

The mic informs us Puerta Vallarta se acerca y vemos que ha cambiado, que estamos en una zona tropical, demasiado verde que más bien diré es selva, cerros tupidos de arbolada y enredaderas. Muy bonito, mas fresco y mas sombra.

I was surprised to see the city more modern and cleaner than where I've been before in Mexico.

We reached the station and began grabbing our luggage, then I'm asked if I have an umbrella. Odd, but I learn sudden downpours occur and one gets soaked. I pay no attention.

While on the bus I had read a brochure or magazine ad about a low-cost hostel that also provided meals and laundry. I inquired further from baggage handlers, taxi drivers and others. The article was accurate and had vacancies.

I picked up a bite on the go- chips, soda, fruit- then hailed a small taxi, showed him the ad and we were soon there, but these risky drivers are wild, take big chances fighting the traffic and putting one's life on the line.

People are constantly self-promoting and it's easy to see why. With poverty, money becomes a must in order to survive and help the family. For example, my driver said he'd be my bodyguard, tour guide, errand boy, chauffer during my stay in Vallarta. I told him yes, up to a point and that I would be calling him. He even had friends for female companionship.

He seemed cordial, maybe honest and offered his assistance, plus advised me to be careful, especially with personnel items- wallets, jewelry and/or papers. Night crawlers were abundant and expert at stealing and thievery.

Further, stay away from scams like 'time shares', he urged because they tended to scam the people, foreigners too, and English is not an obstacle to a sale.

I tipped and thanked him after he placed the suitcases in the courtyard, beautifully accented with lush foliage, mums, geraniums, bougainvillea and some caged birds.

"Bienvenido, Señor", me llamo el mozo.

At the hostel I met unos americanos muy simpaticos y allegras, jovenes, a couple of students or draft dodgers. They asked me where I'd been and I said, "Yale". They couldn't believe I was that smart, at school. I said, "No babosos, I went to where you get handcuffs and an orange jump suit". "Oh, jail", they replied and laughed.

Just a joke to entertain you. Not being a bigot, just Spanish humor, (I can get away with this joke. We can't pronounce the 'J' sound).

Anyways, the humor aside, we met at breakfast and introduced ourselves. I asked them about Vallarta, places to see or visit, the beaches, and so forth. We'd be bumping into each other again, I headed out into the rain.

Another time in Vallarta, I recall with my darling.

We headed out to town, do some sightseeing, that sort of thing when about twenty minutes afterwards a deluge came down. More rain than one can imagine for the next half hour. Something I had never witnessed. I recall this similar incident years later in Vallarta.

The city is surrounded by tall cliffs and when it rains down pours- the water forms strong currents while evacuating to the ocean and takes everything along its way, including the animals from the hills and jungles. One sees snakes, lizards, insects and much worse. Prepare to get soaked.

The best protection is to get to high-ground, or into a building to avoid drowning. The water rises very rapidly, and the uninitiated find their shoes, clothing or other articles or belongings completely ruined from the mud and the high water.

We lucked out by dashing onto a sidewalk, under a veranda and climbing on some metal chairs. This allowed us to remain mostly dry. To be safe, though, I removed my shoes and rolled up my trousers up to my knees. Like many others were doing, we waited until the water receded.

Later we'd see the streets covered with all the mess, from tree trunks to plants, leaves and logs.

The crews would clean up the debris and once dry enough the cobble stone streets would be swept.

Amazingly not too much damage.

The locales are used to this weather.

Not so the tourists.

Before I forget, a thought just popped into my noggin, brought on by the aforementioned reptiles. It's true that they are all over Vallarta and seem to prefer the damp, shady spots and crevices.

Vallarta's one claim to fame is the film, 'The Night of The Iguana'. Do I need to explain: an iguana is an ugly, scaly lizard, a descendent of Godzilla (the Hollywood creation), or Agruntasarous

Rex or one of those horrid mothers from the days of Fred Flintstones: I think the Gila monsters from Tucson are the iguana's brethren.

Anyway, the movie is famous and, I heard, a classic starring Ava Gardner and Richard Burton, made in Vallarta. It figures that Ms. Liz Taylor so fell for Burton's iguana that she married him. "Oh, stop that, Ricky, it tickles". Her 19th marriage.

That evening I met Lourdes and Emma, sister goddesses from Guadalajara on vacation. They'd return home the next day. We had a great time. I saw them when I went to dinner at the coffee shop at the resort they stayed at. Somewhat upscale but not overly done architecture.

The two were educated and classy, with great smiles and perfect teeth- gorgeous. Lourdes had long bronze hair and was slightly taller than sis, whose stature and tanned features made her god-like.

They were relaxed, funny, perhaps from the drinks, and joked quite liberally, even zinging me with their humor, but all in jest, fun. L the physical therapist and E, the accountant, invited me to Guadalajara.

We went to the bar where a trio was playing to the small crowd, with several requests. We stayed late, dancing either as couples or the three of us. Guys paid attention to Lourdes, whose looks drew them like bees to flowers.

All ended well when they returned to their room, but not before providing me their work phones and address.

I informed them I'd likely show up in their hometown in a few days for touring and sight-seeing.

I returned to my pad muy contento y lleno de gusto al conocer estas dos damas.

En la mañana regrese para despedirme, decirles adiós, pero ya habían salido.

We'll meet in Guadalajara.

Having remained in Vallarta meant taking in the port city with its rich history, beautiful vistas and scenic coastline.

Where there are clean, sandy beaches, there are also tall cliffs with jungle vegetation and vines teaming with wildlife and crazies swinging like Tarzan.

In the distance can be seen a Navy ship, probablemente de México, o posible tal vez americano el barco.

The beach goers are- it's packed and the vendors loving it, business is great.

The paragliders, speed boats, scuba divers, jet skis, and those fishing. Simply a fantastic scene with a mixed mass of humanity enjoying itself.

I leave my post, actually an exterior rough looking bar under some palm trees.

I've meandered to a flea market to sample the merchandise and where somebody recognized me and I go along with them, listening to their story about me being "El Coño del Caribe, pal sur, las isles, blah, blah".

He finally realized his mistake and no I don't play "futbol Mexicano", (soccer). He liked the pretend joke I played on him and we parted friends after introducing ourselves, a strong handshake and laughter- no hard feelings, all in jest. His gal is gorgeous in a skimpy string bikini under her see-through shawl, gown, kimono, whatever. Just tight and firm all over, as she giggled with him after the prank I just pulled on them.

This must be the new thing in feminine swimwear. I saw it in Waikiki. I mean dental floss bikini's I've gawked at. Terrific on young beauties, but ugh the unshaven obese septuagenarians.

Same goes for guys in tea bags- get rid of them and shave.

Changes are coming, I guess.

The Navy Days

Como en la linda playa, música, fiesta, licor. Un memento y se prodria cambiar, yeah, into an orgie with the drugs, the culture and the ambiance.

And actually, there would be nothing that law enforcement could do to control the situation.

Que siga la fiesta.

Being too chicken and fearing harm to myself, I backed out of parasailing, water skiing and other water sports though I came close, more so after a drink or two that gave me courage. No thanks, but I thought it through.

MEMO:

TO: Familia Rivera, Douglas, Az.

FROM: U.S. State Department, Counsel of Puerto Vallarta.

Re: Your Son Pancho.

We regret to inform you that your Panchito was found naked (ass up), left hand contents (bottle of Cuervo), three quarters of the way dead, on the beach front in Puerta Vallarto, after an accident water-skiing. However, he will recover.

Mr. Panchito was so pickled that not even the sharks would take a bite, which saved him from more harm.

Please send pesos, trojans and penicillin.

P.S: The U.S. Navy refused to take him back. Heh, Heh, Heh.

What can I say, I made a fool of myself, more than a couple of times (Y.O.L.O) you only live once? Have I mentioned that I am the worst singer- yet I tried karaoke- corridos, romances, Sinatra, and I royally bombed? The audience tossed tomatoes, napkins, foam cups and other shit, just to shut me up, get me off the stage. But I'm telling you, I loved it all.

Like how a guy loves a girl and no is her answer, he tries and fails, but we get used to rejection, we don't lose a woody over it. She's still there, beautiful and gorgeous. Ay Mamasita! As the lust remains.

Now if the guy is a boy and wants to mope, become emotional, suicidal and/or in lock-up at the psych ward. If you want to sit on the porch with the big dogs, you gotta stop running around pissing like a puppy. Oh well, that's a different story. Can't say I'm of much help there. Put him on his mama's Chi-Chi to baby him.

¡Dale Pecho! Este carbón jamás va a ser hombre, buen macho y chyngón.

Lleva una pica diente en vez de un leño semejante, como de un burro.

Así nos criamos en Cumpas según mis primos, Lindolfo, El Chepo y tantos más con esas platicas picaras y sabrosas.

Beautiful Vallarta left such a great impression. As if I'd return and have my honeymoon there, at one of the magnificent resorts on the side of the cliff, overlooking the Pacific. With the waves and white caps rolling in as surfers rode them, the cruise ships sailing by and the yachts in the bay.

I knew I'd be returning, probably in a month, heading north, but much later. The place calls you, grabs you and makes you want to come back.

The courteous staff at the hotel sent me off with smiles y abrazos. Tan lindos y amables estos individuos humildes y respetosos.

Sali de la camionera cerca de medio día para Guadalajara, Jalisco con un intento de volver a ver a esas dos chulas, Lourdes y Emma, además de ver tan hermosa ciudad muy progresiva casi en el centro del país.

No está muy legos de Vallarta, unas cuatro horas y llegamos a la capital del mescal y tequila.

No hay mucho que contar del corto viaje en una carretera muy moderna en comparación a las que he visto.

Llego temprano la camioneta y nos bajamos no muy legos del centro histórico donde se divisaban monumentos, oficinas y el teatro degollado.

Las dos hermanas me recomendaron un apartamento muy bien dispuesto, se rentaba con las tres B- bueno bonito y barato en un lugar central.

Pronto llegue siendo que no tuvo problema el chofer en hallarlo. Un edificio Blanco de dos pisos. Me toco Arriba.

So, I'm in, registered, unpacked, then ready to tour, with spots to see, especially Chapala, but first dinner because my intestines were gnawing my spine.

Andale- lets go and the result was a puesto en el parque nada lejos that the dark clerk pointed out. A friendly couple tended it, I was told.

Sure enough, I saw the young lady preparing the food while her companion handled the money, silverware, customers, etc.

Maximum efficiency by the two with their pushcart. Nothing motorized or electrical, almost all manual, but for propane tanks and water jugs. Backwards and simple worked for them, as it's poorer down south.

Very colorful, the manner they were dressed and by the paint job on their vehicle which both pushed and pulled.

They put out small fold out tables and stools, however, customers mostly ordered to-go.

The food was already prepared, only warmed up and served on Styrofoam with plasticware.

I tried the barbeque pork en tortilla de maíz con salsa que se me hiso diferente. I've been accustomed to Sonoran style Mexican cooking with more wheat and so forth. Here in the central and southern regions the people have more radishes, cucumbers, cebolla Verde with their salsa and vegetables.

I'll be getting ready for some of Montezuma's revenge, maybe, probably, though the water has not yet been any problem whatsoever.

I should add a couple of topics before returning to the main subject. My writing here concerns my travels in Mexico after my release from the Navy near San Francisco in April 1971. Since then, I've returned many times to many areas of Mexico. So, my writing here may be interspersed with what I saw in my travels later, forty-plus years since 1971.

Also, fortunately, illness was rare, and I remained healthy during this time.

Having had dinner al fresco at the park, just sitting on a bench at about six or seven p.m., I met Ruben, an elder, retired jack-of-all-trades- railroad worker, taxi driver, welder, mechanic, block layer, etc. He was almost awarded the Nobel Prize for dedicated worker and lover, he jokingly said.

Ruben was widowed by now and his four or five offspring lived God knows where. He had travelled practically all over Mexico and had loved many pretty girlfriends he related. In California he believed he has a son, maybe two.

We spent nearly two hours getting acquainted y sus cuentos muy divertidos y chistosos.

Guess what, he became my tour guide and volunteered freely his time and energy, however, I got him snacks, drinks and coins.

By now we had taken a short stroll, but we agreed that by morning, early, we'd meet at the same spot and get going, check out Guadalajara, Mexico's second largest and perhaps most charming city.

I returned to my room and inquired about phone service, long distance, which was explained to me, but I could not get through to Douglas. I thought maybe a telegram tomorrow.

Locally, the telephone worked in calling Lourdes and Emma, mostly the former and broached the subject of meeting. They agreed for dinner the next day. Time and place to be arranged when I contacted them back.

Morning soon arrived and Ruben had been waiting at the park, from where we left for a quick breakfast on the go, just coffee and pastries.

Muy platicador Ruben, probably having woke up quite energetic. He seemed younger than sixty-plus, freshly shaved and in clean clothes. He rattled off a list of places to visit, but first was the huge Mercado Central. Estos son muy común en México.

Llego el bus y en ese nos fuimos. Le explique a Rubén mi interés de turista y ver tanto como puedo de México, con intento de ir a la Capital, D.F., en unos cuantos días. El bien comprendió y me aconsejo.

Nos bajamos en una plaza y cerca estaba un motín. Una gente vendiendo y comprando de todo- comida, ropa, muebles, abarrotes y mucho más. Este es el mentado comercio o el mercado, a place unkown to health inspectors. Surprised it has not been shut or torn down. It would be in the USA.

We lingered then ate menudo, which I insisted that my serving be boiled. I mean more flies than those on a herd of dead burros.

I asked Ruben to show me the telegraph office. I believe it was then that I sent a telegram to Cumpas, because for whatever reason it was difficult getting it to Douglas. I asked mis Tias to inform Panchita and Ed that I was okay.

We proceeded to El Teatro Degollado. Guadalajara's top-notch historical museum and public auditorium where the biggies from all over the world perform.

Leaving there, Ruben suggested we buy tour tickets in order to view more of the vast city, otherwise we'd tire and not see as much by walking.

Dicho y hecho. We did just that only after something caught my eye.

It definitely occurred in Guadalajara, but I can't exactly place the location, though it was morning. The event was oratory. Extemporaneous or impromptu speaking of sorts, and Ruben in his smiling content manner assured me I'd enjoy it but warned to only watch and listen. Mostly poetry, singing, comedy, etc.

Very informal, mostly a rag-tag crowd for an audience of around three dozen, mostly men in a competition of sorts with a gentleman, kind of professional, leading us along.

I don't know what to call it, but I had seen it in my hometown of Douglas, en la plaza o los juegos de Beisbol en el barrio los Domingo's donde la plebe se dicen madrasos a lo bruto, but without anger or repercussions and the audience just laughs and goes along with the entertainment. I saw this one, not the poetry readings.

Here we had two or three sides competing for the prize of a few pesos the crowd threw into a hat. The professor would utter a phrase, such as, "Los Mentados Yankees de Nueva York", and one side was pro and the other con, then embellish the argument or debate with personal attacks, such as, " El pinchi Mantle me la mama, vale pura mierda". The response would be, "No tienes nada que te mamen, baboso, tienes un granito, una pinché bellotita". The crowd would roar with laughter and add to the hat.

It was entertaining like you cannot imagine and whoever won that round moved to the next. The applause indicated the winner, on and on until the final round with the champ getting the loot in the hat, not very much. Maybe it lasted an hour.

I felt like volunteering or jumping in, but I listened to Ruben y me quede callado pero muy entretenido. The crowd also liked it and learned a few more insults.

What do you think? Standup comedy. Insults, put-downs and affronts in a comical, joking or humorous manner. Similar to late night television with Carson, Cavette, et al, insulting guests, the

The Navy Days

president, etc. Don Rickles comes to mind but certainly much cruder and more live. Outside. Uncensored.

But talk about a good time, hearty laughter and aching ribs que de la carcajada, te puedes morir de gusto.

I later called Lourdes about our dinner date and she told me. In the meantime, Ruben and I continued sightseeing and wound-up at a leather goods place where purses, boots, belts, and much more were being produced or hand crafted. Fascinating work and terrific, efficient production of great quantities.

These artisans were masters with their tools that were used to decorate the leather goods, which tended to have a male or masculine theme, such as western or cowboy scenes. Maybe if more females worked there this would change, but only if the strong smell of leather disappeared. We moved on.

We saw historical monuments and statues plus many plazas and stopped at a few. We were done at a good time in the afternoon for me to go clean up then have dinner with Lourdes and Emma.

The three of us met at Plaza Garibaldi, one of the muy, muy, most popular spots in Guadalajara.

But first a brief historical note- duh, what for when I am with two most gorgeous women of the evening and everybody was gawking, probably wondering what in heaven are two elegant dames doing, hanging out with the skinny wacho- me.

Who cares, I was gonna have a great time. That's the important reason with my vacación- el buen tiempo y las lindas amistades.

Details almost half a century later are sketchy, but Lourdes y Emma y yo cenamos en un restaurante, no grandioso pero buen lugar que ellas escogieron. Ordenamos tragos, bebidas, aperitivos, mariscos y más. Nos dimos vuelo, luego postre para el café bien fuerte que nos despierte para darle más a los tragos.

Y como Jalisco y Guadalajara son campeones del tequila a esto también le dimos con muchísimas ganas en el ambiente del

Mariachi, a quienes les pedimos lindas piezas; 'Amor Perdido', 'El Moro de Cumpas', canciones de Javier Solís y así.

It's amazing we survived, didn't die right then and there, nor did we become sick.

Emma and Lourdes had a ball and admitted it was more fun with a paying stranger.

They agreed to do it again.

We talked, chatted, discussed, parle vous, conversed and what not. For hours. 'The more we drank, the better we feel, so drink up with every meal'. ¡Ha! ¡Ha!

No beans, but liquor, please.

Cariño, amor, afecto fueron temas favoritos de mis fabulosas compañeras. Tan lindas estas hermanas que tanto aprecio mostraban una a la otra, así como a sus familias.

Me preguntaron de mí y al fin les di la verdad que soy americano nacido en México y no el estudiante de ingeniería, del Norte en Sonora.

Se sorprendieron y no me creyeron hasta que mostré mis documentos. Mucho se interesaron, con miles de preguntas. Les explicó explique mis razones y no se quedaron ofendidas, pero más querían los datos para entrar a los E.U.

Ellas explicaron que la vida es muy limitada en México y más para las mujeres. La iglesia católica influye mucho las costumbres, cultura, sociedad, etc.

Yo más escuchaba para no quedar mal con ellas porque cambiaron las papelas al divulgar mi ciudadanía. Uno ya no se considera muy fiel en los ojos ajenos.

Mucho le gustaron mi 'nueva' vida, como de Cumpas a América y mi educación y desarrollo en Douglas. Luego el colegio comunitario.

The Navy Days

Mas se interesaron con mis episodios militares y dieron gracias a Dios, ellas mismas, al saber que me escape de la guerra en Vietnam.

Al punto que nos salieron lágrimas de gusto y gratitud, y que solamente me vi in the Pacific.

They asked what I'd be studying, and my reply was 'women', starting with the two of them. That went over really well, and we laughed about it.

Guys came to our table to barge-in and get them to dance, but they struck-out while trying to balance the two to one ratio, Pero hasta la vista amigo.

Llego la cuenta, miento, un cuentón, pero para eso, el Navy lo pago y todavía mi cartera bien gorda.

Al terminar con la música, la cena, las bebidas en esta noche inolvidable, lindo hubiera sido ser acompañado con estas dos preciosas damas, tan finas, Cortez y bien educadas, pero se rindió la noche en esa plaza con la música de mariachis.

Platicamos muy agusto, alegres y contentos antes de despedirnos. Sabían que salía yo para la Capital en uno o dos días y me desearon bien, dándome lista de sitios que ver o visitar, como los dos populares volcanes afuera de México, Ixta y Popo.

Llamamos un taxi y en él nos fuimos, primero al hogar de ellas. Nos abrasamos de despedida y sali después yo a mi apartamento. Nos volvemos a ver ya pronto, de acuerdo, nos dijimos.

Sin duda, Lourdes y Emma buscaban más en la vida, un nivel más alto, y un hombre fuerte y responsable con quien hacer vida y tener familia.

Muerto y torpe me hallo la cama- un sueño eterno y en la mañana una cruda superior sin remedio, únicamente café fuerte, aspirinas y pan me aliviaron un poco. Pronto me acorde de Rubén que ya me esperaba.

El ya tenía boletos del shuttle para Chapala, a una distancia de poco menos una hora. pensé dormir en este viaje, pero no pude porque mi guía muy alegre, riéndose de mí, el borracho. Muy bromista mi cuate, que me recomendó menudo.

Chapala is simply beautiful. We rode around and stepped on the shore of Lake Chapala. Very touristy and American with so many of the elder set- retirees.

We went here, we went there, just taking in the sites, but the lake is way too big and we did not go on a launch. Bocaditos y sodas served us well and after a few hours, onto our return trip, very leisurely.

One does not see Guadalajara without visiting the famous Tlaquepaque. It's admired so much that it has been copied or duplicated, but on a smaller scale.

In my home state. Yes, in Sedona, Arizona, exists a replica plaza like Tlaquepaque (TP).

Let's stick to the real thing. TP, a suburb of Guadalajara, gives off the feeling of colonial times and it's vibrant, colorful and very pretty. A great deal of pride can be seen with the clean streets, displays and maintenance.

Ceramics and artwork characterized this city, which has museums displaying the various styles and periods, and it's not just tile. We saw statues, furniture, tableware and more. Amazing!

Disneyland comes to mind upon seeing TP, it's quite whimsical and has so much activity, things to do and places to see. I sensed its youthful ambiance, as did Ruben.

A positive conclusion is that there is too much life in TP, and this was during the day, imagine the evenings or weekends.

We took a break, had razpados and saw folkloric dancers, kids.

Tan cansados que nos parpadeaban los ojos y yo le decía a Rubén que nos faltó la siesta, pero llegamos bien a Guadalajara. Lo lleve a cenar en uno de tantos puestos y platicamos agosto. Este fue el fin de nuestra aventura.

I greatly appreciated his help, wisdom, and guidance, I said, plus I also loved his sense of humor. He responded that he would now add 'tour guide' to his long resume. See what I mean about his sense of humor?

He thanked me as well, adding that he learned a great deal from me and was grateful for the rides, snacks, etc., and would I please be very careful in my travels.

I handed him a couple of Hamilton's. We hugged and shook hands as we bid farewell. He took our departure a bit sad yet really well. What a great guy, a terrific guide and humble human being.

I set for the apartment and my luggage which was already packed, then I got to the train station.

With time to spare. I bought tickets for a late ride to Mexico City, the nation's capital and seat of the federal government.

All aboard we went with a large crowd of pasajeros de todititos tipos. Halle mi asiento.

Pronto me quede dormido por toda la noche.

En la capital en esa linda mañana el tren a la debida hora llego, con más humo que una fundición. Only polluting some more, worsening the heavy smog, so thick you could cut it with a chain saw.

I found my way to a boarding home Ruben had written down for me, with a note to the management to take care of me. The cabbie figured out where I was going, not too long a drive, yet I still thought I'd be killed in the congested traffic with the insane driving I witnessed.

I had never experienced anything like it and had seen it only on screens- movies, television, etc. It was scary crazy and the poverty, which I had not observed much of before, was now just about everywhere with kids begging, the elders as well. Did I just wake up to this or was I still on the train sleeping, having this nightmare, like a Fellini movie?

The driver dropped me off a few yards from my abode so that I could eat breakfast with industrial strength coffee to wake me from this scenario.

I checked in, paid and went to my suite, which, while certainly not five gold stars, maybe two. Okay, maybe one and two-thirds, silver or lead stars. It would do for a night or two. Better by much more than what I had on a Navy ship or the barracks at HEH. From pauper to prince and back to pauper. Heh. Heh. Heh!

Stopping for a moment, I reverted to a previous thought about life, death, family, God and more, such like when I left the airport in Douglas for active-duty on July, '69. My Nina/Tia Ester Acosta presented me with a crucifix which I have since carried with me.

She implored on me to always hold it dear, pray to it and I would always, ALWAYS, be secure and protected.

Había decidido desde aquel tiempo pagar una manda al Señor y rezar por mi niña. Sabía que en este viaje lo iba cumplir. Es un acto católico bastante común que se ocasiona en la capital, especialmente en diciembre cuando celebramos a La Virgen De Guadalupe.

Very similarly, many Catholics, and perhaps other Christians, travel to Rome and the Vatican to pay homage or give thanks for a miracle, a medical recovery, or a safe return from battle and such.

La Basílica en La Ciudad de México Distrito Federal (MDF) presenta tal oportunidad para rezos y ofrendas similares.

Me disculpo, pero quiero seguir uno o dos párrafos más con este tema siendo que en Tucson each December there is a pilgrimage to MDF, by charter plane, to pray a La Virgen De Guadalupe. They travel from San Antonio, San Diego, Tijuana, LA, Phoenix, etc. Check it out and make your reservations now, ahorita. Reservations go fast.

Similarly, on the border in October in Nogales, just south of Tucson, a pilgrimage follows the path to Magdalena to honor San Francisco. I've seen people on crutches, wheelchairs, using Safeway carts, roller skates and bicycles to trek down there from the congested International border. They get their pets blessed too.

I mean Hispanos Catolicos are powerful, strong, a dedicated bunch, so the least this pendejo can do is say are a prayer or two here in MDF, at the Basilica and drop a Hamilton or Jefferson in appreciation for keeping me alive: at Tripler, on the USNCS Holt, in the Navy and much more. Get me home safely Jesus and get me through college. Gracias. Amen.

So, I did. Spent a few hours admiring the famous church, heard some lectures, prayed and read brochures and books until some service started, then I booked.

To where? I didn't know. My eyes were tearing, itchy, como con chiltepines. Hey, cabron! Oops, sorry, I just got out of church, praying. What a hypocrite. Well I couldn't see!

The air was that polluted. I finally cleared mis ojos.

I put myself on a bus after following the crowd that gave me directions. Some street people and/or walkers wanted to hustle me, but it was not even three p.m.

I stopped at the Federal Government Plaza or District, El Zocalo, to admire the architecture, mingle, eat and check my status with the American Embassy. They wanted to lift my U.S. passport because I was AWOL from the Navy and called the guards, the marines.

The Embassy and Navy is just B.S., a bit of humor or a bad joke to keep you interested, see if you are still awake.

At about this point I lost my camera. One of those cheapy Kodak instamatics with a roll for three dozen color prints. I didn't know how it happened, what, when or where. Que Perdida!

The afternoon went by quickly just sightseeing. I grabbed some grub on-the-go and returned to the boarding house where the sweet, pretty lady welcomed us. She picked me out of the group of six or seven lingering in the lobby.

Muy platicadora la bella joven que supongo trabajaba allí. Entre la plática le salió que conocía a Rubén. My antennae went up. We chatted some more, and I had refreshments with Irma.

Then I figured Ruben with his note to the manager likely indicated that I needed to be taken care of. Oh boy, was I ever! Right on point! EVERYTING BUT THE BREATHMINT ON THE PILLOW! Muchas gracias Ruben.

The room may not have been top-notch, but the loving sure was with the svelte, well-endowed and long-haired beauty. Terrific indeed the surprise. If the bad traffic hadn't killed me, she almost did, she was that wonderful. Todo al natural. BEST room service ever!!!

Did I choose a super tour guide in Ruben or were my prayers at the Basilica answered? Gracias Tia Ester.

By morning Irma had to leave for work but promised to meet me for dinner. She handled finance, loans, collections and that sort of thing, plus evening tips it seemed.

The bumpy, three-hour ride took me far into the parks, the volcanos, Popocatepetl (Popo) and Ixtactzeuatl (Ixta), please check the spelling. They are very real, active at times and the legend is something between Romeo and Juliet and Cinderella, or there-in lie the similarities of the love Popo and Ixtab possessed for each other.

I eyed other sites and vistas, all very interesting and entertaining, however, I could not get over the traffic, the mass of humanity, the noise, congestion, poverty and pollution. It was me, not the capital, the people, MDF. My rural background clashed or did not mesh well with the metro lifestyle.

We met for dinner and Irma looked great. Muy preciosa y más preciosa todavía. She was asking for a super performance and we did just that. The cab took us to a fancy, up-scale establishment of her choosing, quite elegant. I'd call it fine dining.

She called it quits early and took us back to my place for a repeat performance of the previous night, which we very gladly, exquisitely enjoyed with her girlfriend joining us, de rigueur.

I was forever spoiled by the best, but very gladly, without burning my wallet for a terrific experience. I leave it to your imagination. The three were all smiling and content.

Onto the next stop on my extended road trip.

"Hon, you're burning", she said as she sprinkled my back with water that felt cool and refreshing. I uncovered my head, threw the towel to the side and turned around.

"Oh, I'm sorry", she apologized, embarrassed.

"Can you get us dos cervezas", I asked. She did and quickly returned with Bohemia's.

Celeste mistook me for someone else, as she strolled the beach by the motel in Acapulco, where I had arrived just hours ago.

Three days of MDF had been enough so I took the short trip straight south and landed on Celeste.

We sat on my straw mat and talked, again she apologized, but I sensed this was her way of meeting someone. Who knows? I was glad she did it.

A slender, tanned, twenty something figure passing the time away from home in California, the bay area.

We BS'd, drank beer and watched Señor Sol sink and disappear.

After an order of chips, salsa y tacos de cena nos despedimos para vernos en la mañana.

Next thing I know is that she wanted to move in together into her place. I passed. Strictly to economize was her thinking.

We had met for coffee the next morning y luego brunch. La doña tristemente estaba de luto. Perdió su marido en la guerra hacía alguno meces. No había matrimonio por mucho tiempo cuando su esposo le llamaron después de terminar el colegio.

He had been trained on the helicopters.

They had married while in college and attempted to avoid the draft, even thinking of going to Canada, but no luck.

She buried him, then got the military lump-sum and wound up down in Mexico. Grieving, naked, in a bikini, guys lusting after her athletic body.

My story convinced her I made the right decision and was alive, never in Viet Nam, but I still served in the Navy, a seafarer. She felt for me.

A widow at near twenty. No kids. She loved him, would give anything to have him back, in her arms, not having to start over.

We were neighbors just a few rooms apart, near the beach.

She'd rise early, jog, do calisthenics and maybe go for groceries, fix her breakfast, what have you or stop by drinking her coffee, bien cargado.

She got by with her Spanish, but she took to me who spoke English equally well. There were few who spoke American.

Cel, not Celeste nor Cely or Sally, progressed and had been coming out of bereavement mode, so much so that by our third evening she, we, us, became one in her bed.

Emotional it was as she cried, thinking about him who coulda, woulda, shoulda, gone Navy, Air Force, Coast Guard, Canada, etc., anything, anywhere, but Nam, combat. Peace Corps even.

More than in a longer relationship, in those few days, we buddied up, gave each other support, talked about the future and our plans.

Walking the beach, admiring sunsets, collecting seashells and all that, we did. She did my laundry also.

A very kind soul who had been crushed by lost love and was now recovering.

We'd take long walks to watch the cliff-divers at La Quebrada, walk to the catch of the day, like maybe a huge shark or grouper.

She claimed to be calm and comfortable with me, at peace, when we talked, as we held each other, and I kissed her lovely, smooth, tight athletic body.

A lot in common we shared: age, being single, returning to school, and such. She'd like grad school, business perhaps or psychologist.

She wished I'd stay and later return to the USA together, but it just wasn't meant to be.

I stayed a week or so with her in Acapulco and when I left, she was there at the bus station to see me off. I know I held back the tears, like she did, after we hugged, kissed and said our long goodbyes.

We promised to correspond, and she sweetly answered my post card. Oddly, eerily she had expressed a thought that I came as a messenger for her deceased husband, to sooth her and to help her in releasing him, let him go, for her to get on with her young life. She put this idea together because I am a Veteran who in MDF visited the Basilica then traveled down to the coast, Acapulco, to meet her, I just listened. Que piensas? Write angel or God's messenger on my resume.

Las siguientes cuatro horas, como doscientas millas, el camión viejo me acarreo a Oaxaca. Raro para mí porque me sentía como mosca en leche. Yo más alto y blanco que el resto de los pasajeros, ellos más trúquenos y chaparros. Bondadosos, muy interesantes, platicadores, campechanos, llenos de gusto. Compartimos de antojitos, dulces, sodas.

Los mismos me dirigieron la iglesia donde había habitación para los que pasaban por esos rumbos. Era una misión.

Fui a la oficina de la parroquia y así fue, muy listos con su ayuda, al menos por esa noche.

El día entrante me cambie a un hotel junto al zócalo.

Surprisingly, people already knew about me. Word got out fast and with my appearance I stood out. For example, dropping in for mid-morning breakfast, the staff readily recognized me, and they treated me like royalty- el Norteño 'or' el Español', etc. Do I dare speak English or Spanglish?

The hostess, the desk receptionist, phone operator, et al introduced themselves very cordially, hell, I started to feel like a Conquistador. They all would gladly provide any service, cabs, linens, newspapers, anything.

I checked the neighborhood, went into a few stores and walked to the mercado.

Before long, shadows grew and the time went by rapidly mientras que turisteaba aquí y allí, comprando chingaderitas, como una botella de vino para más noche.

En una cocina al aire donde come uno de pie ordene un rico mole con arroz, frijoles y tortillas de maíz, recién hechas, con un café marca diablo. Pase al parque, a una banca. Como es el dicho de que están más cerca los dientes que los parientes porque a nadie conocí only the strangers and I sat there munching and making small talk.

I gathered my packages. Also, the utensils and plastics which I tossed in the trash can.

Next was the hotel bar where the waitress/bartender worked the small crowd. She got friendly and suggested a guide, friends she knew para que me accompanie alquien a las ruinas, the ruins I wanted to see.

A common practice for tourists visiting the archeological sites nearby of Mitla y Montauban, if I did not choose the hotel shuttle.

I had not yet decided, I informed her.

The guide picked me up in front of the hotel in the morning. She was the back-up being that the other one woke up sick. She drove a white government pick up, not too clean because of the dust going back and forth to the ruins. She was a very intelligent woman, divorced with her two kids back wherever, with her ex.

She pursued her graduate studies, I think in anthropology and gave up on the big feminine dream, be a mommy, stay at home, blah, blah, blah. Loving the history, digging ancient tombs and such was her thing. Dora quickly figured I was an American trying to pass off as Mexican. No big deal to her.

We were in Monta ban in no time. It's like eight miles outside of Oaxaca. It's something to behold like my driver, who turned me over to the group of sightseers for the time being.

They say Ricardo Montauban (da plane, da plane) of Fantasy Island is a descendant of the first families erecting these structures. I believe it, why not, like I believe flatulence from cows is methane free, won't cause air pollution.

Can you imagine the flame thrower effect of a cow farting over a lit candle or can of sterno? BBOOOOOOOMMMMM!!!!! That's how she jumped over the moon.

But you gotta see this place that mankind walked thousands of years ago. Hell, if Columbus found America, the east Indie's, the new world. He couldn't even find a light for his cigar hanging off his lips.

I got excited. Such fun. We heard a few speeches, such that Monta ban has United Nations protections. Or that artifacts are stolen and sold on the black market.

To be standing where people stood so long ago and erected these beautiful temples, edifices, whatever you call them, to me was very meaningful, spiritual, as if I came from them, had been here before and shared the same blood.

Many years later, 1995 or near then, my wife and I were in Yucatan and visited another archaeological site, Chichen Itza, spent many hours there, mesmerized by its beauty. You can bury the photos, statues, jewelry, I bought, with me when my pine box goes six feet under. This feeling of connection to an unknown part of history is quite strong within me.

I took anthropology courses and greatly enjoyed them and questioned where this civilization disappeared to. Where are their thousand-year-old bones? Were they conquered and killed? If so, by disease or sword? Too many questions.

On another day, meaning the next day or thereafter, forty-five years means a very very long time to dig out all the details. Anyway, we took snacks then Dora drove the Ford truck on the bumpy road to Milta, out near thirty-five miles from Oaxaca. A longer ride in this beautiful country in which we did more than visit Milta.

I vaguely recall some ranching, cattle roundups, branding, una charreada y caballeria. A very rustic, harsh way of life for these people. When we visited Costa Rica last year, 2018, I was reminded of Oaxaca, incluyendo los ranchos.

We'd spent a good part of the day viewing the sites at Mitla. Again, very somber, like at a mausoleum. My untrained eye couldn't differentiate between the two archeological centers of Milta and Montauban.

It seemed Montauban was more level and better maintained or was it vice versa.

Very touching it was for me to see these ancestral places, stand there and have that awesome tactile feeling con tierra sagrada, Santa, first inhabited before the Europeans arrived.

So many different ideas exist, scholarly theories given credence through difficult research and archeological evidence about what may have actually transpired in the past. For example, (and it's something I'd like to do) digging at sites reveals where woolly mammoths perished in huge pits, either in our Southwest or Siberia.

Somebody dug those holes, trapped the animals, killed them with spears and skinned them. The evidence is there and in labs as well as museums. I would have liked to be there, either set the traps, catch the Mastodon or do the archaeological digging.

And my kids and sisters call me nuts when I share these thoughts while reading the National Geographic . What do you think?

On the ride back to Oaxaca we took a slightly different route where nature's pristine beauty could be admired and had a quick picnic, talked, touched, unzipped and kissed.

Daylight started fading when we considered moving on from our hidden rendezvous.

At a very ideal moment we arrived in Oaxaca and at the hotel bar, ordered drinks and dinner, then to our room to drink and kill the wine.

I wouldn't spend another half-day in Oaxaca. I took a ride with Dora who had to work. We went to the mercado y ella compro comestibles y yo de mirón aquí y allá. Tan distinto el sur de México a su norte y la frontera donde la gente tiene más y logra un bien estar más alto y con mejores escuelas.

At the hotel I had cleared my room and my tab right before Dora gave me a lift to the bus for Vera Cruz. We talked briefly while waiting for the time of departure.

She expressed envy at not being entirely free, being still motherly, being tied down with her studies and job. Dora wondered how I did it, a carefree vagamundo.

I shook aside her talking and thoughts to keep her from turning maudlin and offered that I had long desired to cross the isthmus, which I would be doing so from Acapulco, the Pacific side, to Vera Cruz (VC), the Atlantic Coast. What a thought? she was impressed. Entonces nos despedimos.

Bon Voyage! I didn't say much more, simply, "busco a un pariente en VC".

I arrived in Vera Cruz, not late with a case of head lice starting to itch. No sense trying to figure the source, only to get rid of them.

After about a month on the road, something was bound to happen.

Recogi mis maletas y también pedí informe a una farmacia.

En la tienda me dejo el pesero y allí compre champú especial recomendado por el boticario que, entre la plática, me dijo de una casa de huéspedes, limpia y bastante cerca.

Allí fue donde me quede y le di adiós a los come longos que compre en la botica or what I had in my bags. That was dinner.

Called it quits for the day, time to hit the sack, but only after my hair treatment with medicated shampoo.

I also went through my luggage, looking and triple checking, buscando las pinches chinches, liendres y garrapatas.

Según el boticario, él me recomendó una semana de uso con ese champú para quedar sano y limpio. Así fue.

En la mañana salí al desayuno y me sorprendi al ver el cambio de clima. El Caribe/ Atlántico más diferente al pacífica. Mas árido en el Pacifico mientras que Vera Cruz me pareció mucho más tropical y fresco.

They say the western partygoers out do those in Vera Cruz

Tuve o tengo informes o ideas de mis antecedentes. De joven a mí me contaron mis parientes, de mi gran tatarabuelo de hace muchas generaciones. Supuestamente el vino de España al nuevo mundo y empezó su vida bajándose del barco aquí en Vera Cruz hace algunos siglos.

Después de unos años, el rey o el mandamás lo dirijeron al norte, donde se estableció, hizo vida allí por esos alrededores de Montezuma y Cumpas. Se llamaba el Francisco Hoyos, y le decian, "El Tilili". Así es el cuento. Yo no sé.

El intento del gobierno español era de poblar el territorio de norte, y tililí cumplió. He oído que fue muy mujeriego y tuvo un chingo de hijos. Mr. Paridor, they called him, que no?

Me quede satisfecho en ver VC, donde nosotros hace muchísimos años comenzamos al llegar de España. No necesito ni pido comprobantes, para que, lo que paso, paso y no se puede cambiar o mejorar.

El turista en VC tal vez salga desatisfecho o disgustado porque este puerto tiene cuatro hasta cinco siglos de existencia, quizás más. Todo se nota viejo y sucio, a mi vista, pero no anduve ni lejos.

Vera Cruz has a long history as it was here that its colonial period started near 1550, with the initial arrival of Spain's armada and the conquest that followed. The Catholic Church was greatly involved too in spreading Christianism.

I visited the churches, academies, Naval Museum and was lost in artifacts displayed, the logs, the narration of battle, ships lost at sea, the slave trade. Scholars spend days and more time studying records and researching for their theses and doctoral degrees.

Treasure hunters have also combed the libraries for maps, diaries and more in attempts to locate lost treasure from sunken vessels carrying the loot back to Spain. There have been many successes by treasure hunters becoming abundantly rich by finding gold, coins, jewels and much more.

Not only the Native women were raped, Spain performed a major screwing of the land now labelled Mexico, as did the Americans about a century ago in stealing the southwest lands now known as Texas, New Mexico, Arizona and California. The Catholic Church is also culpable.

Vera Cruz esta tupido de selva que ha cubierto muchísimo los templos, pirámides y otras habitaciones de esos tiempos very ancient when inhabitants (Olmeca, Mayans and more) earlier occupied them. En el camion turistico fuimos a visitar estos sitios.

Some of these archeological sites remain to be discovered or even explored further, there are so many throughout the state of VC and the Yucatan Peninsula that circle northward toward Tolum, Cancun and beyond, almost to Cuba.

One can travel beyond Vera Cruz (which means 'true cross') and realize unexplored regions, volcanos and views with year-round snow on their peaks, even though some maybe active.

The entire place is truly amazing, but back in the city after this scenic tour, reality set in, because this became the turning point for me to head north, next morning. I gave some thought to home and the U of A in the fall.

That evening I went for a leisurely stroll, without too much worry and contemplated a brief stop in Puebla, a city not far from VC. A poster about bull fighting had caught my attention. But the stop in Puebla, not on my itinerary, was to check out sites of more pyramids and such, per the librarian's suggestion at the museum.

It took about two- and one-half hours to get to Puebla, and the trip was definitely worth it to view and explore a truly huge and very significant monument that sits five miles from Puebla. It's Cholula.

The gigantic pyramid of Cholula, known as the largest in the new world and maybe the biggest one on earth, makes the stop at Puebla very worthwhile. It was erected as a temple to the gods and as a place of refuge, shelter and worship by the Toltecs, Olmecs, one after the other, but in what order it's not too clear to me. Way before the Spaniards arrived.

The Chichimec's (no, they did not create the chimichanga, as some believe, especialmente las de dulce con platanos- Rivera, te callas por favor) at one point controlled the area and Cholula.

Only thirty-six or so hours I spent in Puebla, which is famous internationally for its Talavera pottery y el rico mole poblano, mucho mejor que el que saborie en Oaxaca.

Puebla es cuidad muy progresiva, más adelante que algunos otros sitios.

The Navy Days

Pushing north, further up.

Would you believe that an hour, almost, separates Puebla from la capital, MDF where I headed for the next day and half as a hitchhiker (the second or third time in Mexico).

A couple in a VW Van felt sorry for me walking to the bus stop and queried me, then offered me not only a lift pero alimento, galletas, fruta, sodas y platicamos. Llevaban un perrito al cual no mucho le agrade.

Parecía que en un instante llegamos a la capital. Le dio gas a su charanga el amigo tan amable. Luego me dejaron no muy lejos de la basílica Guadalupana y nos despedimos de mano. Les di mil gracias al no haber aceptado mi propina. Entre', a la cathedral, prayed and gave thanks.

I took some time, a bit of window shopping, admiring the engineering, artwork and architecture. I made my way back to my former boarding house Ruben had noted, and walking in guess who?

La Bellissima Irma, totally surprised both of us. Her beautiful smile y lindos ojos. Cara muy radiant and flushed.

She registered me, took the key and showed me to my room. We stripped at warped speed. Took it all off, undressing in record time, loving, kissing, hugging.

Later, plans were made to meet, go out to dinner, stroll, talk and to catch up on the past couple of weeks, etc.

We were back at the house that evening, late into the night, both very grateful at meeting once again and greatly enjoying ourselves, our second chance.

Irma knew my voyage north meant home. I told her the truth about being from Mexico, but that I had become a US citizen and was recently discharged from the Navy.

My story turned her on even more, she couldn't get enough of me, calling me valiant, her hero, how courageous and nibbling me all over. She also teased me and made me speak English being she knew it somewhat. This just made her hotter.

We crashed. Upon softly waking up, we held each other then showered, cleaned up, dressed and left for breakfast. She had called her office/work to ask for the morning off. She did not wish to return with me afterwards.

Both of us became melancholic, quiet. The silence overcame us. She seemed honest and would have taken me as hers, but it wasn't meant to be.

Good-byes were in order when she got into the taxi, giving one another compliments and memories to last forever. We waved to each other as the car left.

Me despedí de Irma, pero con mi corazón pesado y luego pensé porque, cuáles son las razones. Una será la esclavitud de ver a mi gente tan trabajadora, fuerte y luchona. determinados al jale y sacrificio. Meten largas horas, como Irma, con dos o tres empleos, tanto, para solo jalarse el pelo y ver muy poco adelanto. Y con cualquier hombre no va a subir más o muy poco. Son pocas las oportunidades en México, ella me contaba al no saber que hacer porque es más difícil para la mujer, más con hijos y familia.

Otra razón sería el empuje de la naturaleza que pide del ser humano to procréate. But why, we of rational, objective, logical perspective ask. Life is very hard and more with children, yet women bear more of the burden in child-rearing and family.

Estos temas los pensaba en el camión hacia Guadalajara donde intentaba estar dos días.

Pero Guadalajara me recuerda de un incidente que ocurrió, yo diré, al empezar 1990. Y casi se me pasaba en mencionárselos, pardon.

Fue una explosión que hubo y causo demasiado daño, muerte and injury. This major gas explosion caused about three and a quarter godzillion dollars or eleven teen point six phoquillion pesos. That bad!!!! All the flatulence and methane of the city's population, pets and disposed waste had accumulated in a poorly constructed high containment sewer line. Some chiquitines jugaban con matches by, close to near a manhole and do I need to explain next, the outcome. Boom! Boom! Boom!

I think my explanation here is about as good as you're gonna get, because the chemists, the investigators, the engineers, bureaucrats et al are still searching for THE cause, virgensitas, etc. are still waiting for a handout and compensation after/from such a tragedy. Thirty years later nothing or next to nothing.

It's reported that over two-hundred-fifty people perished, many more severely, permanently maimed. Over five square miles de la ciudad de Guadalajara were flattened that included businesses, museums, churches, schools, residences, not to mention the many potties that fed the sewer line.

Brisk business in a port-a-Juanito's followed.

Guadalajara nos recibe con mucho fan-fan porque había fiestas esperándonos en al centro de camiones, así como allí también tocaban los Mariachis.

Que palabra es esa, 'Mariachi. En el diccionario se explica que viene del francés, 'marriage', matrimonio. Madre que no.

Alla en mi barrio y en Agua Prieta dicen que no es cierto, no sea 'María Chichona', o corto sea 'Mariachi'. ¿Qué cree usted? Sera la verdad?

Lo que yo me quede sepa dónde, pero si sabía el numero telefónico de Lourdes y Emma y me clave a buscarlas y logre hallarlas a las bellas hermanas que gusto les dio al oír de mí y que regrese bien del sur.

Buena y largas platicas tuvimos con mucha risa, gusto y placer. Nos prometimos juntarnos el día entrante para salir y cenar.

Anduve de tonto aquí y allí por lugares en Guadalajara, un mata tiempo más que nada.

También busque un correo para mandar unos postales a Douglas y darles informe de mi situación y que pronto ya voy a llegar.

I followed them with dinner at a small shopping center with an American imitation or theme. It provided hambuguesa, pizza, fries, etc.

I figured I might as well start getting used to gringo-style cooking or lack of. I think there's more cooking in Mexico, (because of economics, lower incomes, large families, etc.) than up north where take-out, frozen foods and home delivered meals make things more convenient and easier.

Survey says per capita, Hispanics earn less, but spend more on food by forty-two percent than Americans who earn more and spend less on meals, like sixteen percent and in Canada they get it free, just like their medical care. Would you believe those numbers and statistics? Amazing. I don't, I just made it up. Did I fool you?

So, I had dinner then worked it off by walking back to the hotel before it became too dark.

Here is another entry, and off point regarding Guadalajara. A large group of us flew to the sister city of Tucson in December 1979, when we took a troupe of youngsters performing folklorico dancing, to present en el programa navideño en el Teatro Degollado. The youngsters did very well, and our hosts were very gracious. It turned out to be a terrific holiday vacation.

On another note, I often go to Guadalajara, on average I'd say once per month. That is, in Tucson, to say 'vamos a Guadalajara' means the Guadalajara Bar and Grill. Three restaurants, same owners. Great ambiance with music, food, drinks and very festive.

Getting back to the real Guadalajara, Jalisco, 1971, where I found myself on my return to the USA. I had a dinner date con Lourdes y Emma. Nada muy formal. Sería una reunión más bien como una despedida, por la cual ya me sentía muy agradecido.

Ellas salieron del trabajo a su apartamento y se alistaron para luego juntarnos en uno de tantos restaurantes que hoy no recuerdo muy bien.

The Navy Days

Les traje un racimo de flores y al vernos nos saludamos, dándonos abrazos. Tan lindas, finas cordial y atentas las dos como han de ser el orgullo de sus padres.

Empezamos con gusto las pláticas y ordenamos bebidas y unos bocaditos. Al pedirme informe de mis viajes les conté lo bonito que vi al sur y que me encanto más de todo el sitio arqueológicos como Milta y Montalbán. Me quede muy impresionado en ver algo tan antiguo que yo nunca había realizado esto no existe ni se ve en América, donde todo les muy nuevo. In the USA, being a newer nation, its history is not deep.

The waiter interrupted us to take our order, which we agreed would be a parrilada combinada de salsa, pollo, carne asada, frijoles, arros, tortillas y verduras. De esta orden grande nos servimos todos.

Continúe con mis cuentos, diciendo que admire como en México se eleva la historia de las varias gentes indígenas que tanto atrae el turismo cuando recibimos los músicos.

It was a quartet of guitars and violin, plus vocals. They moved from table to table, picking up tips as they went. These were musicians dressed in colorful guayaberas and dark slacks, giving the impression of being from the Caribbean area.

I resumed my chit-chat re: pyramids as an example. I doubt I'll visit there again, but my memory stays with me of thousand-year-old structures from my birthplace. The culture, those people are still here, unlike in America that's so new and old ways are frowned upon.

The dinner looked scrumptious and we served ourselves the deliciously prepared meal. Lourdes y Emma being quite proper and lady-like. They probably figured I was treating, it's my thing, so let's enjoy ourselves while he babbles. They asked polite questions about my return to Arizona, college, work, the Navy, etc.

I serenaded them with my Popeye jingle (not the Spanish one).

I'm Popeye the sailor man

> I sailed in a garbage can
>
> from Japan
>
> To Hilo
>
> and Frisco
>
> I go
>
> I'm Popeye the sailor man, toot-toot.

The two giggled and we toasted. "Have another drink", they urged me.

We were having a very enjoyable time, but they made me the main topic of conversation, about school, I turned the tables on them.

In Mexico, schooling does not take as long as the Americans do, it's more streamlined in just about any field, with some of the best universities right there in Guadalajara, to the point that Canadians and Americans attend medical school, finish as doctors and return north, some to study a specialty.

When queried about my studies, I responded that I had been accepted and would start in September in Tucson to study business and also accounting. Emma took a liking to that. I added I would utilize my Veteran's benefits for schooling and employment, then proceed to explain how that worked.

Plus, I would be purchasing a vehicle stateside when I arrived home. That impressed them, more like wowed them, porque ya figuraron mucha mula tenia yo. Estaban equivocadas.

Pero se llegó el oscurecer.

Tomamos un brindis a nuestra amistad tan corta pero inolvidable. Pagamos le cuenta y pasamos a fuera.

Estas damas tan amables me dieron la despedida y gracias. Nos descontamos después de notar nuestros domicilios para después corresponder.

Así fue porque me llego correo de ellas cuando yo en Tucson, U of A, pero paramos la comunicación dentro de poco.

Regrese a mi apartamento donde recoji mi mochila y sali en el camión para el norte. Había pasado ya como mes y medio casi en México.

En Vallarte dure un día sin mucho que hacer, solo de turista, admirando la belleza del mar, los cerros, la selva y más, todo muy verde.

Mazatlán ya me esperaba y de allí otra vez pensé en viajar al este para el lado de Monterrey, con intenciones de ver el Cañón de Cobre y los Indios Tarahumara.

To travel to the Copper Canyon, preferably by train for me, I would board at Los Mochis, then spend a day or two in the canyon villages to enjoy the experience and the four-hundred-mile trip.

I did not do this, simply fearing I could be delayed getting home in time for Clara's graduation from Douglas High School in late May.

A couple of paragraphs about Copper Canyon. It is internationally recognized and attracts far too many tourists which in turn degrades the canyon's ecosystem. I have heard and read this many times in magazines and television programs.

The canyon is a gem, a gorgeous, scenic, must do item on one's bucket-list as one witnesses nature's beauty of wildlife, waterfalls, forests, canyon walls and mountains.

Another very humble y muy interesante aspecto de esta visita are the Tarahumara. The Natives have occupied the canyon before the Spanish Conquerors arrived, who then enslaved, exploited and then also robbed them of precious silver, gold and such.

The Tarahumara maintain an existence or lifestyle of centuries past and are well known for their running ability as vehicles are minimal in such a harsh environment, I read.

Before long, I intend to return to Mexico for the sole purpose of hopping the train to travel through the canyon.

Con el favor de Dios.

Pronto se llega el tiempo ates con mis tíos.

El camión corrió junto a la costa y pronto Mazatlán se desapareció. Mucha carga llevábamos para Guaymas donde subieron tantos pasajeros como los que bajaron y pronto le dimos a Hermosillo.

Ya sentimos el calor al fin de mayo, cuando cambia el clima en el verano. Muy caliente se pone y debe cuidarse uno que fácilmente se deshidrata, se enferma como nada al punto de gravedad.

Parientes en Hermosillo me esperaban y me toco visitarlos un rato. No dure mucho que pronto me fui a Cumpas, llegando como en tres horas.

Mis tíos sabían de mi porque les había avisado y con mucho gusto y los brazos abiertos me recibieron. Pensaban que venia yo rendido y muy cansado, pero me vieron robusto y sano, con buen apetito. Gracias a Dios.

Muy lindos, atentos todos al verme, como si hubiera sido yo un visitante diplomático o alguien importante, no el sobrino de ellos.

I felt welcomed, loved, admired and more. We met and talked at length, mostly they talked, and I listened. Tias Elisa y Herminia con mi Tio Jesus. They had a good productive life and certainly one more enjoyable than other Cumpeños. They felt, perhaps due to aging and some loneliness, some bitterness and not pleased with the changing times, such as the young having a more privileged existence. They three attributed this to the media, mass communications and the corruptive style propagandized by the USA.

A bit of envy was evident. Here I sat before them, at only twenty-two or so and have seen Mexico, whereas they had lived here all their lives without adventuring much further than Hermosillo. Devoting their lives to the reality of hard work without time-off to stop and smell the roses. Without rising beyond their established status.

Other topics brought up were nieces, nephews, families as well as the tilled fields, harvests, cattle, etc. At dinner, Tio Jesus's lament about the lack of youth in Cumpas. Just about everybody leaves.

We called it a night and being I'd be going to Nacozari to see my Ninos, I also excused myself until morning.

Mi Tio Pedrito y mi tía Ester en Nacozari me dieron la bienvenida. Ya me esperaban hace algunos días, que hasta tenían el almuerzo preparado para solamente sentarnos y comer y listos para conversa, una plática larga y muy linda.

Mi Tio con mucho interés me preguntaba de México, y más de la región central, como MDF, Puebla y Vera Cruz. Él me dijo que, hacía muchos años, cuando de muy joven el había viaja por esos lugares y se encantó. Siempre con muchas ganas de regresar. Parece que nunca se le hizo porque no salió jamás de Sonora.

Confeso que de verdad no está muy encantado con la vida urbana, prefiriendo algo más calmado, especialmente con la edad, años y salud.

Mi Nino no se vencia, he kept at his work, delivering beer and sodas in Nacozari and nearby, as well as handling his investments. Retirement didn't seem to be in the cards for him, not anytime soon anyways.

Mi Tia Ester kept at her wifely duties of caring for Don Pedro and the household. She still prayed daily and was quite involved with the Catholic church and its charity work. A good thing was that the couple had good help, hired for various tasks like chauffeuring, gardening, laundry and more.

Visiting with them reminded me about how much I had enjoyed Nacozari de Garcia ten to fifteen years ago, especially the train. El Cebollero. This clickety-clack on the track, the tooting chimney and the billowing smoke.

I took a ride with my Tio in his truck to make a quick delivery and to see the town. We talked about my past two years in the Navy, what I saw, where I travelled. He inquired about my plans, so he learned that I had returned in time for Clara's high school graduation and that she and I would be in college by September. Both of us already having been accepted, hence we'd have the summer free, waiting for school to start.

We returned to the residence, had some relaxing moments para despuesito cenar a gusto con ellos y también con uno de la ayuda.

Rica y sabrosa la sopa.

Yeah! We had a good dinner, plus a couple of cheves de mi Tio Pete, Carta Blanca.

CHAPTER 25.
Getting Home.

So, stop right here. What happened next I'm not sure, but as Carly Simon sings in 'You're So Vain', about 'Clouds In Her Coffee', well I got clouds in my brain, mind, and noggin, because we took off for Douglas next morning, didn't we? On the train Don Pedro, Ester and me? I think. I don't believe I travelled by myself, but who knows after nearly half a century.

Five hours or so later, the international fence greeted us as did la perra fundición mandando miles de nubes al cielo, el ambiente apestoso de azufre, los ojos de uno quemados y la lengua gruesa con la mierda del PD.

We made it through the crowds, the mooing cows and noisy locomotives to find a cab we dropped into, then to the Customs building on the US side.

"Halt, Mr. Pedro Acosta, you can return to Mexico or be detained for harboring a US Citizen, a Navy sailor wanted for being AWOL!"

"I want my lawyer," I hollered, and then I woke up. Just a thought, a nightmare, or daydream, but it kept you awake, right?

We were easily processed and were home in no time.

Actualmente, I hadn't planned my arrival so exceptionally well with a big welcome from Ed, Panchita and neighbors. Blanca and Clara would arrive later due to their jobs.

Tio Pete was my bodyguard, buffer or bouncer in case my pissed off Parents attacked me. Oddly, no, not too much. Los vecinos were in a celebratory mood, not due to my arrival, but because it was high school graduation week and three or four barrio students were wrapping up their schooling and studies for good. Finished. Todos muy contentos.

Mom too. She coyly asked me, "cuantos hijos dejaste por allá en Vallarta, San Diego, ¿Hawái?"

"No sé, unadocena, ya pronto otra vez serás abuela". Mom did not like my response but smiled when the crowd erupted with laughter.

Not one to be ignored, my Dad beamed, happy, smiling, hugging and kissing me, touching me to prove to himself that I, his son was present, who returned home and raised hopes.

"Gracias a Dios", Ed prayed.

The occasion grew happier, Clara and Blanca arrived with her kids, Tony y Lisa, estos tan chulos y grandes, muy lindos y sonrientes.

El barrio was going to have a week full of cheer, because of the graduations and schools closing for the summer recess. It happened yearly, but now it hit home with Clara's turn, which meant Ed y Panchita no longer had school kids but college students with Clara and I moving on.

I had unpacked and settled in with my Parents and Clara. I got back my bedroom, mostly as I had left it, unchanged except for new linens and blanket.

Everyone peppy, energized and positive with this Traveler's return home to the border, like the Ricky Nelson song, 'Travelling Man', very popular then, at that time.

Adjusting came easy, being idle and sleeping late. I took care of Naval Reserve matters, applied for unemployment insurance and was approved. I visited vecinos, went to A.J. Bayless and stopped to see some friends.

The Navy Days

People said I made the 'two-year Navy stint' look so easy despite the horror, a very dangerous time, especially for young men, because of the Viet Nam War.

That week came to a close on a happy note with Clara's graduation, which we attended along with los Parientes de Cumpas y Nacozari. Clara had many friends and was popular, plus her employer's at Sears Roebuck really liked her, more like adored her. She was greatly appreciated.

I turned down job offers and bought a brand-new VW. Clara did this too, hers was blue, mine tan.

Clara and I tackled the remodeling of our home: painting, new floors, redoing the kitchen, laundry and bathroom, installed new bedroom closets, built a front porch and more. We were young, strong and full of vim, vigor and vitality. I'd work past midnight with music, food, drinks y poca ayuda de los vecinos, who questioned where the funds came from.

From my casino winnings, my drug sales in Mexico, my Navy reenlistment bonus, my gambling in Australia, perhaps from the pimping of the hotties in Hawaii. Anything for a laugh, keep them guessing- he has no job but has brand new cars, is fixing his home, vacationed in Mexico and is paying to go to the U of A. It doesn't add-up they figured, yet it's taking place before everyone's eyes.

Let the rumors fly.

Those first days back weren't mine, but Clara's, being the center of attention with graduation and rightly so. I did not want to steal her thunder she well deserved after working very hard all those years.

I had my share. People welcomed me back.

Friends, neighbors, relatives y conocidos vinieron a celebrar con mi Hermana menor que seguido alumbraba muy brillante y era el orgullo de mis Padres.

With the heat and summer and time to waste, I had laid out my plans for a job and other sundries for my move to Tucson.

A new Veteran has about three months to apply for a Federal Government position. I appreciated the U.S. Post Office in Douglas (at Tenth Street and F Avenue). The Postmaster (whose daughter and I had been classmates in high school and college for years). Served me well from my day's delivering <u>The Douglas Dispatch</u> on the mail route each evening. God Bless him because he came through big-time y me asistio en hallar empleo en Tucson al comenzar en septiembre mis estudios en la Universidad.

Soon after my best friend, brother, paisano, amigo, vecino and all those respective and respectful titles, anyway he came home.

Rafael had his honorable discharge from the military after four years of service. He was soured by being a sailor and greatly looked forward to rest and to civilian life while also, like Raul and I, waiting to start classes at the U of A.

His bitterness showed but slowly went away. No amount of reenlistment bonus would sway him: Ralph craved the freedom.

Those summer days we mellowed. I had changed and was not the same young sailor committing to the regular Navy in 1971. The eager beaver in me gave way to wisdom, caution, wait and see's, I sensed.

Rafael learned I had travelled for about six weeks in Mexico and showed mixed feelings, like 'Why, when the money could be better applied to college', or hailed, 'Que parranda tan chingona con las Viejas'.

Only for us to return to Douglas, our hell hole.

Interestingly, here and there articles appear where one reads that in some places (volcanic areas, gas fields and such,) cracks in the earth emit sulfur and it's strong, nasty smelly fumes, which came from hell. Satan's abode.

In the Bible or other religious writing this is claimed as well.

Then we must be right above hades because Douglas reeks of sulfur from the smog PD belches into the air. We are in hell! Such disturbing thoughts, just crazy ideas among friends. Logical? Hmmmm.

Now it's all over, it's a wrap. We're not taking five. It's finis, no longer a continuation. No need to prolong this. The Trilogy is completed, except to say it all started in Cumpas, Sonora y Mexico and it ended almost similarly upon my return at the end of my travels into Mexico when I stopped to visit mis parientes in Cumpas. It was not planned that way, it just worked out that way. We did a complete three-sixty. Heh. Heh. Heh.

Gracias. Que Dios Nos Bendiga.

Con el favor de Dios.

¿Cuál sería el colmo de mis pasados veinte y dos meces de tanto cambio y riesgo por un mundo extranjero? People say my return to Douglas to see Family in the midst of all this chaos. ¿Sería que salí bien de Tripler después de la cirugía? ¿Tal vez salir completo sin que me maten ya sean las víboras en Australia? ¿Las damas en los noviazgos? ¿Los aviones? ¿Escaparme de la guerra?

Bendito fui porque no hubo ni un gran trastorno. He pensado en el pasado y creo que soy primo de Houdini siendo que han sido varias las veces que me he escapado de varios serios asuntos. Parece ser normal para mí, parte de mi personalidad y al Señor gracias le doy.

La violencia fácil se presentó y ningún pleito o golpe me toco. Al contrario, busco la paz y lo tranquilo y esto me ha salvado.

The Desiderata is wonderful text which provides some guidance to live by.

I like this point: Be your own master and do not live by how others measure or judge you.

Also, try to help others and be kind, however, look out for your own well-being and safety.

Just as I have mulled the above and ventured way out beyond my normal sphere then returned, I'm heading into another adventure, different and more local. Probably much less fearsome and with much greater rewards. I'll be wiser in pursuing my educational experience starting at the U of A this summer.

The past two years of Naval service and travel have served to show me and teach me how life is beyond the horizon, away from my immediate, decadent barrio. Experiencing this first-hand has been very enlightening and far better than books, videos or lectures.

I learned by meeting strangers and as a foreigner being able to adjust, be malleable to given situations or different environments, without negative results.

On this long road trip there were some parrandas, perdition and debauchery, such as in San Diego, in Sydney (King's Cross), Hawaii, fun but part of the maturation and fun for being human amidst the loss of innocence.

Conclusion

Some rambling thoughts to conclude Volume III and then the Trilogy, The Odyssey.

In wrapping up <u>The Navy Days</u>, the last volume of the Odyssey Files, it hardly means finality. I view it, after closer perusal, more as a continuation, telling or description of what happened to me. The experiences, good or bad, that I had while on active duty from about July '69 through mid-April '71, follow me, up to now and in my remaining years.

To this day I am haunted with flashbacks and nightmares of maimed and disabled soldiers I saw, met or helped in the wards of Tripler Army Hospital in Hawaii. But for the Grace of God, he saved me and blessed me. Truly!!

Yet I also recall the terrific times I enjoyed while serving, and such as sipping coffee while sitting in the cockpit, talking with the pilots on the long MAC Flights over the Pacific and admiring the beauty of the skies, the ocean below, earth and vast horizons.

I met many individuals in and out of the military who greatly expanded my perspectives in many areas, thus helping me become well-rounded, insightful and appreciative.

I've had this thought, not unpleasant, after mulling some ideas, that I was a warrior of/in the Cold War, while others were battled tested in the Viet Nam conflict. Also, my active duty seemed more civilian than military.

HEH was a tool keeping check on the Soviet Union, as previously described (tracking its nuclear submarines). I served in a supporting role at the Northwest Cape as a Yeoman in educational services to other sailors- the radiomen, electronic technicians, computer wizards, et al.

I served, fulfilled my obligation and America's call to duty. I gained a great deal and feel thankful yet pray for peace and for my fellow servicemen not as fortunate as me. May the Lord bless them all.

At this point, after my seven decades, I wish not to get negative, though that could easily happen. I did what I could. Que la paz y bendiciones sean nuestra on our way home.

The American Military experience. Hmm. Think Beetle Baily, MASH, Okinawa.

Mas diversión sique para concluir. Reflejo sobre temas incluidos en los tres libros.

Le doy más importancia, sobre todo, en expresar aprecio y gratitud al Divino Ser y a todos, toda la humanidad, muchísimos, quienes me asistieron y prestaron atención durante ese gran viaje que transcurrió durante mis primeros años, como casi a quarter century, así como hasta el presente.

Y en el presente, aquí y ahorita, reflejo en cosas excluidas y que no apunte en estas páginas.

To illustrate, the six years of service to or in the Navy, Reserve and Active, I felt mine was mostly as a civilian and not that much of a military role.

Otro ejemplo, I've described friends and acquaintances from my Douglas days and pointed out that much music was made or played en mi lindo barrio. I give credit to my friend and neighbor whom I grew up with and hangs around this part of the world. A terrific bilingual musician I often see, meet, run into and laugh out loud with. We're about the same age and the crowds love him when he's up on the stage performing his music with his combo-magical! I grew up with him, yet I almost failed to mention him. Sorry.

Dementia happens and fails me. Think of the ship I was on, the Destroyer U.S.S. Evans. An interesting tidbit here. The Evan's was split in half by the Australian aircraft carrier Melbourne in May 1969, killing about six dozen American Sailors. Kind of eerie: I went on active duty July 1969 and served on another Evan's Cruiser around 1970.

So, I guess I am saying that my thousand-page Trilogy doesn't say it all and much has been left out, forgotten.

But another provocative idea follows? Bilingualism is growing, just as biculturalism rises. In Northern Mexico and the American West and the Southwest, trends grow strong, especially with the media, travel, communications and the internet and more.

In a century or less, fusion will occur to give birth/life to a new language similar to today's Spanglish. Linguists, researches, anthropologists and others will seek clues and evidence of this change and may consider my Trilogy as contributing to this transformation with my bilingual format and style of writing. Deep! Indeed. Think about this and I'll bet you never had a clue.

My great, yet different ride filled me with much that life has to offer to a new arrival in this country. But my migration is simply one of millions of those who come to America. Similar to many others but extra ordinary in other ways.

Very many of us, through diligence, sacrifice, stubbornness and more, have found a new home in America. Our niche may be in New York, like the Holocaust victims, or in Miami where Cubans settled, as well as my brethren all over the Southwest.

To say my story was unique, well, maybe, because of the crazy times. I arrived shortly after WWII, and crossed into the US of A- a fantasyland- as it was transforming into a world of power in the fifties and then as I looked at my adulthood, the sixties decade went berserk, nuts, psycho: the assassinations, Viet Nam, Manson, the riots and protests, the moon landing, plus more, then Watergate.

What's an immigrant to do? Get whipped in grade school! Do what I could, not the best nor the greatest, but somehow, I survived, where others did not. Fifty-five thousand perished in Nam. I joined the Navy, but somewhat scared and with doubts. I was puny, undersized, unskilled and had limited English, however, I was accepted, only to realize how terrifying it was. A tin can against the unstoppable, powerful ocean.

Along with all of this, I had strong, supportive, older Parents who amazingly made it happen, despite the humble, impoverished beginnings, giving it their all to succeed in the new land. I believe they departed with happy hearts and joyful minds knowing their success and realizing their legacy: the first generation of the Rivera's in America. A helluva dream. A terrific accomplishment! Heh! Heh! Heh!

Toodle Loo, Folk**s**.

Appreciation

I will say that with a life of seven-plus decades, I feel blessed. I've enjoyed a great ride. I'm thankful as well at having gained perspective and wisdom to be able to put together this Trilogy, which for many years I delayed writing, despite the encouragement of many who have felt I've had an interesting story to tell and describe.

I appreciate daily and forever the hundreds of souls who touched, taught and helped me in my many experiences, such as the doctors at Tripler Army Hospital, the crew of the USS Evans, the departed on the USS Arizona, the fellow mariners at H.E. Holt.

Never can I say I did it by myself. By the grace of God and the many wonderful people, I've travelled this far. A million thank you's I owe.

Thank you all. Gracias mil. Merci Beaucoup.

Que Dios nos cuide, proteja y ayude. Unidos adelantamos.

Doy muchísimas gracias a mis Padres y toda mi Familia.

Mis múltiples recuerdos son demasiados y profundos. Me dan gran paz y bienestar.

Acknowledgements

Frankly, I owe a huge debt of gratitude to the many anonymous donors, who pushed, shoved and not only encouraged me, but helped with admin, clerical, funds, IT and adding much humor to this endeavor.

A mi buen amigo, a squid, Airedale Reid.

Also, from the Bisbee-Naco-Douglas border my publisher Pepe.

My wife Gloria, sisters Blanca and Clara are also very deserving, especially in support of my weirdness.

I alone am responsible for any bloopers, I've erred, and readers note this in the Trilogy.

*In Special Remembrance:

For a Dear Family Friend, Mr. John Luchetti, gracias Amigo.

About the Author

Francisco A. Rivera was born in Sonora, Mexico and immigrated to the United States as a young child with his Family. He grew up and went to the schools in Douglas Arizona. He served in the US Navy during the Viet Nam war and Graduated from the University of Arizona. He worked as a Social worker and in the Educational field until his retirement. He now resides with his wife in Tucson Arizona.

This is his third edition in the Odyssey series covering his Navy Days. Here are links to his other editions in the series. Be sure to check them out.

http://zenbonesproductions.com/

https://www.amazon.com/dp/B086PQKG8P Book II e book

https://www.amazon.com/dp/0999512641 Book II Print book

Original Book in the Odyssey Series

https://www.amazon.com/dp/0999512617

The Navy Days

www.ingramcontent.com/pod-product-compliance
Lightning Source LLC
Chambersburg PA
CBHW022052160426
43198CB00008B/201